Enhancing CAD Drawings with Photoshop®

Scott Onstott

San Francisco   London

Publisher: Dan Brodnitz

Acquisitions Editor: Willem Knibbe

Developmental Editor: Pete Gaughan

Production Editor: Lori Newman

Technical Editor: Ryan Spruston

Copyeditor: Pat Coleman

Compositor: Kate Kaminski, Happenstance Type-O-Rama

CD Coordinator: Dan Mummert

CD Technician: Kevin Ly

Proofreaders: Ian Golder, Nancy Riddiough

Indexer: Nancy Guenther

Book Designers: Maureen Forys, Happenstance Type-O-Rama and Judy Fung

Cover Designer: John Nedwidek, Emdesign

Cover Illustrators: Scott Onstott and John Nedwidek, Emdesign

Library of Congress Card Number: 2004113401

ISBN: 0-7821-4386-5

SYBEX and the SYBEX logo are either registered trademarks or trademarks of SYBEX Inc. in the United States and/or other countries.

Mastering is a trademark of SYBEX Inc.

Screen reproductions produced with FullShot 99. FullShot 99 © 1991-1999 Inbit Incorporated. All rights reserved. FullShot is a trademark of Inbit Incorporated.

The CD interface was created using Macromedia Director, COPYRIGHT 1994, 1997-1999 Macromedia Inc. For more information on Macromedia and Macromedia Director, visit http://www.macromedia.com.

Autodesk VIZ is a 3D solution for modeling, rendering, animating, and creating photorealistic design visualizations. It can be used to explore design concepts, communicate design intent, and share work with clients, colleagues, and consultants. Straighforward modeling features and unique interoperability with other Autodesk design applications add flexibility and efficiency to the creation process. It allows clear and accurate sharing of design ideas with advanced global illumination processes (including the mental ray renderer) to capture even subtle effects for realistic 3D visualizations.

Autodesk, AutoCAD, Design Web Format, and DWF are either registerd trademarks or trademarks of Autodesk, Inc., in the U.S.A. and/or certain other countries. Mental ray is a registered trademark of mental images GmbH & Co. KG, licensed for use by Autodesk, Inc. Certain content, including trial software, provided courtesy Autodesk, Inc., © 2005. All rights reserved.

SYBEX is an independent entity and not affiliated with Adobe Systems Incorporated, the publisher of Adobe ® Photoshop ® software. This is an independent Sybex publication, not endorsed or sponsored by Adobe Systems Incorporated. Adobe ® and Photoshop ® are trademarks of Adobe Systems Incorporated.

TRADEMARKS: SYBEX has attempted throughout this book to distinguish proprietary trademarks from descriptive terms by following the capitalization style used by the manufacturer.

The author and publisher have made their best efforts to prepare this book, and the content is based upon final release software whenever possible. Portions of the manuscript may be based upon pre-release versions supplied by software manufacturer(s). The author and the publisher make no representation or warranties of any kind with regard to the completeness or accuracy of the contents herein and accept no liability of any kind including but not limited to performance, merchantability, fitness for any particular purpose, or any losses or damages of any kind caused or alleged to be caused directly or indirectly from this book.

Manufactured in the United States of America

10 9 8 7 6 5 4 3 2 1

Software License Agreement: Terms and Conditions

The media and/or any online materials accompanying this book that are available now or in the future contain programs and/or text files (the "Software") to be used in connection with the book. SYBEX hereby grants to you a license to use the Software, subject to the terms that follow. Your purchase, acceptance, or use of the Software will constitute your acceptance of such terms.

The Software compilation is the property of SYBEX unless otherwise indicated and is protected by copyright to SYBEX or other copyright owner(s) as indicated in the media files (the "Owner(s)"). You are hereby granted a single-user license to use the Software for your personal, noncommercial use only. You may not reproduce, sell, distribute, publish, circulate, or commercially exploit the Software, or any portion thereof, without the written consent of SYBEX and the specific copyright owner(s) of any component software included on this media.

In the event that the Software or components include specific license requirements or end-user agreements, statements of condition, disclaimers, limitations or warranties ("End-User License"), those End-User Licenses supersede the terms and conditions herein as to that particular Software component. Your purchase, acceptance, or use of the Software will constitute your acceptance of such End-User Licenses.

By purchase, use or acceptance of the Software you further agree to comply with all export laws and regulations of the United States as such laws and regulations may exist from time to time.

SOFTWARE SUPPORT

Components of the supplemental Software and any offers associated with them may be supported by the specific Owner(s) of that material, but they are not supported by SYBEX. Information regarding any available support may be obtained from the Owner(s) using the information provided in the appropriate read.me files or listed elsewhere on the media.

Should the manufacturer(s) or other Owner(s) cease to offer support or decline to honor any offer, SYBEX bears no responsibility. This notice concerning support for the Software is provided for your information only. SYBEX is not the agent or principal of the Owner(s), and SYBEX is in no way responsible for providing any support for the Software, nor is it liable or responsible for any support provided, or not provided, by the Owner(s).

WARRANTY

SYBEX warrants the enclosed media to be free of physical defects for a period of ninety (90) days after purchase. The Software is not available from SYBEX in any other form or media than that enclosed herein or posted to www.sybex.com. If you discover a defect in the media during this warranty period, you may obtain a replacement of identical format at no charge by sending the defective media, postage prepaid, with proof of purchase to:

SYBEX Inc.
Product Support Department
1151 Marina Village Parkway
Alameda, CA 94501
Web: http://www.sybex.com

After the 90-day period, you can obtain replacement media of identical format by sending us the defective disk, proof of purchase, and a check or money order for $10, payable to SYBEX.

DISCLAIMER

SYBEX makes no warranty or representation, either expressed or implied, with respect to the Software or its contents, quality, performance, merchantability, or fitness for a particular purpose. In no event will SYBEX, its distributors, or dealers be liable to you or any other party for direct, indirect, special, incidental, consequential, or other damages arising out of the use of or inability to use the Software or its contents even if advised of the possibility of such damage. In the event that the Software includes an online update feature, SYBEX further disclaims any obligation to provide this feature for any specific duration other than the initial posting.

The exclusion of implied warranties is not permitted by some states. Therefore, the above exclusion may not apply to you. This warranty provides you with specific legal rights; there may be other rights that you may have that vary from state to state. The pricing of the book with the Software by SYBEX reflects the allocation of risk and limitations on liability contained in this agreement of Terms and Conditions.

SHAREWARE DISTRIBUTION

This Software may contain various programs that are distributed as shareware. Copyright laws apply to both shareware and ordinary commercial software, and the copyright Owner(s) retains all rights. If you try a shareware program and continue using it, you are expected to register it. Individual programs differ on details of trial periods, registration, and payment. Please observe the requirements stated in appropriate files.

COPY PROTECTION

The Software in whole or in part may or may not be copy-protected or encrypted. However, in all cases, reselling or redistributing these files without authorization is expressly forbidden except as specifically provided for by the Owner(s) therein.

To Maximilian and Isabella

Foreword

Adobe Photoshop has made an enormous impact on the way architects work. We can now experiment with color schemes with a click of the mouse and have complete control over the colors we use. We can combine computer-generated 3D models with actual site photos to see how a design will look when it's in place. When combined with AutoCAD, presentation material can be generated faster and with greater accuracy. Cut-away views of 3D plans can be rendered and colored in hours instead of in days.

But Photoshop is a complex program with a lot of depth. Until now, the unique methods that architects need to employ with Photoshop had to be learned through trial and error, or by gathering knowledge from disparate sources. Enter Scott Onstott's *Enhancing CAD Drawings with Photoshop*.

When I first heard about this project, I was very excited because it's the book I've been wanting in my own library for some time. And having worked with Scott, I have no worries about the quality and content; I know how Scott works, and he leaves no stone unturned. His writing is thorough yet easy to understand. Those qualities combined with his professional experience using Photoshop in an architectural setting make *Enhancing CAD Drawings with Photoshop* a killer book. I don't think anyone could have found a better combination of knowledge, experience, and writing skill for this project.

He starts out with a chapter for complete beginners, to help you understand how Photoshop works and how it differs from CAD software. Next, he delves into the all-important topic of color and all its ramifications. This chapter alone is worth the price of admission as it covers color calibration; understanding calibration can save your office hundreds of hours in wasted time. Next, Scott shows you the tools that let you fine-tune color, sharpness, and other effects. Chapter 4 covers one of my favorite topics, entourage, where you learn how to add life to a computer-generated 3D model. Later chapters discuss methods for rendering 2D images from CAD plans, such as floor plans and elevations, and get into the nitty gritty details of combining images from different sources. Scott presents some great information on alpha channels and layers—key tools when combining 3D and 2D images. Finally, Chapter 9 covers the all-important methods for getting consistently great hard-copy output.

If you are an architect looking to get the most out of Photoshop, look no further; it's all here in Scott's book. You could probably buy five or six other general Photoshop books and still not find the gems that are pressed between these pages. Great work, Scott!

Regards,
George Omura
Author, *Mastering AutoCAD 2005 and AutoCAD LT 2005*

Acknowledgments

First I'd like to thank my wife, Jenn, for her loving support and encouragement throughout this project.

I'd like to thank all those at Sybex who worked on this book for their help in publishing this, my first book as sole author. Although I've worked on numerous Sybex books in various supporting roles, and I self-publish many digital books and video courses, it is quite an honor for me to see this book in printed form.

Thanks to Willem Knibbe for believing in me and presenting the opportunity to write this book. Thanks go to Pete Gaughan for his unfailing support and excellent editorial feedback, making this a much better book. Thanks to Ryan Spruston for being a great technical editor and to Pat Coleman for very helpful copyediting. Lori Newman also deserves thanks for keeping all those working on this project on track.

Special thanks to Richard Trueman, Stephane Osmont, Christian Sterner, Chan Lee, Michael Sechman, and David Wright, who have all taught me a lot and offered their support over the years.

Contents at a Glance

Contents

Introduction

Adobe Photoshop is the program of choice for dealing with still images and photographs. Photoshop has been around since the dawn of time in computer years, so most people picking up this book have probably used Photoshop before to resize and print photos at least. If you are one of the few who has not used Photoshop before, never fear: no experience is assumed or required in this book.

You can use Photoshop for so much more than resizing and printing images; Photoshop is an indispensable tool for enhancing the level of your graphical communication.

This book is for architects, designers, engineers, industrial designers, builders, real estate developers, web designers, artists, students, and anyone who communicates with drawings in their work. Each chapter exposes you to concepts and techniques that you can integrate into your digital work flow in conjunction with other software such as AutoCAD and Autodesk VIZ. You will find step-by-step tutorials that reveal a wide variety of techniques built on many years of real-world experience. You'll learn how to enhance your graphical presentations and gain important marketing benefits for your practice.

How to Use This Book

The first three chapters teach essential concepts: the basics, working with color, and digital darkroom skills. Absorb the concepts in these chapters in a linear order before taking on the tutorials in the rest of the book. If you have been using Photoshop for years and feel that you are well aware of how it all works, feel free to jump ahead.

Chapters 3 through 9 are self-contained, so you can read them in the order you prefer. These chapters feature tutorials that take you step by step through many complex procedures. The goal of performing these steps on your own is to aim for an understanding that you can abstract into real-world situations.

Since every project presents different obstacles and opportunities, I urge you to focus on the concepts and techniques presented, rather than memorizing the specific steps used to achieve the desired result.

The best way to build skills is to perform the steps on your computer exactly as they are presented in the book during your first reading. After you achieve the desired result, start over and experiment using the same techniques on your own project (whether invented or real). Only after you have practiced can you abstract the techniques performed; then you really begin to own the knowledge.

What You'll Find

In Chapter 1, you'll get a quick introduction to the basic concepts and tools used in Photoshop. You'll learn about pixels, modes, bits, channels, layers, painting, adjusting, filtering, text, shapes, paths, transforming, and more.

Chapter 2 delves into the subtleties involved in working with color on a computer. You'll learn about modes, gamuts, color spaces, calibration, characterization, and device profiles. In addition you'll learn how to plan your work flow to ensure consistent color printing, and you'll learn professional tips for managing color.

Chapter 3 introduces you to the digital darkroom and teaches retouching skills that you can use to improve every photo you take. You'll learn how to work with digital film, adjust tonal range, balance color, strategically sharpen and blur, and more.

Chapter 4 shows you how to extract entourage objects from photographic backgrounds to be used in architectural illustrations, renderings, plans, or elevations. You'll clean up the entourage and assign alpha channels to preserve the object boundaries and learn how to use entourage in a 3D model using Autodesk VIZ.

Chapter 5 looks at how to enhance AutoCAD plan drawings with the power of Photoshop. You'll add tone, color, pattern, gradient, transparency, and shadow to line drawings that pop the presentation up to a new level.

Chapter 6 examines the traditional elevation line drawing and dresses it up with Photoshop's layer style effects, shadows, reflection and refraction, and entourage. Your clients will understand your colorized elevations much more readily after you master the techniques presented in this chapter.

In Chapter 7, you'll learn the art of compositing whereby you transfer 3D objects in Autodesk VIZ to image layers in Photoshop. You'll then use Photoshop to make the objects appear realistic with real-time layer style effects, adjustment layers, and clipping groups.

Chapter 8 opens the door to non–photo-realistic illustrations that you can make in Photoshop based on a 3D model from Autodesk VIZ. Illustrations stimulate the imagination and can have a range of appearances from pencil sketches to watercolors and painted looks.

Chapter 9 prepares you to show digital work to your clients by producing prints, e-mailing images, generating a web photo gallery, creating optimized web pages, and presenting slide shows. You'll finally learn strategies for protecting and cataloging your intellectual property with metadata, watermarks, and passwords.

What's on the Companion CD

The CD that accompanies this book includes all the files you'll need to use the tutorials and exercises throughout the chapters. The CD contents include native CAD and Photoshop files plus various types of image formats.

The companion CD also contains AutoLISP and MAXScript programs used in tutorials involving AutoCAD and Autodesk VIZ. Screen-captured computer videos are included that briefly describe techniques for each chapter.

The free Acrobat Reader and a trial version of Photoshop CS are also included on the companion CD.

How to Contact the Author

Sybex strives to keep you supplied with the latest tools and information you need for your work. Please check their website at www.sybex.com for additional content and updates that supplement this book. Enter the book's ISBN—4386—in the Search box (or type **enhancing cad**), and click Go to get to the book's update page.

If you have any questions or comments about this book, feel free to contact me by e-mail at Scott@ScottOnstott.com or by visiting my website—ScottOnstott.com—and using the web contact form there.

Chapter 1

The Basics

Color is represented by computers in unique ways. The relationship between bit depth and storage space is important. Photoshop's layer, paint, and filter tools have a wealth of features and options. You must be at least familiar with just a few of these basics before you can start to work creatively in Photoshop.

Fundamentals such as anti-aliasing, vectors, and additive versus subtractive color are also basic concepts that you need to know to help build a solid foundation for a broad understanding of digital imaging.

If you are familiar with Photoshop, you can go through this chapter quickly, skipping sections that present material you already know well. However, be sure to understand the basics before you dive into tutorials in the following chapters.

- ◆ Color vs. Number

- ◆ Understanding Modes, Bits, and Channels

- ◆ Using Layers

- ◆ Painting, Adjusting, and Filtering

- ◆ Text, Shapes, and Paths

- ◆ Sizing and Transforming

Color vs. Number

Computers store data in two basic ways: in colors and in numbers. Ultimately, computers reduce everything to ones and zeros, so you could say that, in the end, computer operating systems simply crunch numbers. However, at a higher level, what that data represents becomes important because the data relates to what you can do with it in a program.

When data fundamentally represents numbers, a program can easily apply math to manipulate the data set. All computer-aided design (CAD) programs are *vector based*, meaning they fundamentally manipulate numbers behind the scenes.

The term *vector* literally refers to a mathematical object that is defined at a point in space (implying a coordinate system), with a given magnitude (shown by the length of a line segment) and direction (indicated by an arrowhead at the end of the line). You might have dim memories of vectors from those math classes you once took in school. So what does this have to do with CAD anyway?

In a way, vectors have everything to do with CAD, because CAD is based on points, lines, angles, coordinate systems, and so on. The word *vector* was sort of chosen as a mascot for this type of euclidean geometry/Cartesian coordinate type of linear mathematical system. Let's take a quick look at how this works in AutoCAD.

1. Launch your CAD program. This book will use AutoCAD 2005, but many of the concepts are similar in other CAD programs.

2. Open `SimpleDrawing.dwg` from the CD. Figure 1.1 shows the CAD drawing.

3. Click one of the lines. The line highlights and three blue grips appear, indicating this entity is selected. You can select an entity like this because CAD is object based: AutoCAD actually "thinks" and stores information on a per–object basis.

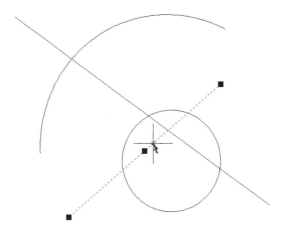

4. Click the Properties button on the main toolbar or type **Properties** on the Command line, and then press Return or Enter to open the Properties palette (see Figure 1.2). (You may have to hover your mouse over the vertical palette title bar to get it to fly out if it is set to Auto-hide on your system.) Under the Geometry heading in the Properties palette, notice numeric values in the Start X, Y, and Z and End X, Y, and Z fields. These numbers are the coordinates of the selected line's start and end points.

This line is represented by start and end points because AutoCAD uses a three-dimensional coordinate system to locate entities in space—an important feature of the program. AutoCAD doesn't "understand" anything about the space surrounding the objects. Instead, it only "knows" about the entities that are stored in its database; the spatial relationship you see between the objects is controlled by their numerical coordinate system.

5. Zoom in closer toward the center of the drawing; you can click the Zoom Realtime tool and click and drag up to do this. Observe how the line work does not get any thicker as you zoom in; the coordinates of this line do not change either. When you zoom in AutoCAD, you are using math to manipulate the display of the coordinate system. You could zoom in forever and still never get to an "end."

6. You can close your CAD program now, and there is no need to save the example drawing.

FIGURE 1.1
A simple drawing in
AutoCAD

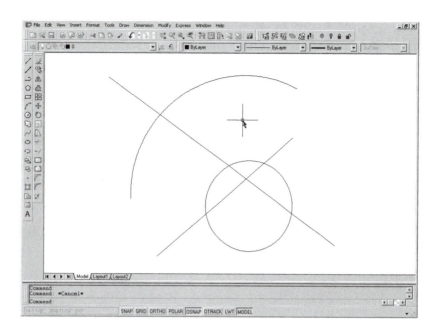

FIGURE 1.2
Clicking the Properties
button opens the Proper-
ties palette.

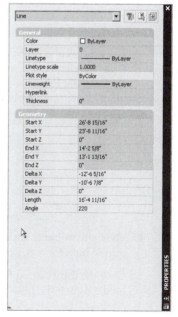

NOTE AutoCAD objects are independent of resolution.

On the other hand, data that represents color is more difficult to manipulate using math. In point of fact, colors are ultimately represented by numbers on a computer. However, the way color data is stored and manipulated is far less efficient than the way numerical data is stored and manipulated with math. Let's take a look at Photoshop to see how it fundamentally handles data.

1. Launch Photoshop.

2. Choose File ➢ New to open the New dialog box (see Figure 1.3). Click the Width and Height drop-down lists and change the measurement to pixels. Type **600** in the Width text box, and type **450** in the Height text box. Set the Resolution to 72 pixels/inch, and choose White from the Background Contents drop-down list. Click OK to create a new image document with these settings.

FIGURE 1.3
Creating a new Photoshop document

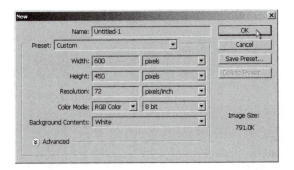

The process of creating a new document shows how Photoshop works; it stores data as *pixels* ("picture elements" that are tiny squares of color). You have to choose exactly how many pixels you want to work with right from the beginning. The *resolution* is the pixel density, or how many pixels appear per unit length.

3. Click and hold the Rectangle icon in the toolbox to display the hidden tools. Select the Line tool.

4. The Options bar is at the top of the interface (see Figure 1.4) and displays context-sensitive information for many of the tools in the toolbox.

Click the third button from the left, Fill pixels, to directly create pixels using the tools shown on the right. (The Line tool is selected.)

FIGURE 1.4
The Options bar when
the Line tool is selected

5. Before you draw a line, you need to select the relevant options on the Options bar:

   ◆ Set the width to one pixel by typing **1 px** in the Width text box if it is not already set to 1 pixel.

   ◆ Make sure the blending mode is set to Normal.

   ◆ Also leave the opacity at 100%.

   ◆ Finally, make sure the Anti-aliased check box is unchecked.

6. Draw a line by dragging and releasing the mouse in the left side of the document window.

7. Hold down the Shift key and draw more lines. Notice that while Shift is held, you can only draw lines that are horizontal, vertical, or on a 45-degree angle.

8. Toggle the Anti-aliased check box on and draw a few more random lines on the right side of the document. Use Shift to draw horizontal, vertical, and 45-degree lines also. Figure 1.5 shows aliased lines on the left side and anti-aliased lines on the right.

FIGURE 1.5
Aliased and anti-
aliased lines

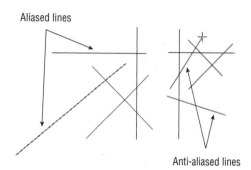

Aliased lines

Anti-aliased lines

9. Press Z or click the Zoom tool in the toolbox, and then zoom in to the left side of the document where you drew aliased lines, to 600% magnification. (The zoom amount is shown in the title bar of the document window, as shown in Figure 1.6.)

At this magnification, you can see that the lines are made of square pixels. Unlike AutoCAD, in Photoshop the closer you zoom in, the larger the line work becomes because the pixels get bigger. These "lines" are merely black pixels in a matrix of white pixels that form the overall image. Photoshop doesn't record these black lines as entities, but alters the appropriate pixel colors already stored in memory.

Also, notice how the horizontal and vertical lines look smooth: the pixels are in a regular grid that aligns with this horizontal/vertical orientation.

FIGURE 1.6
The relationship of pixels
to grid

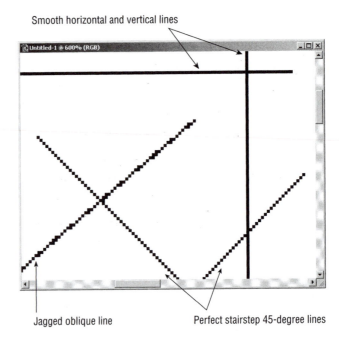

Smooth horizontal and vertical lines

Untitled-1 @ 600% (RGB)

Jagged oblique line

Perfect stairstep 45-degree lines

NOTE   The relationship that pixels have with their implied grid determines how jagged they appear.

The 45-degree line also has a clean look because it is made of a perfect stairstep of pixels. Only the oblique line seems jagged because it must be represented on this grid of pixels.

10. Hold down the spacebar and drag the mouse to the left in the document window to pan over to the anti-aliased area of the image (see Figure 1.7).

The horizontal and vertical lines are perfectly represented because they align with the grid of pixels. The 45-degree and oblique lines get an anti-aliasing treatment that blends the adjacent pixel colors to make the edge seem softer. Notice how the 45-degree anti-aliasing is symmetrical and that the oblique blending is a bit more complex.

11. Double click the Zoom tool in the toolbox to return to 100% magnification. Save this file as Linework.psd. This file is also provided on the CD for your convenience.

Let's compare a few items in Figures 1.6 and 1.7. First, the aliased oblique line in Figure 1.6 is unacceptable because it is clearly jagged. Oblique lines therefore benefit from anti-aliasing. The horizontal and vertical lines appear the same whether they are anti-aliased or not because they align with the grid of pixels in the image. Finally, the lines that are at a 45-degree angle actually look better in Figure 1.6 because they appear thinner than the anti-aliased lines in Figure 1.7.

FIGURE 1.7
Anti-aliased pixels

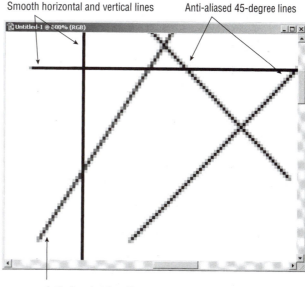

Smooth horizontal and vertical lines

Anti-aliased 45-degree lines

Anti-aliased oblique line

Anti-aliasing and Resolution

The scale of anti-aliasing is tied to resolution. Holding all other variables constant, increasing the number of pixels in an image makes the effect of anti-aliasing more subtle. Let's take a look at an example of this phenomenon.

1. Open the file Linework2.psd from the CD (see Figure 1.8). This file is similar to the Linework.psd image you have been working on except Linework2.psd has greater resolution.

FIGURE 1.8
Line work with greater resolution

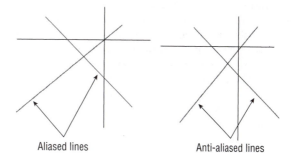

Aliased lines

Anti-aliased lines

2. Zoom out to 25%. To do this, choose the Zoom tool in the toolbox or type **Z** on the keyboard. Hold down the Alt key on the keyboard and click the center of the image until you reach a magnification of 25%. This sizes the image in the Linework2.psd window down to a similar size as the Linework.psd window.

3. With the Linework2.psd window selected, choose Image ➢ Image Size. There are 2000×1500 pixels in this image.

4. In the Image Size dialog box, uncheck Resample Image.

TIP   Only use Resample Image when you want to change the number of pixels in the image.

5. Change the height to 6.25 inches. The width and resolution are automatically calculated from this number. The resolution is 240 pixels/inch. Click OK to close the dialog box.

6. Select the Linework.psd window, and choose Image ➢ Image Size. This image has exactly the same document size, but its resolution is only 72 pixels/inch. Therefore, the pixels in Linework.psd appear more than three times bigger than the pixels in Linework2.psd.

    Notice how the lines in Linework2.psd appear thinner and less jagged than the lines in Linework.psd. You perceive the lines to be smoother when the pixels are smaller. The lines on the left side of Linework2.psd (shown earlier in Figure 1.8) appear smooth, even though they are aliased, because of the higher resolution.

7. Close both Linework.psd and Linework2.psd.

Raster Data Storage and Compression

Raster data is the color of pixels stored on a hard drive. Each pixel is given a color number, and these numbers are stored in a matrix of columns and rows, called a *raster*.

The amount of raster data stored can be large for high-resolution images. When you store more pixels, you need more disk space and memory. Data compression schemes are often used to cope with the demands placed on storage and memory systems. Compression algorithms look for patterns in the data (recognized by repetition or similarity) and can more efficiently represent patterns in a file as compared with the raw, uncompressed data. Furthermore, compression schemes fall into two categories: lossless and lossy. Lossless compression preserves 100% of the original data, whereas lossy compression is a trade-off between much smaller file sizes and degraded data.

Consequently, many file formats have arisen over time that deal with the compression issue in different ways. For example, the Windows bitmap (.bmp) format is uncompressed and therefore takes a large amount of memory and disk space. An example of lossless compression is the Lemple-Zif-Welch (LZW) method used in the Tagged Image File Format (.tif). The Joint Photographic Experts Group (.jpg) format is lossy; it was designed to greatly reduce the size of photographic images, but the trade-off is reduced quality. You will learn how to prepare and optimize compressed images for the Web in Chapter 9, "Showing Your Clients."

Understanding Modes, Bits, and Channels

To understand how images are stored on a computer, we will take a mental journey from the simplest beginnings toward greater complexity. This journey will give you a solid foundation for working with digital images in the future.

Bitmaps and Grayscale Images

The fundamental unit of information on a computer is called a bit. A bit can either be 1 or 0 and is the basis of binary computing. Figure 1.9 shows the simplest kind of computer image, a bitmap.

NOTE   There are 8 bits in a byte. Bytes are a common measure of information in a computer. Most files are measured in kilobytes (KB) or megabytes (MB). Hard drives currently store many gigabytes (GB), or billions of bytes of data.

You will open a bitmap and examine it in detail.

1. Open the file `StreetBitmap.psd` from the CD.

2. Zoom in to the image a few times until you clearly perceive the individual black and white pixels that make it up.

   The reason digital imaging works at all is that the human visual system undergoes a figure/ground shift in perception when presented with a pixel image of sufficient resolution. When you zoom in the image on the right of Figure 1.9, you might not understand what all the pixels represent. It is only when the pixels become small enough and dense enough, that your mind perceives the illusion of the continuous picture.

   Each of the pixels in Figure 1.9 is either black or white. This visual information is stored in the computer as either a 1 (white) or a 0 (black). In other words, each pixel is represented by a bit. As such, the bits in memory map directly to the visual image that we perceive, and thus the name *bitmap* is apt.

NOTE   Fax machines transmit bitmap images.

3. Zoom back out to 100% magnification (as shown in Figure 1.9). You can double-click the Zoom tool in the toolbox to do this quickly.

4. Open the file `StreetGrayscale.psd` from the CD. This image (shown in Figure 1.10) contains far more information than the bitmap in Figure 1.9.

FIGURE 1.9
Bitmap image: viewed at (left) 100% and (right) 500% magnification

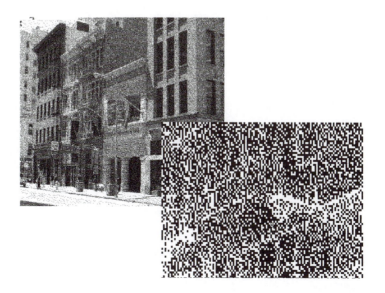

5. Zoom in to the image until you reach the maximum magnification of 1600% and can clearly perceive the individual grayscale pixels.

6. Click the Eyedropper tool in the toolbox. Select Point Sample from the Sample Size drop-down list on the Options bar.

7. Click a light pixel in the image to sample its color in the foreground color swatch in the toolbox (see Figure 1.11).

FIGURE 1.10
Grayscale image: viewed at (left) 100% and (right) 1600%

FIGURE 1.11
Sampling colors with the Eyedropper

Notice the RGB values for the sample.

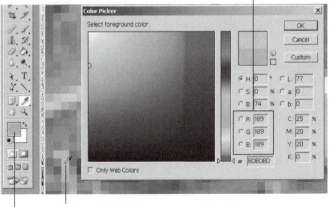

Click a pixel in the image to sample its color.
Click the foreground color swatch to open the Color Picker.

8. Click the foreground color swatch to open the Color Picker, and then observe the RGB values for the sample. The pixel sampled in Figure 1.11 has a numerical value of 189.

9. Select a darker pixel in the image while leaving the Color Picker dialog box open. Figure 1.12 shows a darker pixel selected whose value appears as 57 in the Color Picker.

10. In the Color Picker, drag the color selector in the color ramp along its left edge from the top, down to the bottom (see Figure 1.13). As you drag the selector, observe the color numbers changing. By dragging along the left edge, you select only grayscale values when the R, G, and B values are all equal.

   Figure 1.13 shows the relationship between grayscale value and number. At the extreme ends of the scale, white is represented by 255 and black by 0. All the shades of gray fall somewhere in between.

11. Close StreetBitmap.psd and StreetGrayscale.psd without saving.

Grayscale allows exactly 256 possibilities (including zero) for the value of each pixel. As you probably are aware, 256 is a special number that is a power of 2. More specifically 256 is 2 to the 8th power (2 multiplied by itself 8 times).

It is no coincidence that the number of shades of gray in a grayscale image is tied to powers of 2. The number 2 is important in computers because it is the basis for binary mathematics (ones and zeros). Table 1.1 lists the powers of 2.

FIGURE 1.12
Sampling a darker color yields a lower number.

Notice the corresponding color shown here.

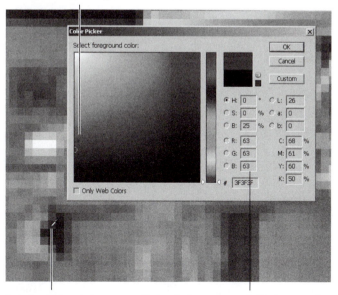

Sample a darker pixel.   Darker pixels are represented by lower numbers here.

FIGURE 1.13
Understanding
color values

Drag selector from here…

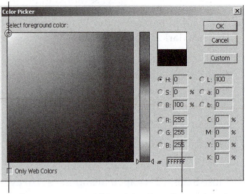

…to here…   …while noticing the color numbers here.

TABLE 1.1:   Powers of 2

POWER OF 2	NUMBER OF VALUES	BIT DEPTH	NOTES
2^1	2	1	Bitmap mode
2^2	4	2	
2^3	8	3	
2^4	16	4	
2^5	32	5	
2^6	64	6	
2^7	128	7	
2^8	256	8	Grayscale mode
2^9	512	9	
2^{10}	1024	10	
2^{11}	2048	11	
2^{12}	4096	12	
2^{16}	65,536	16	Limit of human perception of tonal differences
2^{24}	16,777,216	24	RGB (8 bits/channel)
2^{32}	4,294,967,296	32	CMYK (8 bits/channel)

At the top of the table, notice that 2 to the first power yields two possible values: 1 or 0. Bitmap images have pixels that fall into this category because there are only two possibilities for their pixels: black or white.

You can visualize grayscale images as a composite of 8 bitmaps laid on top of each other in imaginary transparent planes called *bit planes*. When 8-bit planes are overlaid, there are 256 possibilities for each pixel in the resulting image (2 to the eighth power). Grayscale images are known as 8-bit images because 8 is their *bit depth*, or number of overlaid bit planes.

NOTE Images with greater bit depth require more memory and storage space because they contain more information.

Color Images

Color is a complex subject that you will learn more about in Chapter 2, "Working with Color." For now, let's start by taking a look at how color images are stored in computers. Color is represented digitally by combining a few basic or elementary colors to obtain others. For example, in the RGB color mode, there are three component colors: red, green, and blue. A large range of color can be produced by combining the elementary or component colors in differing amounts. Color is stored in *channels* that correspond to each of the components. Let's see how this works with an example.

1. Open the file `StreetRGB.psd` from the CD.

2. Choose Edit ➤ Preferences ➤ Display & Cursors to open the Preferences dialog box, as shown in Figure 1.14.

3. Check Color Channels In Color in the Display group, and then click OK. This setting will help you initially visualize the way channels work.

4. Click the Channels palette, and then click the Red channel. The other channels are turned off, and you see only the selected channel in the document window, displayed as shades of red.

5. Zoom in to the full magnification of 1600% with the Zoom tool.

6. Using the Eyedropper tool, take a point sample of the red channel (see Figure 1.15). Notice that the color sample appears in gray in the foreground color swatch in the toolbox.

7. Click the foreground color swatch to open the Color Picker. Observe that the color sample you selected with the Eyedropper is a shade of gray.

8. Drag the Eyedropper around on the image, and verify that all the samples it takes are shades of gray, even though the image in the document window appears in shades of red.

FIGURE 1.14
The Preferences
dialog box

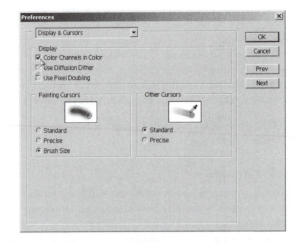

FIGURE 1.15
Sampling the Red
channel

9. Close the Color Picker and double-click the Zoom tool in the toolbox to return to 100% magnification.

10. Choose Edit ➤ Preferences ➤ Display & Cursors again to open the Preferences dialog box. Now that you have seen how the data in the channels is actually grayscale, you can uncheck Color Channels In Color in the Display group and click OK.

11. In the Channels palette, click the green channel. The image in the document window changes.

12. Click the blue channel. Once again the image's tonality changes as you are now viewing only the blue data that the digital camera's blue sensor captured.

13. Finally, click the RGB channel to turn on all three color channels. Now you see the composite color image in the document window.

What this procedure should teach you is that although color is stored in channels, each channel by itself has only tonal information (light/dark) and can be represented as a grayscale image. Only when the channel data is reproduced with colored light does the true color image emerge.

A traditional cathode ray tube (CRT) monitor has three electron guns inside—a red gun, a green gun, and a blue gun. Each gun is fed the corresponding grayscale channel data by Photoshop. When the colored light emerges on the screen, it combines to form the color image that you perceive.

Color Bit Depth

Traditionally, each channel in a color image is an 8-bit grayscale image. Therefore, an RGB image has a bit depth of 24, or 8 times 3 (see Table 1.1). If you do the math by raising 2 to the 24th power, you will get more than 16 million possibilities of color for each pixel in the image.

That sounds like a lot, and it is a lot because our human ability to perceive differences in tonality fails in the range of a few million possibilities per pixel. In other words, 24-bit images have more gradations of color than our eyes can perceive.

For a long time in the history of digital imaging, 8-bits/channel has been sufficient for all but the most discerning professionals. However, when you manipulate images you lose some of the data in the process (see Chapter 3, "Retouching Photos," for more on this subject). The differences in tonality post-manipulation often fall below our perceptual threshold—in other words, we can see problems with heavily manipulated images.

The solution some photographers are adopting is to shoot in 16 bits per channel. This is currently possible only on prosumer or high-end professional digital cameras. Photos with 16 bits per channel have 65,536 possibilities per pixel per channel (refer to Table 1.1), and in RGB color mode this equates to 48-bit images (16×3). The benefit to shooting in 16 bit is that you can heavily retouch photos without being able to perceive *banding* (imperfections) in the result.

WARNING   The downside to shooting in 16 bit/channel is the huge volume of data that your system then has to handle. Much larger images require expensive digital cameras with huge storage space available. In addition, your computer must have more than a gigabyte of memory, huge hard drives, and fast processors to reasonably manipulate the data sets.

You can check an image's bit depth by choosing Image ➤ Mode and seeing whether 8 Bits/Channel or 16 Bits/Channel is selected.

To arrive at the total bit depth stored in an image, see how many channels appear in the Channels palette and multiply this number by your bits per channel. For example, if your image has 4 channels (CMYK) and it stores 16 bits/channel, multiply 4 by 16 to arrive at a composite 64-bit image.

NOTE   Photoshop CS now offers greater ability to work with images containing 16 bits per channel.

Additive versus Subtractive Color

RGB color mode was designed with light in mind. It is a fact of physics that when you shine three beams of red, green, and blue light together, they combine into white light. RGB color is an additive color system because when these components are added together, they yield white. Therefore, RGB is an ideal way to represent color on a computer monitor, which shines light directly into your eyes.

When you look at printed matter, the color you see comes from the illumination in the space where you are. This light reflects off the surface of the page before entering your eyes. This situation is physically quite different compared with directly viewing colored light on a computer monitor.

For printed matter, the component colors are cyan, magenta, yellow, and black (abbreviated as CMYK). When cyan, magenta, and yellow are combined and viewed with reflected light, they should make black. These three components theoretically subtract all the hue from the light source, leaving only black (in what is called a subtractive color system).

In practice, no inks or dyes are perfect, and the combination of these primaries usually results in a muddy brown. Black is added as a fourth color to give a boost to the shadows, making the practical closer to ideal color rendition.

NOTE Some printer manufacturers have now moved to a seven-ink system for even better color rendition. These systems use cyan, light cyan, magenta, light magenta, yellow, light black (gray), and black as components. The printer driver converts the RGB components in your image to the seven-ink system automatically, and no adjustment is needed from Photoshop.

Selecting Pixels

In a vector program such as AutoCAD, selection is trivial because the data is stored as objects in the first place, and AutoCAD merely has to select one of the objects it already has in memory to operate on it.

Since Photoshop is not primarily based on objects but rather on pixels, selection is an important issue. Selecting pixels is an art you will become more proficient in the longer you use Photoshop. Unless you want to alter the entire data set, careful selection of pixels is the first step before manipulation becomes possible.

NOTE Photoshop also has vector-based objects that you can easily select, such as shape layers, paths, and text. These work more like entities do in AutoCAD.

Marquee, Lasso, and Magic Wand are three groups of tools you'll use the most to make selections. The Marquee tools offer simple shapes for selection such as squares, circles, rectangles, and ellipses. The Lasso tools let you draw selections freehand and can be curved, polygonal, and even magnetic (automatically adjusting the selection boundary to match features of the image). The Magic Wand is in a class by itself and allows you to select pixels based on the similarity of their color.

Saving and Loading Selections with Channels

After you spend a lot of time creating and refining a complex selection, it hurts to see it lost. You can always undo or use the history to retrace your steps up to a certain point, but what if you want to reselect something you were working on yesterday?

A sure way of keeping a record of your important selections is to save them as channels. Then, you'll always be able to go back and reselect by loading the selection from these extra channels of information that are stored with your image file.

The only downside to storing selections as channels is they increase file size because more bits have to be recorded. As long as the situation doesn't get out of hand because you are saving too many channels, your file will stay a reasonable size.

You will open a sample file and learn how to save and load selections with channels.

1. Open Cafe.psd from the companion CD.

2. Make a careful selection using any of the selection tools.

3. Choose Select ➤ Save Selection to open the Save Selection dialog box (see Figure 1.16). Type **MyFirstSelection** in the Name text box and click OK.

FIGURE 1.16
The Save Selection
dialog box

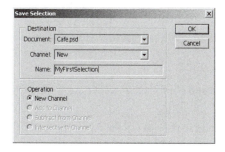

Your selection is saved as a channel.

TIP   It is possible to save and load selections into and from other open documents using the Save Selection dialog box. This is a powerful way to exchange data between documents.

4. Press Ctrl+D to deselect your important selection made in step 2.

5. Click the Channels palette, and you'll see a new channel at the bottom of the list. Click the MyFirstSelection channel to view it in the document window.

6. The channel displays in grayscale. If you want to load the stored selection from this channel, click the Load Channel As Selection button along the lower edge of the palette.

7. Click the RGB composite channel, and you will see the marching ants, indicating that your saved selection has been reloaded from its channel.

8. Close the file without saving.

Using Layers

Think of layers as invisible planes stacked on top of each other. The pixels you place on any one layer do not interfere with the others, so you can manipulate each layer independently. Layers are viewed from top to bottom, and their stacking order determines what is visible in the resulting composition. In addition, styles can be associated with layers that offer a wealth of creative possibilities.

Organizing Layers

In complex projects, you might well end up with dozens or even hundreds of layers. If it weren't for organizing techniques, you would spend most of your time trying to find the proper layer to work on.

Fortunately, you can organize your layers in several ways and keep them tidy and well identified for future use. It all starts by understanding the Background layer.

Every new file starts with a single Background layer. By definition, this layer must remain at the bottom of the stack, so its contents remain in the background of your composition. Let's take a look at an example.

1. Open the file Layers.psd from the CD (see Figure 1.17).

2. Click the Layers palette. The Background layer is at the bottom of the stack. Notice the padlock icon to the right of the name *Background*, meaning this layer is locked. Also, the controls at the top of the Layers palette are all grayed out for this layer.

WARNING You cannot change the blending mode, opacity, or fill percentage of the Background layer. These attributes let you see through the layer, and by definition, the Background is opaque and immobile at the bottom of the stack.

3. Now that you are aware of these limitations, let's exceed them. Hold down the Alt key and double-click the Background layer in the Layers palette. Its name automatically changes to Layer 0, and now it's just like any other layer.

NOTE You can make any layer the new Background layer by choosing Layer ➢ New ➢ Background From Layer. Having a Background layer is entirely optional.

4. Drag Layer 0 on top of Layer 1, as shown in Figure 1.18.

FIGURE 1.17
The Layers.psd file and its layers

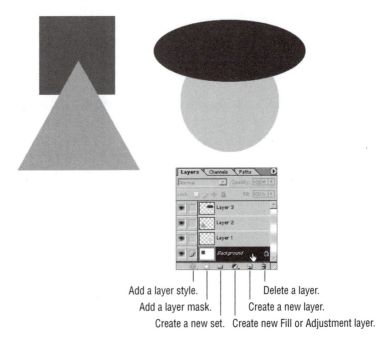

Add a layer style.
Add a layer mask.
Create a new set.
Delete a layer.
Create a new layer.
Create new Fill or Adjustment layer.

FIGURE 1.18
Dragging layers to
reorder them

This bar highlights as you drag.

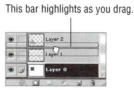

A bar appears between layers as you drag Layer 0 in the stack. Release the mouse when the bar appears between Layer 1 and Layer 2. Observe that the yellow circle disappeared from the document window.

The yellow circle on Layer 1 is now obscured by the white pixels on Layer 0, which is now higher in the stack. You can use layers to obscure each other like this.

5. Click Layer 0 in the stack to select it. Press W to choose the Magic Wand tool and uncheck Use All Layers on the Options bar. Now the magic wand affects only the current layer. Click anywhere on the white pixels to make a selection.

6. Press the Delete key to erase the white pixels, and then press Ctrl+D to deselect.

   The yellow circle is now visible (see Figure 1.19) because it is no longer obscured by white pixels that were originally part of the Background layer. Notice that the background in the document window looks like a pattern of gray and white squares. This checkerboard pattern is used in Photoshop to indicate transparency.

7. Drag Layer 0 onto the Create New Layer button along the bottom edge of the Layers palette to duplicate this layer. A new layer called Layer 0 Copy appears above Layer 0 in the stack (see Figure 1.20).

NOTE   If you click the New button, a new blank layer appears above the selected layer in the stack.

FIGURE 1.19
The layers image with a
transparent background

FIGURE 1.20
Duplicating a layer

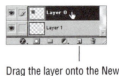

Drag the layer onto the New
button to duplicate.

8. Press V to choose the Move tool and drag the new red box on top of the yellow circle.

9. Select Layer 3 and drag it onto the Trash icon on the bottom edge of the Layers palette. The layer is deleted. You can also select a layer and click the Trash button, but then you are also asked to confirm (Yes or No) in a dialog box (an extra step).

10. Click the Create A New Set button, which is third from the left along the bottom edge of the Layers palette, whose icon looks like a folder. Layer sets are folders that appear in the layer stack simply for organizational purposes. Double-click Set 1 and type **Straight** as the new name.

11. Drag the layers whose shapes have straight edges into the Straight layer set. Just drag each one of these layers and drop it right on the Straight folder icon.

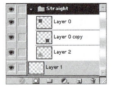

The layers are indented as they are added to the layer set, so you can see which layers belong to the Straight folder.

12. Click the arrow to the left of the Straight folder icon to minimize the set. Now the Layers palette is tidier.

TIP You can now nest layer sets within layer sets in Photoshop CS. This is wonderful for projects with hundreds of layers because you can now stay organized much more effectively.

13. Double-click Layer 1 to highlight its name. Type **Circle** and press Return or Enter to rename this layer. To make this layer more distinctive, you can add color. Right-click (or Control+click in Mac OS) the Circle layer and select Layer Properties from the context menu. Choose yellow as the color in the dialog box and click OK.

Now the Circle layer is identified by the yellow color in the Layers palette. Color coding makes it much easier to find this layer in a large list of layers.

14. Close the file without saving.

Layer Attributes

Each layer has simple attributes that include its visibility, blending mode, opacity and fill percentages, and three kinds of locks. These attributes are controlled from the top of the Layers palette. You will open another sample file and explore layer attributes.

1. Open the file Lagoon.psd from the CD (see Figure 1.21). This file contains two layers: Background and Clouds. The visibility of the Clouds layer is currently off.

FIGURE 1.21
Let's play around in
this lagoon.

2. Click the eye icon on the left side of the Clouds layer to make it visible.

3. Click the Clouds layer to make it current. The tools at the top of the Layers palette are enabled. These controls are grayed out for the Background layer.

4. Click the Blending Modes menu at the top of the Layers palette. You have many choices of blending modes.

TIP Choose Help ➢ Photoshop Help and look up Blending Modes in the Index to get more information about each mode.

5. Choose Lighten as the new blending mode. Blending modes affect the way the pixels in the layer are blended with the layers below it in the stack. In this case, Lighten ensures that the pixels on the Clouds layer only lighten the existing sky that is part of the background.

6. Click the small arrow to the right of the Opacity control to display a horizontal slider. Drag the indicator to the middle of the slider to 50%, and then press Enter or click anywhere outside the slider.

Notice that the clouds got lighter because the pixels on the layer are now more transparent.

7. Press 7 on the keyboard. This is a shortcut that changes the opacity of this layer to 70%. The clouds are a bit more opaque now.

TIP Press 0 to change the current layer's opacity to 100%.

Notice the Fill opacity control below the standard Opacity control. Fill works much like Opacity for pixels on the layer. However, Fill does not affect the opacity of layer *effects* (see "Layer Styles" later in this section).

8. Three lock options are available for each layer: Local Transparency, Lock Image, and Lock Position. Four buttons are to the right of the word *Lock* on the Layers palette. Click the Lock All button to display the padlock icon after the layer name.

◆ The Lock Transparency button locks the transparent pixels, meaning you won't be able to add pixels to the already transparent areas of this layer.

◆ The Lock Image button locks the image pixels (the opposite of transparent pixels), so you can't alter the existing pixels; however, you can still add more pixels in transparent areas of the layer.

◆ The Lock Position button locks the layer so it can't move.

◆ Finally, the Lock All button applies all three locks together.

9. Close the file without saving.

NOTE Layer locks are provided only as a convenience for you, so you don't inadvertently alter a layer you want to preserve. Be aware that layer locks don't provide security, as they can easily be unlocked at any time in the Layers palette.

Layer and Vector Masks

Masks are used to selectively block out portions of a layer. Unlike visibility (which controls whether an entire layer is on or off) or opacity (which affects an entire layer in a gradual or partial way), masks can be used to selectively hide or display portions of a layer without changing other areas.

There are two types of masks in Photoshop: layer and vector. Layer masks are made of pixels, and vector masks are made of paths. Both are separate entities that are linked to the layers they mask. Let's explore examples of each type of mask.

1. Open the file Masks.psd from the CD. This file contains two layers: Background and Gradient. Background is all white pixels, and Gradient is a linear color ramp.

2. Select the Gradient layer. Type L to choose the Lasso tool. Draw an irregular, organically shaped selection, like the one in Figure 1.22.

FIGURE 1.22
I've lassoed an irregular
selection.

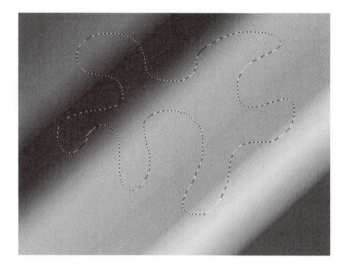

3. To create a layer mask from this selection, click the Add Layer Mask button. This button is second from the left across the bottom edge of the Layers palette. Clicking this button creates the layer mask and links it to the Gradient layer.

The Layer thumbnail on the left side of the Gradient layer contains the actual pixels of the layer. The Layer mask thumbnail on the right is a grayscale channel acting as a mask. The layer mask is linked to the layer by the small link icon between the two thumbnails.

4. Click the Channels palette. Notice that the Gradient layer's mask is stored as a grayscale channel.

5. Switch back to the Layers palette. Click the Layer thumbnail. A white border surrounds this thumbnail showing that it is active. Press B to choose the Brush tool. Paint a black brush stroke across the entire image, from left to right (see Figure 1.23).

The brush stroke appears in the Layer thumbnail, and parts of it are hidden in the document window by the mask. You can now clearly see how the mask is hiding what lies behind it on the Gradient layer.

6. Click the Layer mask thumbnail on the Gradient layer. A white border surrounds this thumbnail, indicating that it is now selected. Paint another black brush stroke across the image, just above your initial brush stroke made in the previous step, like the one in Figure 1.24.

FIGURE 1.23
The shape has a black
stroke across it.

FIGURE 1.24
Drawing in black on a
mask hides part of your
layer.

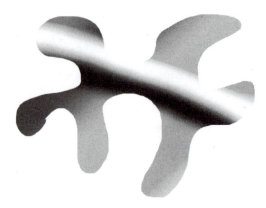

This time, the black brush stroke was painted on the mask. Black pixels on the mask hide the gradient layer.

7. Press X to exchange the foreground and background colors. Paint yet another brush stroke across the mask (see Figure 1.25).

This time you were painting with white on the layer mask. This exposes the Gradient layer. Most important, notice that by painting with a soft brush, you can get partial exposure through the mask, leaving a soft edge. This occurs because there are some gray pixels on the mask at the edges of the brush stroke, partially revealing the Gradient layer.

FIGURE 1.25
Drawing in white on
a mask reveals layer
content.

8. Press V to choose the Move tool. Drag the image a short distance, and notice that the mask and underlying layer move together because they are linked.

9. Unlink the mask from the layer by clicking the link icon in between the two thumbnails on the Gradient layer.

10. Using the Move tool again, drag the layer a short distance. You should see that this time, the layer mask moves relative to the Gradient layer because it is no longer linked with the layer it is masking.

11. Drag the Layer mask thumbnail to the Trash icon at the bottom of the Layers palette. A small dialog box appears asking, "Apply mask to layer before removing?" Choose Discard to erase the mask without changing the content of the layer.

    Now that the layer mask is gone, we will explore vector masks.

12. Choose the Ellipse tool (press Shift+U to cycle through the shape tools, or press U and click the Ellipse icon on the Options bar); then click the Paths button (second from the left) on the Options bar.

13. Draw a large horizontal ellipse path in the middle of the image.

14. Hold down the Ctrl key and click the Add Layer Mask button at the bottom of the Layers palette. Ctrl+clicking the button creates a vector mask instead of a pixel-based layer mask.

    The vector mask hides with a crisp edge, as shown in Figure 1.26, because the mask is controlled by the path, not by pixels as in a standard layer mask. This strength of a vector mask is also its limitation, as you cannot soften the crisp vector edge. Therefore, use vector masks if you want crispness of edge.

FIGURE 1.26
A vector mask has
sharp edges.

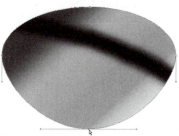

15. Press Shift+A to choose the Direct Selection tool. You use this tool to manipulate the shape of the path. You will learn more about paths in the Text, Shapes, and Paths section later in this chapter.

16. Click the bottom handle of the elliptical path, and drag it downward to create an eyeglass lens shape, as shown on the right in Figure 1.26. No painting is necessary when working with vector masks. Instead, you can directly alter the path to control the shape of the vector mask itself.

17. Close the file without saving.

Clipping Groups and Knockouts

Clipping groups and knockouts are advanced masking techniques involving multiple layers. Clipping groups allow you to use one layer as a mask for a group of layers. Knockouts allow you to use the content of one layer to "tunnel through" a stack of layers, knocking out pixels on each layer along the way. Let's take a look at how they work with a couple of example files.

1. Open the file ClippingGroup.psd from the CD. It has three layers: Sky, Get Away (rasterized text), and Lagoon (off).

2. Turn on the Lagoon layer. It obscures the layers below it in the Layers palette, so now you see only the Lagoon image. You will first create a clipping group so the Lagoon image shows through the Get Away text.

3. Hold down the Alt key and hover your mouse in between the Get Away and Lagoon layers. Your cursor changes into the Clipping Group icon.

4. While you see the Clipping Groups cursor between the layers, click the mouse. The bottom layer in the new clipping group acts as a mask which the other layer(s) in the clipping group show through.

The Get Away layer is underlined, indicating that it is acting as the base (which functions as a mask) of the clipping group. The Lagoon layer is indented and has a downward facing arrow to indicate its new status as member of the new clipping group. The Lagoon image now shows through the text, as shown in Figure 1.27.

TIP On your own, try to rearrange the clipping group so that the Sky layer shows through the text on a Lagoon background.

5. Close the file without saving.

6. Open the file Knockout.psd from the CD (see Figure 1.28). There are three layers: Background (Lagoon image), Brush Strokes, and Get Away (rasterized text). We will use the Get Away layer to knock out the Brush Strokes layer and show through to the Background layer underneath.

FIGURE 1.27
Creating a clipping group

FIGURE 1.28
The knockout image

7. Double-click the Get Away layer, just to the right of its name to open the Layer Style dialog box (see Figure 1.29). In the Advanced Blending group, change the Knockout drop-down list from None to Deep. Also in the Advanced Blending group of this dialog box, change Fill Opacity to 0%, and click OK.

FIGURE 1.29

The Layer Style dialog box

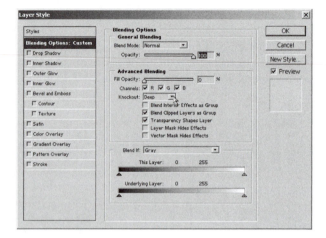

By turning the Fill opacity down to nothing, the pixels on the Get Away layer no longer obscure what they are on top of. Now the text knocks out the pixels down to the Background as shown in Figure 1.30.

Layer Styles

Each layer can be assigned a variety of creative blending effects that are stored in a style. Layer style blending effects include: drop shadow, inner shadow, outer glow, inner glow, bevel and emboss (with contour and texture subeffects), satin, color overlay, gradient overlay, pattern overlay, and stroke. All these blending effects are controlled through the Layer Style dialog box that is accessed via the Layers palette. Let's take a look at a few key blending effects now.

1. Create a new file by choosing File ➤ New, or press Ctrl+N.

2. In the New dialog box, select 640×480 from the Preset Sizes drop-down and click OK.

3. Click the Create A New Layer button on the bottom edge of the Layers palette.

WARNING You can't apply blending effects to the Background layer.

4. Press D to set the default colors in the foreground and background color swatches in the tool-box (black and white).

5. Press B to choose the brush tool. Paint a few soft black brush strokes on the image.

6. Click the Add A Layer Style button on the bottom edge of the Layers palette. A menu appears (see Figure 1.31) that contains all the blending effects. You will open the same dialog box no matter which blending effect you choose.

7. Choose Stroke from the menu to open the Layer Style dialog box (see Figure 1.32).

FIGURE 1.30
Creating a knockout

FIGURE 1.31
The layer style choices

FIGURE 1.32
The Layer Style
dialog box

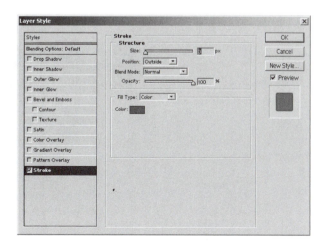

You navigate this dialog by clicking the blending effects in the table on the left. The dialog box is context-sensitive; currently Stroke is selected, so you see the Stroke controls on the right side.

8. Change Size to 1 px, and change Position to Inside.

9. Click Color Overlay on the left side of the Layer Style dialog box, and then click the color swatch on the right side to open the Color Picker. Choose a dark blue color and click OK to close the Color Picker.

10. Click the Bevel And Emboss effect on the left. In the Structure group on the right, change Depth to 100%, and change Size to 18 px.

11. Click the Drop Shadow effect on the left. Then, in the Structure group to the right, change Distance to 17 px, and change Size to 27 px.

12. Click OK to close the Layer Style dialog box. Each blending effect is accessible now through the additions made in the Layers palette. You can double-click any of the round *f* icons in the Layers palette to open the corresponding effect page of the Layer Style dialog box. Figure 1.33 shows the transformation the black brush strokes took after the application of a few blending effects. (Many are visible only in color.)

13. Close the file without saving.

TIP You can create an amazing variety of looks by applying blending effects. Try experimenting on your own with the various tools in the Layer Style dialog box.

FIGURE 1.33
Blending effects

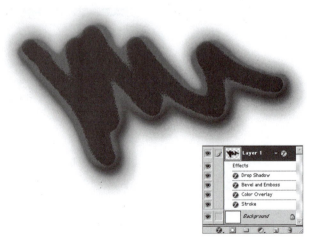

Painting, Adjusting, and Filtering

Painting, adjusting, and filtering are major classes of tools that you will be using in Photoshop. Using all three requires skill and lots of fine-tuning to achieve the results you want. As is often the case, "trial and error" is a time-tested method for achieving success. With that in mind, this section concludes with a discussion of Undo, Fade, and History: three tools that make the "error" part of this process less painful.

Using Brushes

You can use brushes for a lot more than painting in Photoshop. As you will see in Chapter 3, you often use brushes in the digital darkroom to edit images in many ways. Choosing a brush shape is the most important decision in determining the character of its stroke, but this is only the beginning. Brushes have numerous parameters that affect their stroke's appearance, including hardness, spacing, textures, dual brush tips, scattering, and many dynamic properties that occur in time.

You will create a new file to experiment with brushes.

1. Create a new file by choosing File ➢ New, or press Ctrl+N.

2. In the New dialog box, select 640×480 from the Preset Sizes drop-down list, and click OK.

3. Type **B** to choose the Brush tool. Click the popup on the Options bar to open the Brush palette, or Brush Preset picker (see Figure 1.34) in which you can see a list of preset brushes.

TIP You can enlarge the Brush pop-up palette by dragging its resize handle in the lower-right corner.

Scroll through the list to see which presets are available in the default brush library. The list starts with a series of hard, round brushes and continues with a number of soft, round brushes. Near the bottom of the list are many brushes with custom tips and advanced features.

FIGURE 1.34

The Brush pop-up palette, or Brush Preset picker

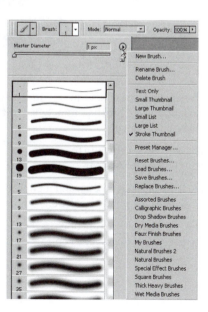

4. Click the round button with the right-facing arrow to open the Brush pop-up palette menu (shown on the right side of Figure 1.34). This menu includes a listing of brush libraries in the group at the bottom. Choose Calligraphic Brushes from this menu.

5. A small dialog box will appear, asking "Replace current brushes with the brushes from Calligraphic Brushes.abr?" Click OK.

NOTE   The .abr file type is used for brush libraries in Photoshop. These files are stored in the C:\Program Files\Adobe\Photoshop CS\Presets\Brushes folder and its subfolders. You can share your libraries with others by putting custom .abr files in this folder and restarting Photoshop.

Now the preset brushes are different in the Brush pop-up palette.

6. Double-click the 20-pixel flat calligraphic brush to close the Brush pop-up palette. Press D and paint some black strokes in the document window.

7. Repeatedly press the right square bracket key to enlarge the brush. Paint another stroke.

8. Hold down the Shift key and press the left square bracket key three times to soften the brush. Paint yet another stroke.

The square bracket keys in conjunction with the Shift key are convenient shortcuts to the two most important brush parameters. For greater control and far more options, we will explore the Brushes palette.

The Brushes palette is in the palette well in the default workspace. The palette well is on the far right of the Options bar.

9. Click the Brushes palette, and it pops up within the well. Drag this palette out of the well, and it becomes the floating palette, as shown in Figure 1.35.

The Brushes palette functions in a way similar to the Layer Style dialog box. The categories on the left side of the palette control which parameters are accessible on the right.

FIGURE 1.35
The Brushes palette

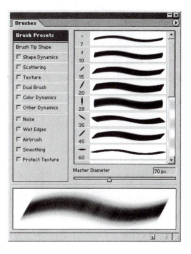

10. Click Brush Tip Shape to display the corresponding parameters on the right of the palette. Change Angle to 120 degrees, Hardness to 50% and Spacing to 300%. Paint a stroke in the document window.

11. Click the Shape Dynamics category. Change Jitter to 30% and Angle Jitter to 5%. Paint another stroke in the document window.

You can combine an almost limitless number of parameters in the Brushes palette to create a variety of strokes. Spend some time exploring all the various parameters.

12. Click the round button with the right-facing arrow icon in the top-right corner of the Brushes palette to open the menu, and choose Reset Brushes.

13. A small dialog box will appear, asking "Replace current brushes with the default brushes?" Click OK, and the brushes you saw in step 3 return to the Brushes pop-up and palette.

NOTE   The default brushes are part of Photoshop itself and cannot be altered by overwriting an .abr file.

14. Drag the Brushes palette back into the palette well to save room in your workspace. Close the current document; it was just for your experimentation.

Making Adjustments

Adjustments allow you to alter color and tonality within a selection or an entire image. The many specialized adjustment tools available include Levels, Curves, Color Balance, Brightness/Contrast, Hue/Saturation, and many others.

You will open a sample file and make some adjustments.

1. Open the file Adjustments.psd from the CD.

2. Click the Channels palette and select the Alpha 1 channel. This grayscale channel contains a saved selection.

3. Click the Load Channel As Selection button at the bottom of the Channels palette to select the red brick portion of the building on the street corner.

4. Select the RGB channel to toggle the Red, Green, and Blue channels on and at the same time toggle the Alpha 1 channel off.

5. Press Ctrl+H to hide the selection. The marching ants disappear. Be aware that the hidden selection is still active, and you can toggle the marching ants back on at any time by pressing Ctrl+H again.

6. Choose Image ➢ Adjustments ➢ Levels, or press Ctrl+L to open the Levels dialog box, which appears (see Figure 1.36) showing a histogram of the image.

NOTE A *histogram* is a graph of the pixel intensities in an image, reading left to right from shadows through midtones to highlights.

7. Drag the midtone arrow to the right a short distance until you see the Input Levels midtone text box read 0.70. Click OK to close the dialog box.

   By dragging the midtone arrow to the right, you darken the selection because more of the histogram data ends up being on the shadow side. Notice how the red bricks deepen in tone.

8. Choose Image ➢ Adjustments ➢ Hue/Saturation (or press Ctrl+U). Drag the Hue slider to +75 and Saturation to –60. The bricks are adjusted to a less saturated dark green color. Click OK.

FIGURE 1.36
The Levels dialog box

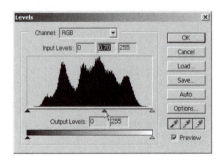

9. Choose Image ➤ Adjustments ➤ Color Balance (or press Ctrl+B). Drag the Yellow/Blue slider a short distance in the Blue direction to shift the color balance until the corresponding Color Levels text box reads +70. Click OK.

10. Choose Image ➤ Adjustments ➤ Brightness/Contrast. Drag the Brightness slider to +30 and Contrast to –20 and click OK.

Each of the adjustments offers its own specialized set of features that often overlaps with other adjustment tools. For example, you can adjust color using Hue/Saturation or Color Balance, each in different ways. Take some time to experiment with some of the other adjustments, and refer to Chapter 3 to see how you can use adjustments in the photo retouching process.

Using Adjustment and Fill Layers

Adjustment layers are different from adjustments in one important respect: they remain editable as layers, so you can try out adjustments without having to commit to them. You can turn off Adjustment layers or throw them away later if you deem them inappropriate. You can also modify the parameters of the Adjustment layer if you change your mind later on.

NOTE Adjustment layers affect all the layers below them in the Layers palette. You control which pixels an Adjustment layer affects by using a mask.

1. Choose File ➤ Revert to start over with the `Adjustments.psd` file.

2. Click the Create New Fill Or Adjustment Layer button at the bottom of the Layers palette.

3. Choose Hue/Saturation from the menu that appears. Drag the Hue slider left to –100, giving the entire image a violet cast. Click OK.

   The Adjustment layer appears above the current layer in the Layers palette. You can access the Hue/Saturation dialog box by double-clicking the adjustment thumbnail shown in Figure 1.37. Notice that the mask shown is completely white, meaning it is not hiding anything.

4. Click the Channels palette. Note that our new Adjustment's layer's mask appears as an extra channel. Select the Alpha 1 channel, and click the Load Channel As Selection button at the bottom of the Channels palette.

5. Click the RGB channel to return to the color image. Return to the Layers palette.

FIGURE 1.37
An Adjustment layer

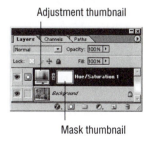

Adjustment thumbnail

Mask thumbnail

6. Press Ctrl+H to hide the selection, and then add another Hue/Saturation Adjustment layer, as you did in steps 2 and 3.

7. Drag the Saturation slider to –100 and click OK. The bricks turn gray as they desaturate.

8. To reverse the effect of the last Adjustment layer, you will invert its mask. Press Ctrl+I to invert the mask, which is currently selected in the Layers palette. Now the desaturation applies to everything but the bricks.

   The image now appears in grayscale except for the violet bricks. To show how Adjustment layers always remain editable, you will change the color of the bricks again.

9. Double-click the adjustment thumbnail of the Hue/Saturation 1 layer to access its parameters in the Hue/Saturation dialog box. Drag the Hue slider to +25 to make yellow bricks.

Fill layers are like Adjustment layers in the way they remain editable in the Layers palette. Fill layers also have mask thumbnails that allow you to control which areas of the image are affected. You will experiment with Fill layers.

1. Select the top layer in the stack. Then click the Create New Fill Or Adjustment layer button at the bottom of the Layers palette.

2. Choose Solid Color from the menu that appears.

3. Select a medium red color from the Color Picker. This color fills the screen.

4. Apply a Gradient Fill layer. Click the Gradient drop-down list, and select the second gradient thumbnail (Foreground To Transparent) and click OK.

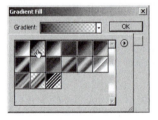

5. Apply a Pattern Fill layer. Click the Pattern Picker arrow, and choose any pattern. Click OK.

6. Change the blending mode of the Pattern Fill 1 layer to Overlay to see through it. Note that all the Fill layers obscure the layers below; you used the Overlay blending mode to see through one of the Fill layers.

7. Close the document without saving after you experiment with Fill layers.

NOTE   Unlike Adjustment layers, Fill layers do not affect the layers below them in the Layers palette. Fill layers are straightforward in how they simply fill the image with a color, gradient, or pattern.

Applying Filters

Filters are algorithms that affect pixels. You can test and apply a wide range of filters using the Filter Gallery, new in Photoshop CS. The Filter Gallery brings many of the filters together into a single dialog box interface where you can create a stack of effect layers and see their cumulative effects in a preview window. Let's see how it works.

You will open a sample file to try out the Filter Gallery.

1. Open the file `Street.psd` from the CD.

2. Choose Filter ➢ Filter Gallery to open the Filter Gallery.

3. Expand the Artistic folder, and click the Poster Edges filter thumbnail, as shown in Figure 1.38.

4. In the effect control area, change Edge Thickness to 1, Edge Intensity to 3, and Posterization to 3. Each filter will have its own parameters that control the algorithm.

TIP The best way to interact with filters is to experiment with the effects by dragging the parameter sliders back and forth and observing the changes in the preview area.

5. Click the New Effect Layer button. Click the Artistic folder in the thumbnail area to close it, and then click the Brush Strokes folder to open that category of filters.

6. Click the Angled Strokes thumbnail. The second filter's parameters appear in the control area. Change Direction Balance to 75, Stroke Length to 10, and Sharpness to 8.

Notice that the second effect appears above the first in the effect layer stack. The effect layer stack is built from the ground up, and each layer has a cumulative effect that you can see in the preview area.

FIGURE 1.38
The Filter Gallery

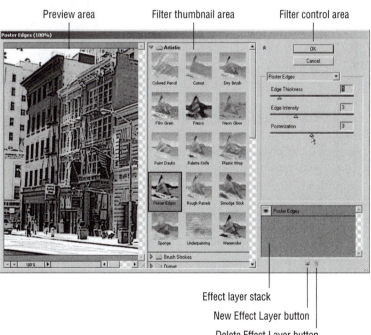

7. Click the New Effect Layer button again. Click the Texture folder to expand its contents in the filter thumbnail area.

8. Click the Texturizer filter thumbnail to apply it as your third effect layer. Change the Texture to Canvas (if it's not already), Scaling to 50, Relief to 6, and Light to Top Right.

9. When you are satisfied with the overall effect in the preview area, click OK to close the dialog box and apply the changes you have made to the document. Figure 1.39 shows the result of the filters on three effect layers you applied to this image. Leave this file open.

FIGURE 1.39
A filtered image

NOTE   You can edit the parameters on any effect layer and experiment with many filters before apply-ing the cumulative changes to the image. The order in which effect layers are applied is significant.

Reversing Changes: Undo, Fade, and History

As you have seen with painting, adjusting, and filtering commands, it usually takes a great deal of experimentation to create a composition from your mind's eye. Fortunately, several tools make it easy to play around without worrying too much about the consequences.

Undo is an obvious lifesaver. If you make a mistake, just choose Edit ➤ Undo or press Ctrl+Z to undo it. However, Undo isn't as helpful as it might sound. Pressing Ctrl+Z remembers only one level of history. Pressing Ctrl+Z again redoes your undo, leaving you back where you started.

If you press Alt+Ctrl+Z, you can move backward through Photoshop's history, one step at a time. On the other side of the coin, press Shift+Ctrl+Z to progress forward through the history one step at a time.

Better yet, use the History palette to see a listing of a great number of steps you have taken, called *states*. To change the length of your history, press Ctrl+K to open the Preferences dialog box. If you increase the number of History states (default is 20), more steps are recorded in your History palette, and you'll have more time to catch a mistake before it's too late. Figure 1.40 shows the History palette.

FIGURE 1.40
The History palette

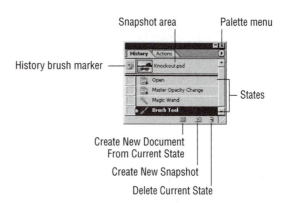

WARNING   Increasing the number of History states increases the amount of memory needed to remember them. If you use too many, Photoshop will run out of RAM.

Relying on history isn't always the cure for your forgetfulness. For example, you are using the Brush tool. You are happily painting and clicking away when you pan over and realize you painted over something in the image you meant to protect. You go to the History palette and start rolling back 20 states until you realize that you are too late; you must have painted over that important feature 40 states ago. (That's before recorded history in Photoshop-time.)

NOTE   History evaporates when you close a document because it exists only in the computer's memory and not on its hard disk.

If you are one to learn from mistakes, you might be proactive and protect important moments in your document's history by intentionally saving *snapshots*. There are three buttons on the bottom of the History palette: Create New Document From Current State, Create New Snapshot, and Delete The Current State. When you create a new snapshot, it is saved as a thumbnail at the top of the History palette, and the state is permanently saved as part of the file.

WARNING   Snapshots increase file size, so be selective when saving them.

Undo, history, and snapshots can do a lot to prevent you from losing hours of work whenever you discover mistakes. Fade is another timesaver, because it works like a partial Undo. If you like an effect but think it is too much of a good thing, Fade can help tone it down more to your liking. Let's fade the Filter Gallery effects you made in the last section.

   1. Choose Edit ➢ Fade Filter Gallery.

WARNING   Fade only works immediately after you apply a filter or adjustment. If Fade isn't available on the Edit menu, try going back in the history and then reapply the Filter Gallery before choosing Fade.

   2. Drag the Opacity slider to 60% in the Fade dialog box. The Filter Gallery effects are toned down. Click OK.

3. Choose Image ➢ Adjustments ➢ Desaturate to remove all hue from the image.

4. Choose Edit ➢ Fade Desaturate.

5. In the Fade dialog box, change the Mode pop-up to Color. Drag the Opacity slider to 50% and click OK.

   You are fading the removal of color back to 50%, so the image is half-desaturated. Fade gives you the power to partially undo filters and adjustments.

6. Close the file without saving.

Text, Shapes, and Paths

Text, shapes, and paths are related because they are all based on mathematical objects. Being math based, these objects have crisp, clean edges that are ultimately anti-aliased as Photoshop turns them into the pixels of an image. Working with shapes and paths is a lot like working in a drawing program because each object has handles and anchor points that can be altered to control their forms.

Creating and Editing Text

Let's first take a look at text and how to create it and modify it in Photoshop.

1. Create a new file by pressing Ctrl+N to open the New dialog box.

2. Select 640×480 from the Preset Sizes pop-up and click OK.

3. Press T to choose the Horizontal Type tool, or select it from the toolbox. All the controls you need to work with text appear on the Options bar as shown in Figure 1.41.

4. It is best to set all the options before you start typing. Start by selecting the Times New Roman font from the first pop-up on the Options bar.

5. The second pop-up on the Options bar may show a few options that are defined by the font you have chosen. Not all fonts offer options in this pop-up. In the case of Times New Roman, the choices are Roman, Italic, Bold, and Bold Italic. Select Italic.

6. Type **55 pt** on the Options bar to set the font size.

7. The last pop-up has a list of anti-aliasing options. Select Smooth.

8. Click the middle justification button to center the text.

FIGURE 1.41

Text tools on the Options bar

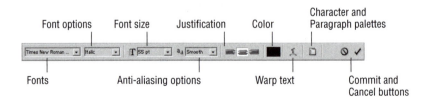

Font options   Font size   Justification   Color   Character and Paragraph palettes

Fonts   Anti-aliasing options   Warp text   Commit and Cancel buttons

9. Change the color swatch to black if necessary. This color will initially be the same as your foreground color, but after you make your first text object, the text color swatch will maintain the same color you used the last time you made a text object.

10. Click a point in the middle of the document window. Type the phrase **The quick brown fox**, press Return or Enter, and then type **jumped over the lazy dog**. Multiple lines of text are handled within the same text object.

11. Click the Commit button on the Options bar to complete the command. Notice how a new text layer automatically appears in the Layers palette.

TIP You use the options on the Character and Paragraph palettes to control the spacing in between letters, words, lines, and paragraphs, as well as control many advanced options. Warp text is used to bend text in a variety of ways.

WARNING Photoshop is not a good program to lay out lots of text. You are better off using QuarkXPress, Adobe InDesign, or another page layout program for this purpose.

Editing text is easy and intuitive. You can change many options on a character-by-character basis simply by selecting the character or words you want to change and then applying appropriate settings from the Options bar:

12. Still using the Type tool, drag your cursor over the word *jumped* to highlight it.

13. Change the color to red by clicking the color swatch on the Options bar. Choose Bold Italic from the Font options pop-up. Finally, click the Commit button.

The quick brown fox
jumped over the lazy dog.

NOTE Notice how the text color swatch displays a question mark after the last step was performed. The question mark appears when there is more than one color per text layer.

14. Right-click the text layer name in the Layers palette, and choose Rasterize Layer. Notice how the thumbnail changes from the T icon to a standard layer thumbnail. The text converts from a mathematical description to a pixel-based one. Notice how the thumbnail changes from the T icon to a standard layer thumbnail.

WARNING When text is rasterized, you can no longer edit it using the Type tools. Rasterize text only when sending your artwork to someone who may not have the fonts you used.

15. Press Ctrl+Z to undo step 14 and restore editability to the text object.

Once again, if you're going to continue working through the following sections, you can leave this file open for now.

Creating and Editing Shapes and Paths

You use shapes to create simple geometrical forms such as those you might see in Adobe Illustrator. Shapes have three modes: shape layers, paths, and fill pixels.

Shape layers are like having a solid color Fill layer but with a vector mask containing the shape's path. Shapes can also be created in Paths mode, where only a working path is generated. This path can later be combined with other path objects, stroked, or filled. Finally, Fill Pixels mode is a way to use shapes to make pixels on the current layer without any fuss.

Resuming from where I left off in the preceding section, follow these steps:

1. Click the foreground color swatch in the toolbox, and choose a medium blue using the Color Picker. Click OK.

2. Press U, and click the Rectangle tool on the Options bar.

3. Select the Shape Layers button on the left side of the Options bar.

4. Drag out a rectangle surrounding the word *fox*. Notice that a new layer is created in the Layers palette called Shape 1.

5. Drag the Shape 1 layer below the Text layer. Now the blue rectangle appears below the text in the document window.

6. Press A to select the Path Selection tool (black arrow in the toolbox). Drag a window around the blue rectangle, and drag it under the word *dog*. You move the entire path with this tool.

   You use the Direct Selection tool to change the form of a shape object by moving individual anchor points:

7. Press Shift+A to select the Direct Selection tool (white arrow in the toolbox).

8. Drag a window around the left two anchor points of the blue rectangle to select them (see Figure 1.42).

FIGURE 1.42
Selecting with the Direct Selection tool

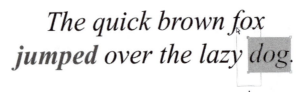

The quick brown *fox* jumped over the lazy *dog*.

Drag a window surrounding the left two anchor points.

9. Hold down the Shift key to constrain motion horizontally and vertically, and drag one of the rectangle's left handles toward the left so the rectangle underlays the words *lazy dog*.

10. Press U and choose the Rounded Rectangle tool. Set Radius to 20 px on the Options bar.

11. Click the Paths Mode button, which is the middle of three buttons on the left of the Options bar. The color swatch on the Options bar disappears because it not relevant to creating paths.

12. Drag a rounded rectangle around the word *quick*. As a path, this shape is not filled with color.

13. Click the Paths palette. You should see two paths listed here: Work Path, and Shape 1 Vector Mask. The rounded rectangle you just created is the Work Path. The blue rectangle you made earlier is the Shape 1 layer's vector mask.

14. Manually create a new layer before you stroke or fill this path. Click the Layers palette, and click the Create A New Layer button along the palette's bottom edge to create Layer 1. Double-click to rename Layer 1 to Stroked Path.

15. Click the Paths palette and notice Work Path is the only path listed. You will see only vector mask paths in the Paths palette while the corresponding layer is current.

16. Click the foreground color swatch in the toolbox, and choose a green color in the Color Picker. Click OK.

17. Press B to choose the Brush tool. Click the Preset Brushes pop-up, and select the 5-pixel round hard brush.

18. Back in the Paths palette, click the second button from the left, along the palette's lower edge. This button is Stroke Path With Brush. A green stroke appears around the Work Path, as shown in Figure 1.43.

FIGURE 1.43
Stroking a work path
around the word *quick*

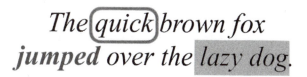

19. Change the foreground color swatch to bright yellow.

20. Choose the Ellipse tool (press U and click the Ellipse icon on the Options bar, or cycle through Shift+U). Click the third and final mode button on the Options bar, which is Fill Pixels.

21. Create a new layer to accept the pixels you will be creating in the next step. Rename this layer Filled Pixels.

22. Drag an ellipse under the word *over*. These pixels are put directly on the layer.

You have now created shapes using all three modes. Each mode has its merits and potential liabilities:

Shape layers are the best for displaying colored forms that need to maintain editability as a layer with a vector mask.

Paths mode offers the most options but is the most difficult to use.

Shapes made in Fill Pixels mode are the easiest to create, but they lose their vector editability because they are created directly as pixels.

If you have something more elaborate in mind than just a simple geometric shape, you can draw from libraries of custom shapes or create your own. You will work with custom shapes now.

1. Press D to set the default colors.

2. Press U, and click the Custom Shape tool on the Options bar.

3. Click the Custom Shape pop-up and select the Fleur-De-Lis icon.

4. Click Shape Layer Mode and drag out the custom shape in the document window. Hold down the Shift key before you release the mouse button to maintain the custom shape's aspect ratio.

5. Notice that the shape's edge appears highlighted because the vector mask is selected. Rename its layer Fleur-De-Lis. Click the vector mask's thumbnail to deselect it. The shape appears crisp and clean in the document window.

6. Photoshop comes with a large number of custom shapes. These are arranged in libraries according to subject matter. You can access the library menu by clicking the round arrow button in the Shape pop-up (see Figure 1.44).

7. Select Objects Library from the custom shape pop-up menu. Click OK when the small dialog box appears asking you to confirm replacing the library.

8. Double-click the "left foot" custom shape icon in the Shape pop-up.

9. Hold down Shift and drag out a left foot custom shape in the document window. Rename its layer Foot, and click its vector mask thumbnail to deselect it.

10. Close the file without saving. (I've provided a Shapes.psd file on the CD for you to compare.)

TIP Explore all the custom shape libraries on your own.

FIGURE 1.44
Accessing the custom
shape pop-up menu

Click here to open the menu

You can create your own custom shapes and even save them in your own libraries for future use. You can share shape libraries with other people because they are stored as files by Photoshop. Refer to Chapter 5, "Presenting Plans," in which you will create a graphical scale bar and save it in your own custom shape library.

Sizing and Transforming

Images can be stretched and shrunk, rotated and resized, and otherwise transformed to fit your needs. All these transformations are mathematical manipulations of the pixels in your image. As such, extreme manipulations tend to alter the original data so much that image quality and believability can be lost. On the other hand, more conservative changes can help improve an image while maintaining its "truth" as a representation of reality.

Setting Image Size, Resolution, and Document Size

Image size, resolution, and document size form a trinity of factors that are involved in a relationship. Changes to any of these three factors affect the others. You manage this relationship from the Image Size dialog box.

You will open a sample file to explore the Image Size command.

1. Open the file Lunch.psd from the CD.

2. Choose Image ➢ Image Size to open the Image Size dialog box.

3. To begin with, make sure the Resample Image checkbox is unchecked. While this setting is off, the relationship mentioned earlier is made simpler.

4. Note that the Document Size is currently more than 11 by 8 inches while the resolution is 72 pixels per inch. Change the resolution to 200. The width and height automatically adjust to 4 by 3 inches.

NOTE Traditionally screen resolution is either 72 or 96 pixels per inch (ppi). Most web design work is done at 72 ppi.

5. Change Width from 4 inches to 8. As you do this, the other two parameters (Height and Resolution), automatically change, so the image now measures 8 by 6 inches with a resolution of 100 pixels per inch.

NOTE Resolution and document size are inversely proportional; you trade one for the other.

6. Place a check in the Resample Image check box. This enables the 2-pixel dimension parameters (see Figure 1.45).

7. Change Width in the Pixel Dimensions group to 1000. As you do this, notice that the document size has increased (10 by 7.5 inches) while the resolution remains constant. Also note that the file size has increased because more pixels must now be stored.

8. Click the Cancel button in the Image Size dialog box to discard the changes you made while experimenting.

FIGURE 1.45
The Image Size
dialog box

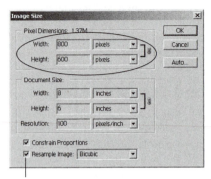

This check box enables the Pixel Dimensions boxes.

WARNING Resampling an image to much larger pixel dimensions does not increase the quality of the image. The extra pixels are merely resampled and interpolated from the existing pixels. If you really want a much larger, higher-quality image, you must start with an image of higher resolution. If you are using a digital camera, for example, you must use a camera with more megapixels.

When you start with more pixels in an image (by using a 5-megapixel camera, for example), you can make larger prints of a high quality. Less-expensive digital cameras (2 megapixels, for example) cannot produce high-quality prints of the same size because less information is captured from the real world.

TIP A rule for reasonable resolution is not to print images at less than 200 pixels per inch; 72 pixels per inch is sufficient for display on a computer monitor.

Straightening Images

You can transform images that were captured at some angle to the horizon or photos that were scanned at some oblique angle in several ways. We will take a look at straightening issues in this section. The first two methods apply when you want to straighten photos that were taken with a tilted camera.

You will straighten the sample file you have been working with.

1. Continuing with the Lunch.psd file, notice that it could benefit from straightening.

2. Expand the document window by dragging its corner, giving the image more space within its own window. You will need extra room in the next step.

3. Press Ctrl+A to select all. Then press Ctrl+T to start the Transform command. Handles appear along the image border.

4. Position your mouse outside the handles but still inside the document windows, as shown in Figure 1.46.

5. Drag your mouse in a clockwise fashion to rotate the selection in that direction. Manually rotating is easy to do, but is not as accurate as other methods.

6. You could complete the rotation transform by clicking the Commit button on the Options bar. However, let's cancel by pressing the Esc key and try another more accurate way to straighten this image. Press Ctrl+D to deselect.

7. Press Shift+I repeatedly until you see the Measure tool appear in the toolbox. (Its icon looks like a ruler.)

8. Drag out a measuring line across the top horizontal surface, as shown in Figure 1.47.

9. Choose Image ➢ Rotate Canvas ➢ Arbitrary to open the small Rotate Canvas dialog box, which has a number of degrees already entered. This information was entered by the Measure tool. Click OK.

The image is rotated accurately according to the measurement line you drew in step 8.

FIGURE 1.46
Rotating an image manually

Position your mouse here, and drag in a clockwise fashion.

Drag a measurement along this horizontal surface.

The Crop And Straighten Photos tool is new in Photoshop CS. It is helpful when scanned photo prints were not aligned carefully on the scanning bed. It doesn't help with photos that were captured at an angle with respect to the horizon (such as when the camera was tilted as in the earlier example). Let's see how Crop And Straighten Photos works.

1. Open the file Lunch2.psd from the CD. This photo print was scanned without regard to its orientation. You don't have to worry about it in Photoshop CS because you can rely on the Crop And Straighten Photos command to fix it for you.

2. Choose File ➤ Automate ➤ Crop And Straighten Photos.

3. A new document window appears with the—you guessed it—cropped and straightened photo. Photoshop is now "smart" enough to deduce the image's edges and does the tedious work for you. This is wonderful if you are scanning dozens of photos because you can forget about trying to carefully align them with your scanner bed as Photoshop takes care of it for you.

4. Close the open documents without saving.

Correcting for Two-Point Perspective

Photos of tall buildings tend to have walls that lean inward, especially if taken with wide-angle lenses. If you extend lines along all the wall edges, they converge at three points in the distance (two on opposite sides of the horizon, and one directly above), technically called three-point perspective.

In architectural illustration, it is common to draw tall buildings with straight vertical walls because we "know" in our minds that walls are vertical. In two-point perspective, objects along the horizon diminish in size with distance from the camera (as they appear to our eyes), but objects running in the vertical dimension remain straight up and down (not exactly true to our eyesight but intellectually pleasing nevertheless).

We can simulate a two-point perspective in a photo by skewing the pixels using the transform tool:

1. Open the file `Street.psd` from the CD.

2. Press Ctrl+A to select all.

3. Click the Channels palette and click the Save Selection As Channel button (second from the left along the lower edge of the Channels palette).

4. Press D to set the default colors.

5. Choose Image ➤ Canvas Size to open the Canvas Size dialog box. Click the Relative check box in the New Size group.

6. Select Inches from the Width and Height drop-down lists if these are not already selected. Enter **2 inches** in both Width and Height text boxes and click OK. The canvas is increased in size so that a 2-inch white border surrounds the image; the overall image size has increased.

7. Press Ctrl+R to turn on the rulers.

8. Drag a guide from the vertical ruler and release it where it meets the bottom edge of the building wall, as shown in Figure 1.48.

9. Drag another guide out from the vertical ruler, and release it along the street corner on the right side of the image.

FIGURE 1.48
Dragging guides to building edges

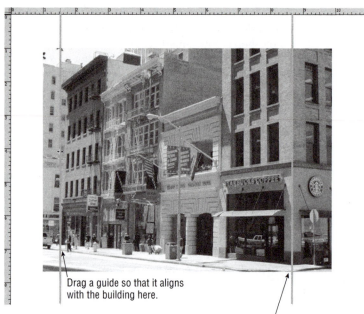

Drag a guide so that it aligns
with the building here.

Align another guide to meet the bottom corner here.

Notice how the vertical walls lean inward in three-point perspective. You can see this lean as the distance between the guides and the upper portion of the vertical walls. The guides help establish a visual vertical reference line.

10. In the Channels palette, click the Alpha 1 channel. Click the Load Channel As Selection button (leftmost button along the palette's lower edge). Click the RGB channel again.

11. Press Ctrl+T to start the Transform command.

12. Right-click anywhere inside the document window to open a context menu that lists specialized transform tools. Choose Skew from this menu.

13. Hold down the Shift key to constrain motion horizontally. Drag the upper-left handle to the left until the vertical building wall aligns with the guide. Do the same by Shift-dragging the upper-right handle to align with the guide on the right, as shown in Figure 1.49. Click the Commit button on the Options bar.

14. Press Ctrl+D to deselect. Press Ctrl+H to hide the guides. Press Ctrl+R to hide the rulers.

15. Press C to choose the Crop tool. Drag a crop window around the image, and click the Commit button on the Options bar. Figure 1.50 shows the completed two-point perspective image. The building walls are truly vertical.

FIGURE 1.49
Skewing the image

Drag these handles horizontally outward, and align the vertical walls to guides.

FIGURE 1.50
Two-point perspective

Summary

This chapter has been a whirlwind tour of the most important tools and concepts in Photoshop CS. If you are new to Photoshop, or even if you have been using it a while, this chapter should provide you with a solid foundation. In the next chapter we will work with one of the most interesting and challenging concepts in digital imaging: color.

Chapter 2

Working with Color

As you learned in Chapter 1, color modes (RGB and CMYK, for example) were developed to deal with the optics of additive and subtractive color in the real world. However, you know that the color of a document you see on a computer monitor often appears differently when that document is printed.

Color varies between makes and models of monitors, scanners, cameras, printers, and printing presses. Color rendition can change on the same device over time. People even perceive colors a bit differently, and this effect can be pronounced under different lighting conditions. Therefore, it is impossible to perfectly represent the same color everywhere.

The best we can shoot for is to produce consistent color and to make its representation as accurate as possible on every device. You should be able to get close to the ideal of "what you see is what you get." To effectively work with color in Photoshop, you need to understand the following concepts and techniques:

◆ Modes and Gamuts

◆ Color Spaces

◆ Calibration and Profiles

◆ Consistent Color Printing

◆ Professional Color

Modes and Gamuts

You have already been introduced to RGB and CMYK color modes. These modes represent *color models*, or basic assumptions we make when dealing with color. In the RGB color model, red, green, and blue are the three components. These are stored as three channels that combine to represent a wide range of colors. The complete range of colors that a mode can display or print is called a *gamut*.

Each mode offers a different gamut of colors. Although there is a lot of overlap between color models, some RGB colors cannot be represented in CMYK, and vice versa. Colors that can be represented in a given mode are considered "in gamut," and those that can't be represented are considered "out of gamut."

Photoshop's internal color conversion engine uses a third color mode called Lab because it has a larger range of colors encompassing both RGB and CMYK's entire gamuts.

NOTE   Lab color is actually an abbreviation for the CIE L*a*b* color model that was created by the International Commission on Illumination (CIE is its French acronym), an organization devoted to the issues relating to the art and science of lighting.

Every color that can be represented in RGB and CMYK can be represented in Lab mode. Lab color represents more colors than the human eye can perceive, so it is often used as an absolute color standard. Unfortunately, no devices can reproduce the full gamut of Lab color. To get started, let's take a look at an example.

1. Open the file `LabColor.psd` from the CD. This is the Lagoon image from Chapter 1, in Lab color mode.

2. Choose Edit ➢ Preferences ➢ Transparency & Gamut to open the Preferences dialog box:

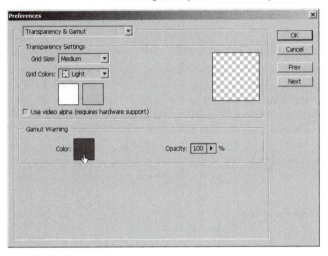

3. Click the color swatch in the Gamut Warning section. Choose a bright red color and click OK to close the Color Picker. Click OK again to close the Preferences dialog box.

TIP Choose a hue that is not present in the image as your gamut warning color.

4. Choose View ➢ Gamut Warning to display the gamut warning image, as shown in Figure 2.1.

   The red pixels displayed on the screen are out of gamut for printing in CMYK mode. If the gamut warning shows extensive out-of-range pixels, correct the color before converting the image to CMYK. This example shows minor gamut warnings.

NOTE See Chapter 3 for color correction techniques.

5. Click the Channels palette. There are three channels in Lab color: Lightness, a, and b.

FIGURE 2.1
The lagoon image with the gamut warning turned on. Some pixels in the sky are out of gamut—red on screen but black here.

6. Click the Lightness channel. This channel carries the grayscale detail in the image, so it should look like a desaturated version of the image.

7. Click channel a, shown on the left in Figure 2.2. The a channel carries the green-to-red color component in Lab mode. This channel appears mostly gray with very little contrast.

FIGURE 2.2
The Lab color "a" channel (left) and "b" channel (right) each carry a portion of the image's color information.

8. Click channel b, which carries the blue-to-yellow component. By itself, channel b isn't much use. Channels a and b together carry all the color information in the image.

9. Click the Lab composite channel to turn on all three channels at once.

10. Choose Image ➤ Mode ➤ CMYK. Photoshop mixes the colors that were out of gamut from Lab to CMYK when you change color modes.

11. Make sure Gamut Warning is checked in the View menu again, and see the change in the image. No red pixels are shown in the image this time; all the pixels now fit within the CMYK gamut.

12. Press Shift+Ctrl+Y to toggle Gamut Warning display back off.

13. You can close this file without saving.

Be aware of the potential for out-of-gamut colors so you don't get any color surprises when you print your images.

> **NOTE** You can convert directly from RGB to CMYK (or vice versa) without manually entering Lab mode as a separate step. Photoshop automatically makes the color conversion using Lab color internally. You can use Lab color intentionally in advanced retouching, as you will learn in Chapter 3.

Color Spaces

To make matters more complicated, each color model has many *color spaces* that can be used. Color spaces are narrower portions within a color model representing a specific gamut.

For example, millions of colors can be stored in a 24-bit RGB image. However, a specific RGB print device might only be capable of reproducing several hundred thousand colors. Each device's gamut defines its own specific color space within the RGB model.

Every device operates within its own color space. Every type of paper also has its own color space, because media absorb color differently. Color spaces that characterize devices or media are stored in *profiles*.

> **NOTE** You will learn how to calibrate your monitor and create its color profile in the next section.

Since each device has its own color space, you might be wondering how Photoshop can ever maintain consistency in this cacophony of color. The real secret is Photoshop's Color Management Module (CMM). If color spaces are languages, the CMM is the universal translator. The CMM's job is to translate the gamut of one color space into another by matching colors as closely as possible.

Color spaces can also represent device-independent standards called *working spaces* that are used while you edit images in Photoshop. Working spaces describe absolute color, referencing Lab color for best possible accuracy. The working space you choose depends on the type of work you are doing—whether it is destined for a printer, a printing press, or the Web. Let's explore color spaces through another example.

1. Choose Edit ➢ Color Settings to open the Color Settings dialog box, as shown in Figure 2.3.

FIGURE 2.3

Photoshop's Color Settings dialog box: (left) the North American General Purpose defaults, and (right) the U.S. Prepress defaults

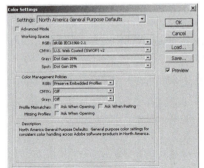

2. Click the Settings pop-up and choose the U.S. Prepress Defaults from the list. The settings you choose change some of the parameters in the dialog box. For example, in the Working Spaces section, the RGB standard changes to Adobe RGB (1998). This working space defines a large gamut that is well suited to documents that will eventually be converted to CMYK. Click OK to close the dialog box.

TIP   The Adobe RGB (1998) working space is a good general-purpose standard to use for all print work.

3. Open the file `Street.psd` from the CD. The Missing Profile dialog box opens, as show in Figure 2.4.

FIGURE 2.4
Here are your choices when you set Preserve Embedded Profiles and you open an image that doesn't have one.

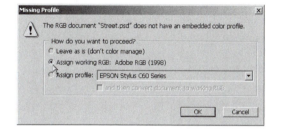

4. Click Assign Working RGB: Adobe RGB (1998), and then click OK to close the dialog box.

   The document window displays the image via its working color space. No further color management is necessary because the working space profile is now embedded in the document.

5. You can change the embedded profile at any time by choosing Image ➢ Mode ➢ Assign Profile to open the Assign Profile dialog box, as shown in Figure 2.5.

6. Click the Profile radio button, click the Profile pop-up, and choose ProPhoto RGB from the list. Experiment with each of the listed profiles in turn and preview the results in the document window in real time. Finally, click Working RGB: Adobe RGB (1998) and then click OK to close the dialog box.

NOTE   ProPhoto working space is an alternative to Adobe RGB (1998). ProPhoto is best for digital dye-sublimation and high-end inkjet photo printers.

   Notice how each working space displays the image slightly differently in the document window.

FIGURE 2.5
Assigning a profile to embed in an image

7. Some file formats let you tag (also called associate or embed) a color profile onto the data. Choose File ➢ Save As to open the Save As dialog box. Make sure ICC Profile (Windows) or Embed Color Profile (Mac OS) is checked as shown in Figure 2.6. Type the filename `StreetEmbed.psd` and click Save.

FIGURE 2.6
When saving, check the box to tag the file with the associated ICC profile.

Check here to tag the file with the associated profile

The image data records only relative colors, but the way you actually see the image (in absolute colors) depends on the profile you choose.

WARNING You can embed color profiles only in PSD, PDF, JPEG, TIFF, EPS, DCS, and PICT formats.

8. You will select color management policies for consistent handling of color issues in Photoshop. Press Shift+Ctrl+K to reopen the Color Settings dialog box. In the Color Management Policies section, click the RGB pop-up and select Convert To Working RGB from the list.

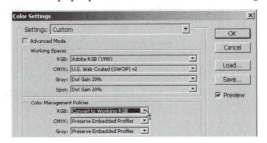

Images that you open will now be converted to the Adobe RGB (1998) profile automatically.

9. Clear Ask When Opening and Ask When Pasting For Profile Mismatches. Also clear Ask When Opening For Missing Profiles.

Now you won't be bothered by having to confirm your decision to assign the working profile to all your documents, and Photoshop will handle this automatically on all documents you open or paste into the current document.

10. Click OK to close the Color Settings dialog box.

WARNING Be aware that by clearing the Ask settings you override a document that already has a profile assigned to it without knowing it. If you work in an office that agrees to use only one profile, this is not a problem. If you work with multiple profiles, it is best to have Photoshop ask for confirmation in every situation. This book will consistently use the Adobe RGB (1998) profile.

Calibration and Profiles

To maintain consistent color between your computer's peripherals, it is essential that you create a profile for each device. Because every device has its own color space, each device is characterized by a unique color profile. The CMM uses these profiles to translate between all the color spaces used throughout your workflow—from the working space you use when importing from digital cameras and scanners, to the one used when editing, to the output you see in monitors and printers.

If you are working without profiles, there is no consistency between your input and output devices, and color will almost certainly be off. In this case, color "corrections" that you make may be a waste of time because what you see on the screen is not representative of what will be printed, for example.

In this section you will learn to calibrate your monitor and thus generate its color profile. You will also decide how you will work with your printers and change profile settings specific to your printer drivers.

Profiling Your Monitor

When you *characterize* a monitor, you tell the computer how the device performs and store that information in a profile. In contrast, when you *calibrate* a monitor, you actually change the device's performance. You'll learn to characterize in this section.

NOTE The subject of calibration is beyond the scope of this book; you can read more on critical color in Tim Grey's *Color Confidence* (Sybex, 2004) for real, advanced fine-tuning.

Each monitor can be characterized by an International Color Consortium (ICC) profile developed by its manufacturer. You can usually download such profiles from the manufacturer's website or load them from the disc that shipped with the product. Once you have an appropriate profile on hand, here's how to set it up:

1. Choose Start Control Panel to open Control Panel.

WARNING   The following procedure uses the Adobe Gamma control panel and is for Windows users. The procedure on the Mac OS is essentially the same, although the actual steps are different. Refer to the Mac system help for more information on using the Monitor Calibrator utility.

2. When you install Photoshop on your computer, the installation program also adds Adobe Gamma to Control Panel. Double-click Adobe Gamma to open a dialog box that asks if you want to use the Step by Step (Wizard) version of the Control Panel version.

3. Choose Control Panel and click Next to open the Adobe Gamma dialog box:

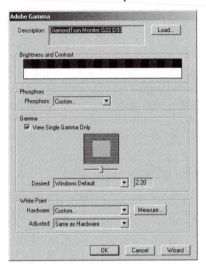

NOTE   The intent of the ICC profile format (.icc and .icm) is to provide a cross-platform device profile format for more reliable color. Unfortunately, manufacturer profiles do not account for variations that occur among the same models or changes that occur from age. See the "Professional Color" section later in this chapter to learn how to profile individual devices and media using measurement hardware.

4. Click the Load button to open the Open Monitor Profile dialog box (see Figure 2.7), in which you can browse to the profile you need. I'm using a Mitsubishi Diamond Pro monitor, so I select the Diamond Compatible 9300K profile; select the profile that matches your hardware, and click the Open button.

5. Change the brightness and contrast using the controls on your monitor until the color bars in the Brightness and Contrast section shown in the Adobe Gamma dialog box in step 3 appear as black and white to your eyes.

6. The Phosphors and White Point: Hardware pop-ups (see Figure 2.8) contain various standard values that the product literature that comes with your hardware may advise you to select. My ICC profile automatically set these, so Custom was automatically selected for both.

FIGURE 2.7

Browse to your monitor's profile.

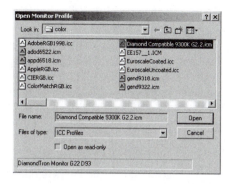

FIGURE 2.8

Set the Phosphors and White Point: Hardware values according to the manufacturer's directions.

 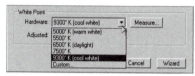

7. Gamma is the middlemost gray color that your monitor can produce. Use the slider under the graphic in the Gamma group, as shown in Figure 2.9, to adjust the midtone. The goal is to have the least amount of contrast that can still be discerned between the center box and the horizontal lines.

FIGURE 2.9

Gamma adjustment

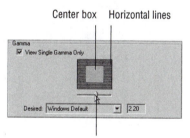

TIP If you don't know what color temperature to set, click the Measure button in the White Point group to display three neutral gray squares. You can also click the Wizard button at the bottom of the Adobe Gamma dialog box and use it to step through the settings.

8. Click OK at the bottom of the Adobe Gamma dialog box to open the Save As dialog box.

9. Save your profile setup as **My Monitor.icm** and click Save.

Congratulations! You have just generated your monitor's profile.

Disabling a Printer's Color Correction

Now that you have profiled your monitor, it is time to think about your printers. Every printer has *drivers* that let it communicate with your computer. The drivers are written by the manufacturer (available on their website) and have controls specific to your device.

Many drivers have built-in color correction software that you can use, or you can disable that software and let Photoshop take over the color management issues. Become familiar with the options available in your specific printer drivers. It will be helpful to take a look at driver options found in a common Epson inkjet printer, even if you use a different printer, because many of the options are similar.

In Windows, follow these steps to disable your printer's color correction :

1. Choose Start Printers And Faxes to open the Printers And Faxes folder.

2. Double-click a printer to open its folder. In this case, we will be looking at an Epson Stylus C60. The driver is installed when you connect the printer to your computer for the first time and remains thereafter.

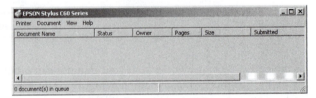

3. Choose Printer ➢ Printing Preferences to open the Printing Preferences dialog box:

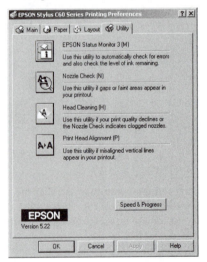

The options in the Printing Preferences dialog box depend on the manufacturer and model of your printer. Just follow along with the steps even if you don't have this specific device, as the concepts are similar for all printers. I'll describe a typical set, from my Epson model.

4. Find the printer utilities. (I clicked the Utility tab.) Epson provides status monitor, nozzle check, head cleaning, and print head alignment utilities. Using these is essential to maintaining the "health" of the device.

5. Find the part of the dialog box in which you can set media type and color mode. (I clicked the Main tab.) This is one of the most important parts of the driver as the choices you make here have a huge impact on the printed results.

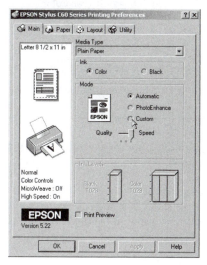

6. You usually must hunt for more advanced controls to change the color space. In this case, I click the Custom button in the Mode section and then click the Advanced button to open the Advanced dialog box:

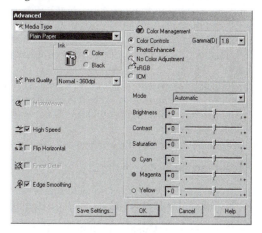

7. This driver provides many options for managing color, and these are probably great for most applications. However, because Photoshop is such an advanced tool for manipulating color, I click No Color Adjustment and then click OK and OK again to close the dialog boxes and disable color correction in the driver.

CALIBRATING MONITORS

Here are some recommendations for achieving the best results when calibrating your monitor:

◆   Make sure a cathode ray tube (CRT) monitor has been on for at least 30 minutes prior to creating a profile. CRTs need warm-up time to produce stable color.

◆   Set your graphics card's color depth to 32-bit True Color.

◆   Set your desktop background to a neutral 50% gray.

◆   Match the lighting in your studio to the lighting where your output will be viewed.

◆   Calibrate your monitor every month, because performance declines over time.

◆   Use calibration hardware to create more accurate profiles. (See the "Professional Color" section later in this chapter.)

If possible, you should disable color management in your printer driver. Let Photoshop do this work. It is a mistake for both Photoshop and a printer driver to try and take over this important job, because conflicts will arise. You must decide which software will manage color and stick with this decision throughout your workflow.

If you have other peripheral devices, such as digital cameras, scanners, and printers, disable color correction in their drivers also. In this book, Photoshop will be entirely responsible for color management.

Consistent Color Printing

Now that you have accurately profiled your monitor and output devices, your infrastructure is set up to maintain consistent color. Earlier in this chapter you set up your working space and set color management policies, so you are also ready to work consistently with color in Photoshop.

Using a printing press can be an expensive proposition. Before you make color separations and produce the CMYK plates, print a *hard proof*, or color-accurate hard copy, on an inexpensive printer (an inkjet, for example). That way, you can spot potential problems before they become expensive mistakes.

To save even more, you can make a *soft proof* on the screen without actually printing anything. However, soft proofs are only accurate if your system is already color-accurate throughout. Soft proofs can show you on screen how your image will look on a specific printing press, desktop printer, or operating system before you print.

You'll make a soft proof and then print the image.

1.   Open the file StreetTagged.psd from the CD.

2.   Choose View ➤ Proof Setup ➤ Working CMYK if this is not already selected. The colors may shift slightly as the image displays with U.S. Web Coated (SWOP) v2 color space.

3.   Choose View ➤ Proof Setup ➤ Custom to open the Proof Setup dialog box, as shown in Figure 2.10.

FIGURE 2.10

Setting the paper and
profile for consistent
color

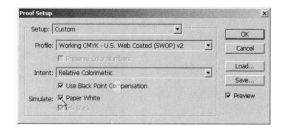

4. In the Simulate section, check Paper White to simulate the way the image will look on paper (according to the paper that is defined in the working CMYK space).

5. Click the Profile pop-up, and select one of your printers from the list. Click OK. Notice that the profile you selected appears in the document's title bar.

6. Press Ctrl+Y to toggle Proof Colors off. The document's title bar now shows the parenthetical information (RGB/8), meaning it is in RGB mode with 8 bits per channel.

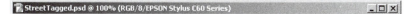

7. Choose File ➢ Page Setup to open the Page Setup dialog box, as shown in Figure 2.11. Here you can choose the print device (click the Printer button), paper size, and orientation of the print. Click Landscape and then click OK. (This step doesn't have anything to do with producing consistent color, but should be done before the following Print With Preview step.)

8. Choose File ➢ Print With Preview to open the Print dialog box shown in Figure 2.12. Check Show More Options if it isn't already checked.

FIGURE 2.11

Changing the page setup

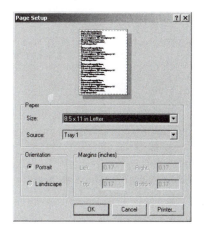

FIGURE 2.12
Accessing more options
in the Print dialog box

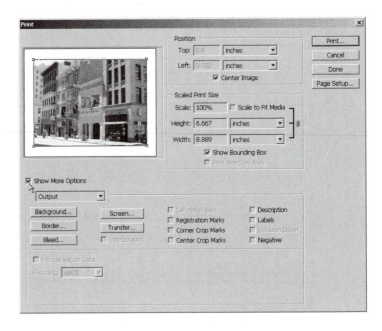

9. Change the pop-up underneath Show More Options to Color Management. Change the Profile pop-up in the Print Space section to the profile of your printer. In this case, it is changed to Epson Stylus C60 Series. You can select your own printer driver in this step.

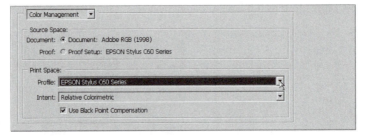

Now Photoshop will convert the document from the source space of Adobe RGB (1998) to the color space of the Epson Stylus C60 Series profile when the document is printed.

TIP To rely on your printer driver for color correction, change the Print Space Profile pop-up to Printer Color Management.

10. Finally, click Print to send the document to the printer. The desktop printing workflow is complete.

PRINTING PRESS CONSIDERATIONS

If you want to print on a printing press, your workflow may be different than if you print on a desktop printer. You can use Photoshop to manipulate the image and then import the .psd document into a more specialized printing program such as Adobe InDesign or Illustrator. These programs are better designed to work in CMYK mode for printing presses.

On the other hand, you might want to send your documents to a service bureau for four-color printing. In this case, one option is to tag your image with a working space profile. The service bureau should then be able to produce the exact colors referenced in the profile.

If you want the greatest control over a print sent to a printing press, manually convert your image to CMYK in Photoshop and then do any last-minute color correction you deem necessary post conversion. See Chapter 3 for more about color correction using Levels, Curves, Hue/Saturation, and other tools. If you decide on this option, coordinate which CMYK working space your printing press is using, and match your color settings in Photoshop.

Professional Color

If maintaining precise and consistent color throughout your workflow is critical to your business, you might want to invest in several technologies that go beyond Photoshop: design considerations for your studio environment, calibration systems, display devices, RGB printers, multicolor ink systems, archival pigments, and specialty papers.

Studio Environment

The first place to start when thinking seriously about color is in the environment where you work on the computer and view printed output. If you work by a large window, you may have problems with glare. The changing intensity and color of sunlight throughout the day has a large influence on how you perceive color on a monitor. It is best to keep the blinds closed or even consider working in a windowless (and, hopefully, temperature-controlled) room.

The color of the walls, objects in your immediate environment, and even the clothes you are wearing can influence the colors you perceive. Ideally, everything surrounding your monitor should be matte polychromatic gray, like the background in Photoshop itself. Although it is a bit overboard to wear a gray jumpsuit, wearing a Hawaiian shirt or sitting in front of a saturated red wall isn't the best idea when looking at critical color proofs.

If your printer room has fluorescent lighting, it really is no wonder that your prints have a blue-green cast when you look at them emerging from the printer. Remember that we see printed matter with reflected light, and this light has a tremendous effect on the colors we perceive. It is best to examine your prints under the same lighting in which they will ultimately be displayed.

If you are truly serious about color, install proper lighting in your work area. The best luminaire on the market is the SoLux MR-16 halogen bulb (comes with a special filament and reflector). The SoLux bulb simulates the D50 illumination standard of 4700 Kelvin. Installing these bulbs is an affordable way (about $200 U.S. for one workstation) to help turn your work area into a professional proofing room.

TIP See www.soluxtli.com and www.gtilite.com for D50 luminaires.

Calibration Systems

Calibration systems feature a scientific measuring instrument, called a spectrophotometer, that measures the light intensity emitted from a monitor, plus software that interfaces with Photoshop. Hardware-based calibration solutions are more accurate than software-only methods.

WARNING   Do not calibrate twice with different systems, as errors will result. Do not use the Adobe Gamma or Monitor Calibrator utilities if you are using calibration hardware, for example.

If you decide to invest in a hardware-based calibration system, why not calibrate your monitor every day? Monitors change over time, and daily or weekly profiles ensure that what you see on the screen is accurate. Make calibration part of your morning coffee ritual, or write it on your calendar.

Every type of media that you print on reflects color uniquely. In addition to profiling the direct light of monitors, the best calibration hardware can measure color on different kinds of media under reflected light. You can create a profile for each type of paper that you print on for the very best in color output.

GretagMacbeth offers profiling and calibration products of the highest quality. Their Eye-One Photo system costs about $1500 U.S.; it offers digital color management for CRT and LCD displays, plus RGB printers. You can upgrade the system with add-ons that allow you to calibrate and profile digital cameras, scanners, CMYK presses, and digital projectors as your needs grow.

Photo courtesy of GregtagMacBeth, LLC

TIP   See www.gretagmacbeth.com and www.colorvision.com for professional color calibration systems.

Display Devices

Monitor quality varies, and you usually get what you pay for. If you can afford it, invest in large 21˝ displays and graphics cards that support high resolution and color depth. Monitors usually last through at least two or three computer replacement cycles, so their value can be amortized over a longer period. (A seven-year service life is safe to assume for top-level manufacturers.) Flat-panel liquid crystal displays (LCD) render sharpness more clearly, while cathode ray tube (CRT) monitors render blurriness more effectively; each type has its strengths and weaknesses, so having both is the best option.

TIP   The Cintiq interactive pen display is the ultimate display device, combining input and output technologies. It features a pressure-sensitive tablet transparently overlaying an 18″ color LCD display (about $2500 U.S.). Find out more at www.wacom.com.

RGB Printers

A common misconception is that you should convert an image to CMYK color mode before printing on a desktop inkjet printer. However, all desktop printers are designed to receive RGB color data, so you should keep your images in RGB color mode in Photoshop. Convert to CMYK only when using a professional printing press that uses four separate plates (excellent for high-volume printing).

The best RGB printers as of this book's publication use high-end inkjet technology. In the past, Iris printers or dye-sublimation machines were the best in the business, but experts now agree that more affordable inkjet technology has taken over the industry.

NOTE   High-end RGB prints are sometimes called *Giclee* or *Piezo* prints in the art world.

Epson and HP are among the most respected inkjet printer manufacturers. In particular, Epson has built a solid reputation among fine art printers and professional photographers. If color is critical to expressing your design vision, consider purchasing a studio-quality color printer. For example, Epson currently makes top-quality printers ranging from $700 to $8000. The ultimate would be to have a smaller desktop model for hard proofs (13″ wide) and a larger floor model that handles 24″ wide media for presentations.

Inks

When it comes to inkjet ink, you need to take several items into account. Many high-end printers use more than the traditional four inks that emulate traditional printing presses (cyan, magenta, yellow, and black). For example, Epson currently uses the seven-color ink system mentioned in Chapter 1 that includes light cyan, cyan, light magenta, magenta, yellow, light black, and black. HP currently has an eight-color ink system in some models.

The actual ink droplet size is critical in how much resolution can be achieved with inkjet technology (the smaller, the better). Look for inks with droplet volume in the range of 5 picoliters for best results.

Many printers can be retrofitted with continuous-flow ink systems that connect the moving print head with flexible tubes to bottles of ink outside the printer. The advantage here is economy because bottled ink can save you up to 90% on ink costs compared with single-use cartridges.

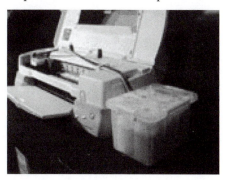

TIP   Learn more about the Niagara continuous-flow ink system at www.mediastreet.com.

Ink itself can be classified as either a dye or a pigment, depending on whether it is water-soluble. Dyes have a larger gamut but fade more quickly than pigments. On the other hand, pigments tend to have a greater archival quality. The choice depends on your needs and is affected by the paper used.

Specialty Paper

The type of paper you use makes a huge difference in the quality of the resulting print. Do not sell yourself short by printing an important presentation on inexpensive bond paper. You can print on a wide variety of substrates, including canvas, textured watercolor paper, satin, rag, velvet, glossy and matte finish photo paper, and more. Consult a service provider, paper companies, or your printer manufacturer for media options that are designed to work with your printers.

TIP   Different ink, paper, and framing combinations have varying archival qualities. See www.wilhelm-research.com for estimated longevity test results of popular inks, printers, and media.

Summary

Your relationship with color can be as amateurish or professional as you desire. Although amateurs tend not to be able to print color consistently or to be able to make effective color corrections on a monitor, they also do not spend any energy on the subject (and may not need to). In this chapter you have seen how you can tighten up your color workflow so that what you see on the monitor is exactly what you get in your output.

Although the learning curve may be steep in producing professional color, its benefit may be well worth the effort. Color is a beautiful dimension that greatly adds to your work if you choose to embrace what it takes to work with it effectively on a computer.

Chapter 3

Digital Darkroom Skills

Thankfully, you do not have to subject yourself to toxic chemicals to develop and print photos like traditional film photographers; you can do it all in Photoshop. Perhaps Photoshop is best known for its ability to function as a digital darkroom. This chapter teaches essential darkroom skills that you can use to improve every photo you take:

◆ Working with Digital Film

◆ Adjusting Tonal Range

◆ Balancing Color

◆ Replacing the Sky

◆ Sharpening and Blurring

◆ Simulating Camera Effects

Working with Digital Film

As you are probably aware, the term *digital film* is an oxymoron. Thinking of your raw data as digital film may be helpful, however. New technology is often understood using the metaphors of the technology it replaces.

Traditional photographers had the advantage of the film itself—a persistent record of their shooting. Unfortunately, most of the raw data taken by digital photographers is lost or is stored in a manipulated form.

Start thinking of your digital photos as "film" that must be "developed" on a read-only medium like a CD-ROM or DVD-ROM. If you get in the habit of burning a disc as a "roll," you will have a persistent record of your shooting experience. Years from now you will be able to access the light recorded on your camera's sensor plate, and the "truth" of your shot will be preserved for posterity.

WARNING If you work directly on your original image data, any mistakes that you save into the file are permanent and destroy the truthful record of your shooting experience.

Once your digital film is developed, the images burned on the disc are like "negatives" that you can manipulate in Photoshop. Because you will access the originals from a read-only medium, there is no danger of overwriting your shooting data with work you do in Photoshop.

Photoshop CS's File Browser has been greatly improved. Let's see how to use the File Browser to access and organize your digital film.

1. Press Shift+Ctrl+O, or click the Toggle File Browser button on the options bar, just to the left of the palette well, to open the File Browser. Figure 3.1 shows the DVD drive selected (the E drive in this case) in the Folders palette; the disc is called Film Roll 0001.

FIGURE 3.1

The Photoshop File Browser

NOTE The File Browser is no longer a palette as it was in Photoshop 7. You cannot dock the new File Browser in the palette well; instead toggle it on and off as needed.

2. Notice that the File Browser now has its own menu and palettes. Using the file system tree in the Folders palette, navigate to a folder on a disc you have burned or to a folder on the CD that comes with this book. You will see image thumbnails on the right.

TIP You can drag the palettes within the File Browser around and dock them where you want.

3. Hold down the Ctrl key and single-click a few thumbnail images to select them. Then click the Flag File button on the options bar within the File Browser (shown in Figure 3.2). Tiny flag icons appear on the thumbnails of flagged images.

4. Choose Flagged Files from the Show pop-up. Only the files you flagged in step 3 now show up. This is a great way to select a few choice photos you'd like to work on from all the photos you shot on your "roll" and hide the rest.

FIGURE 3.2
Flagging files

Flag File

5. Navigate to the Chapter 3 folder on the companion CD and double-click the file IMG_1959.JPG to open it in a document window. Figure 3.3 shows the original photo that you will be working on later in this chapter.

WARNING Thumbnail images that show padlock icons in the File Browser were stored on a read-only medium and cannot be altered. However, you can open these images and save a copy.

FIGURE 3.3
The original photo

6. Choose File ➤ Save As to open the Save As dialog box. Navigate to a project folder on your hard drive, change the Format pop-up to Photoshop's native format, and save this file as `Sidewalk.psd`.

7. You can create a printable contact sheet that has the thumbnails and filenames of all the images on your digital film roll. Choose Automate ➤ Contact Sheet II to open the Contact Sheet II dialog box (see Figure 3.4).

FIGURE 3.4

The Contact Sheet II
dialog box

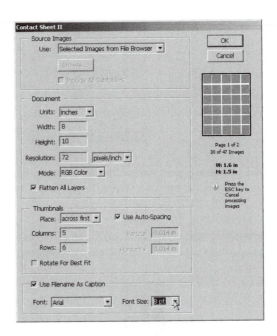

8. Change the Font Size pop-up to 8 pt and click OK. Smaller font sizes allow lengthy filenames more space to fit on the sheet.

   Photoshop begins the lengthy process of resizing and transforming the thumbnails—thankfully it all happens automatically. Figure 3.5 shows a typical contact sheet image. Press the Esc key to stop the process if you want.

TIP   Put a printed contact sheet in the disc's jewel case and you won't have to put the disc into the computer to know what's stored on it.

9. Close the contact sheet without saving the file when you're finished.

Most low- and midrange consumer digital cameras have options to save photos as Joint Photographic Experts Group (`.jpg`) files or in Tagged Image File Format (`.tif`). The problem with the former is its blurriness (due to lossy compression), and the latter format has enormous file size (although no data is lost). Less-expensive cameras often force color correction and exposure control within the camera itself, so the actual light hitting the camera sensor is not preserved.

FIGURE 3.5
A contact sheet

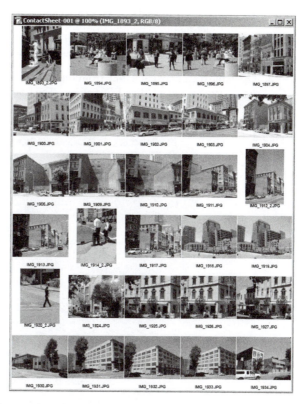

Many "prosumer" and professional quality cameras offer raw formats that preserve 100% of the original data that was captured by the camera sensor. These cameras also have many options for tweaking images within the camera itself, but people who are serious about shooting prefer to leave that task to Photoshop. It is better to adjust tonal range and color balance of your images at a color-corrected workstation (see Chapter 2, "Working with Color"), and under proper room lighting, rather than in the field with your camera. As you develop digital darkroom skills, you will want to leave these tasks up to your trained eye, rather than entrust the "development" of your photos to some in-camera presets.

NOTE   Camera raw images have smaller file size than uncompressed TIFF images of the same pixel dimensions.

Photoshop CS now has raw image file support built in as a standard plug-in. (It was initially available as a free download for Photoshop 7.).The Camera Raw plug-in is much improved in CS and offers many options for working with digital film. You will be using Camera Raw to develop your digital negatives before bringing them into Photoshop.

1. Point your browser to www.adobe.com and select Downloads from the Support group. Click the link for Photoshop (either the Macintosh or Windows version) and then download and install the updated Camera Raw plug-in version 2.2 or later. The new version of Camera Raw includes bug fixes and supports many more makes and models of digital cameras.

TIP It is a good idea to periodically check Adobe's website for free updates to Photoshop.

2. Follow the download instructions given in the `.pdf` file that accompanies the plug-in. You will be required to move two files and restart Photoshop.

3. Open the file `Landscape.NEF` from the CD. This file is in Nikon's raw format and was taken with a professional Nikon D70 camera. The Camera Raw dialog box (see Figure 3.6) automatically appears as Photoshop senses raw image data.

FIGURE 3.6
The Camera Raw
Interface

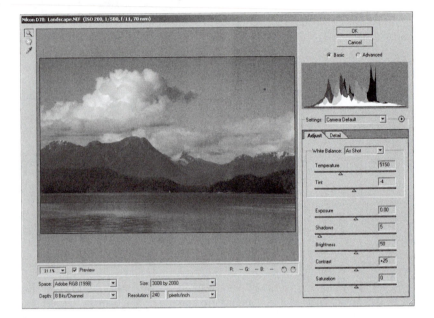

4. Click the Settings pop-up and select Camera Default from the list if it isn't already selected. The preview image gets darker and bluer. A colorful *histogram* within the dialog box changes in real time to give you more detailed information about the image.

NOTE The Camera Raw dialog box shows the camera and shot statistics on the title bar. This image says "Nikon D70: Landscape.NEF (ISO 200, 1/500, f/11, 70mm)," indicating the model, filename, film speed equivalent, shutter speed, f-stop, and digital film size equivalent.

5. Click the Adjust tab if it is not already selected. Click the White Balance pop-up and select Auto. Then drag the Exposure slider to the right until its value reads +0.70. The image brightens, and the color balance shifts away from the blue tint that was initially visible.

6. Click the Advanced radio button at the top of the dialog box and notice that two additional tabs are added below: Lens and Calibrate (see Figure 3.7). You can experiment further by clicking each one of the tabs, dragging the sliders, and watching the preview image change accordingly.

7. Click OK to "develop" your image and open it in a document window in Photoshop.

FIGURE 3.7
Camera Raw settings

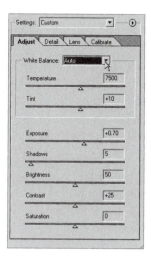

8. Save the new image as Landscape.psd on your hard drive. Note that the native Photoshop file is more than six times the size of the raw file format.

9. Close the Landscape image. As you have seen, Camera Raw is like your own photo processing center for professional-quality images inside Photoshop.

Not everyone has access to a high-end digital camera that supports a raw data type. The good news is you can "develop" photos in other formats by learning to manually adjust tonal range and balance color. Histograms give you valuable feedback that aid in this process.

This Histogram palette is new in Photoshop CS. This palette shows real-time information about your image as you are working.

A histogram is a graph of the tonal range of the image. The left side of the graph represents the darkest parts of the image (shadows), the middle displays the midtones, and the right side shows the highlights. The height of the graph reveals how much detail is concentrated in the corresponding key tonal areas. Images with full tonal range have pixels in all areas of the histogram. You can tell a lot about the quality of an image by studying its histogram.

NOTE The Levels dialog box shows a histogram that you can manipulate (see the tutorial in the next section).

Every time you manipulate pixels with the tools in Photoshop, you lose some of the original data as the pixels abruptly change colors. Data loss is called *banding* and is visible in a histogram as gaps in the graph (shown in Figure 3.8). Banding can appear in an image as discrete jumps in what ought to appear as continuous color.

FIGURE 3.8
Histogram banding

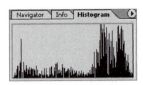

High-quality images tend to preserve as much original data as possible. Images that have been heavily altered may show a great deal of banding, and many small gaps will appear in the histogram. You will get less banding generally by slightly adjusting your images; extreme changes in the data set are usually perceptible in the final result.

One way that the pros decrease banding is by working in 16-bit color (see Chapter 1, "The Basics"). When images start with twice as much information per channel, you can manipulate a lot more before image quality visibly suffers.

Photoshop CS now works better with 16-bit images with full support by layers, painting, text, and shape tools. If you have a camera that can create 16-bit raw files, Photoshop is finally ready to work with them.

Adjusting Tonal Range

The first change you should make to a photo once it has been opened in a document window is to adjust its tonal range. Proper tonal range makes an image appear balanced in light and shadow, and more detail can be discerned.

WARNING If you adjust tonal range before you calibrate your monitor, the adjustments you make may be a waste of time (see Chapter 2).

1. Open the file Sidewalk.psd if it is not already open (see the last section). A color "before" version of this image is included in the color section.

2. The basic tool to adjust tonal range is called Brightness/Contrast. This tool shifts the entire tonal range at once. Click the Create New Fill Or Adjustment Layer button along the bottom edge of the Layers palette to open the pop-up and choose Brightness/Contrast.

3. Drag the Brightness slider to the right to a value of +60. Drag the Contrast slider to the left until the value reads –35. Click OK to create the Adjustment layer.

   Figure 3.9 shows the resulting image. Although you can now see into the shadows, the overall image appears overexposed and muddy. The entire tonal range shifted to the right, and you lost a great deal of data as many pixels washed out to pure white.

   Brightness/Contrast is not an effective tool here. It is the most primitive tool available to you to adjust the tonal range; I applied it to this image primarily to warn you about its limitations.

4. Click the eye icon next to the Brightness/Contrast 1 Adjustment layer to turn it off. Click the Background layer to select it.

WARNING The Shadow/Highlight tool is a wonderful new addition to Photoshop CS. Unfortunately, it is only available as an adjustment, not as an Adjustment layer (see Chapter 1 to understand the difference).

FIGURE 3.9
The brightness/contrast
adjustment

5. In order to leave the pixels on the Background layer untouched, make a duplicate layer before using the new Shadow/Highlight adjustment: make sure the Background layer is selected as the active layer in the Layers palette, and then choose Layer ➢ New ➢ Layer Via Copy (or press Ctrl+J).

6. Rename the new layer Shadow/Highlight to be clear about what you will be doing to this layer.

7. Choose Image ➢ Adjustments ➢ Shadow/Highlight to open the Shadow/Highlight dialog box. Check Show More Options to expand the dialog box (see Figure 3.10).

8. In the Shadows section, change Amount to 70% and Tonal Width to 40%. This brightens the shadows and constrains the brightening to slightly darker shadows. Don't click OK yet because once you do, you will no longer have access to this dialog box.

9. In the Highlights section, change Amount to 35% to darken the highlights. Change the Color Correction slider in the Adjustments section to –10 to slightly desaturate the colors that were altered in both the shadows and highlights. Click OK to apply the changes to the current layer.

Figure 3.11 shows a much-improved image with brightened shadows and toned-down highlights.

FIGURE 3.10
The Shadow/Highlight
dialog box

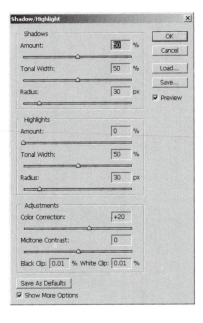

FIGURE 3.11
Shadow/highlight
adjustment

You will have to experiment with the Shadow/Highlight parameters on each image you adjust, and getting real-time visual feedback as you drag the sliders makes it easy. As you can see, Shadow/Highlight is like Brightness/Contrast on steroids because you can focus its effects right where you want them within the tonal range.

10. Toggle the visibility of the Shadow/Highlight 1 layer on and off. You can see the effect of the adjustment by comparing the altered layer with the Background layer. The only downside is you can't access the parameters in the dialog box again if you want to tweak them. Instead you can throw away the layer, duplicate the Background again, and reapply the adjustment. Leave the Shadow/Highlight 1 layer on in the end.

11. Now let's use a layer technique to adjust the exposure of the image. Make sure the Shadow/Highlight layer is selected in the Layers palette and press Ctrl+J to duplicate it. Rename this new layer Exposure.

12. Change the blending mode of the Exposure layer to Multiply and change the opacity to 25%. The image darkens slightly as you compensate for slight overexposure. The shadows are more believable while still maintaining the detail that was brought out in previous steps. You can adjust the strength of the effect by changing the opacity value of the Exposure layer.

TIP Use Screen blending mode to compensate for underexposed images.

13. To make selective exposure adjustments, let's use another layer-based technique. Click the Create A New Layer button on the lower edge of the Layers palette. Rename this layer Dodge And Burn. Note that unlike the Exposure layer, this layer is empty to start with.

14. Change the blending mode of the Dodge and Burn layer to Soft Light and change its opacity to 50%. These settings allow you to paint in black to burn (darken) and to paint in white to dodge (lighten) the image.

15. Press B to choose the Brush tool. Select a large soft brush and press D to set the default colors.

16. Paint in black over the sidewalk area in the foreground of the image with a few quick brush strokes. The area visibly darkens as you burn with black.

17. Press X to exchange the color swatches so you will be painting in white. Make a few quick brush strokes along the left edge of the image, dodging the masonry building. The areas you paint in white get visibly brighter. You can tune the overall effect of this layer by adjusting its opacity.

18. Select the Brightness/Contrast 1 adjustment layer and drag it to the Trash icon in the Layers palette. Apply a Levels adjustment layer to open the Levels dialog box.

19. Drag the Shadow Input slider to the right until it meets the darkest pixels in the histogram. This adjusts the darkest pixels to pure black. Drag the midtone input arrow slightly to the left. This adjustment brightens the image overall by shifting the middle of the tonal range. Figure 3.12 shows these adjustments. Click OK.

FIGURE 3.12
The Levels adjustment layer

Drag the midtone arrow to the left

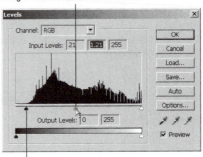

Drag the shadow arrow to the right

TIP When using levels, make your adjustments subtle to reduce banding.

20. Save your work as SidewalkWorking.psd.

The histogram shows some banding where data loss has occurred. This is unavoidable because we are working with an 8-bit image, but the quality is still acceptable, and the tonal range is greatly improved from where we started. The details in the shadows are visible, and the histogram shows a relatively even spread with a concentration in the midtones, which makes for a well-balanced image.

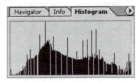

You can toggle off each layer made in this section to compare the effect of each adjustment with the original Background layer. Most important, using the techniques presented here you can fine-tune the image by adjusting the parameters and opacities of layers.

Balancing Color

Many digital cameras and artificial lights add a colorcast to images. For example, photos taken under fluorescent lighting have a blue-green cast. Photos shot with a particular digital camera may always seem a bit yellow if the camera's sensor was not properly color balanced at the factory. You can easily correct these issues in your digital darkroom.

TIP It is best to balance color in the image only after you have adjusted the tonal range to your liking, because further tonal adjustments may tip the color balance.

In some cases, you might want to intentionally change the mood of an image by shifting its color balance slightly. A bright sunny day might seem psychologically warmer if the image has an orange cast. Color influences emotions, and people's perceptions can be shifted with careful color balancing.

1. Continue from where you left off in the last section, or open the file SidewalkWorking.psd from the CD.

2. The primary tool for color balancing images that have easily identified neutral tones is Curves. Apply a Curves adjustment layer to open the Curves dialog box as shown in Figure 3.13.

FIGURE 3.13

The Curves dialog box

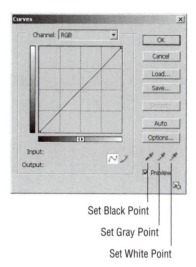

Set Black Point
Set Gray Point
Set White Point

TIP You can use many other specialized tools to work on color in Photoshop. Choose Help ≻ Photoshop Help for more information on the following adjustments: Hue/Saturation, Color Balance, Selective Color, Match Color, and Replace Color.

3. You can use the Curves dialog box in a couple of ways: by manually creating your own custom curve, or by using the eyedropper tools shown in Figure 3.13. In these steps, you will use the latter approach to remove any color cast in this image. Start by double-clicking the Set Black Point eyedropper to open. the Color Picker dialog box.

4. Set the target shadow color by dragging along the left edge of the color ramp until RGB values all read 20. You are setting the grayscale level to which you want this eyedropper to map. It is a good idea to map your blacks slightly brighter than pure black so you still have some wiggle room. Click OK.

WARNING Once pixels are pushed to either pure black or pure white, any tonal information that may have once been stored in them is lost.

5. Double-click the Set Gray Point eyedropper and verify that its RGB values are set to 128 (middle gray). Click OK.

6. Double-click the Set White Point eyedropper and set the RGB values to 235. This is a bit darker than pure white so that you'll avoid washout when you map the colors of your image to this value in subsequent steps.

7. Click OK to close the Color Picker, and then click OK to close the Curves dialog box. A small dialog box asks, "Save the new target colors as defaults?" Click Yes. You won't have to repeat steps 3 through 6 in the future. So far you have set up the target values to which you want to map colors, but you haven't yet selected the corresponding colors in your image.

8. Apply a Threshold adjustment layer (see Figure 3.14). Threshold displays high-contrast black-and-white images; all pixels darker than the threshold are converted to black, and all pixels whiter than the threshold are converted to white. Moving the slider helps determine which are the very darkest and brightest areas of your image.

FIGURE 3.14

The Threshold adjustment layer

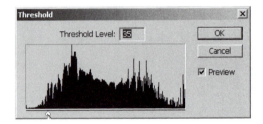

9. Drag the arrow at the bottom of the Threshold dialog box all the way to the left; the image in the document window becomes pure white. Then slowly drag the arrow to the right until you start to see some black areas, as shown in Figure 3.15. Click OK.

FIGURE 3.15

The threshold showing the darkest areas

10. Press Shift+I until you see the Color Sampler tool 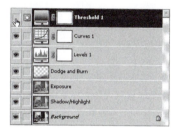 in the toolbox.

11. On the options bar, change the Sample Size pop-up to 3 by 3 Average. This allows you to take a more representative color sample of a tiny area by averaging across 9 pixels.

12. Click to place a sampler in the center man's shadow, which is one of the darkest areas in the image.

13. Double-click the Threshold layer thumbnail and drag the arrow all the way to the right. The image turns pure black. Then drag the arrow slowly to the left until some white areas appear in the document window; these areas are the brightest in the image. Click OK.

14. Choose the Color Sampler tool again, and click the minivan's hood to place your second sampler. This locates the brightest part of the image.

15. Turn the Threshold 1 layer off. This adjustment layer was used only to identify the brightest and darkest areas of the image and is no longer needed after you have placed both samplers. You can optionally delete this layer if you prefer.

16. To determine where middle gray is in this image, you use the Info palette. Click the eyedropper button in the upper-left portion of the Info palette. Choose Total Ink from the pop-up menu. Total Ink gives you a total percentage value instead of individual RGB component values.

17. Choose the Color Sampler tool again, and drag in the document window without releasing the mouse button yet. Release the button when the total ink value is as close to 50% as you can get it and the area you are over is a neutral gray if possible. Figure 3.16 shows where the samplers in this image might be chosen.

FIGURE 3.16
Placing color samplers

Gray sampler #3

White sampler #2   Black sampler #1

WARNING   Using the eyedroppers to remove a color cast is not appropriate in images without any neutral grays (for example, graphic illustrations using only bright colors).

18. Double-click the Curves adjustment layer thumbnail to reopen the Curves dialog box. This time, single-click the Set Black Point eyedropper. You will now map the sample you select in the image to the black point of your image (previously set in step 4). Carefully click the tip of the eyedropper inside sampler #1.

TIP   The RGB values for each numbered sampler are shown in the Info palette.

19. In the Curves dialog box, click the Set Gray Point eyedropper and click inside sampler #3. Click the Set White Point eyedropper and click inside sampler #2. Click OK to close the dialog box; your image is now color balanced.

    You can apply one of Photoshop CS's new photo filters to intentionally shift the color balance, in the way that traditional photographers do when they screw lens filters onto their cameras to "warm" or "cool" the image. This is done more for psychological effect rather than to achieve true color balance.

20. Apply a Photo Filter adjustment layer. Select Warming Filter (81) from the pop-up, and drag the Density slider down to 15%. Click OK. The image warms noticeably.

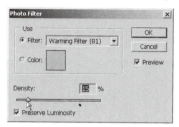

21. Save your work as Sidewalk2.psd (also provided on the CD). Figure 3.17 shows the final corrected image. Compare the before and after images on screen and in the book's color section. You've certainly come a long way in your digital darkroom!

22. Close the file without saving when you're finished.

FIGURE 3.17
The corrected image

Replacing the Sky

Often times you take pictures of architectural subjects when the sky is evenly overcast or completely cloudless. Rather than go back to the site and reshoot when the weather is more interesting, you can use Photoshop to replace a mundane sky in your original image with, for example, more dramatic billowing white clouds or a beautiful sunset.

1. Open the file House.psd from the CD. Figure 3.18 shows the original image with a rather boring blue sky.

FIGURE 3.18
A house with a blue sky

2. To begin the process, select the sky, and then choose Select ➢ Color Range to open the Color Range dialog box, as shown in Figure 3.19.

FIGURE 3.19
The Color Range
dialog box

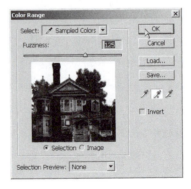

3. Click a point on the left side of the sky in the document window. The preview image in the Color Range dialog box shows some of the sky selected in white.

4. Click the Add To Sample eyedropper tool in the Color Range dialog box. This allows you to add colors to your range. Click a point on the right side of the sky in the document window. More of the sky should appear in white within the Color Range dialog box.

5. Drag the Fuzziness slider to the right until the entire sky area shows in white within the Color Range dialog box. A setting of 125 is about right for this image. Click OK.

6. The marching ants appear in the documents window showing what has been selected. Not only is the entire sky selected, but portions of the house that have a similar paint color compared to the sky are selected. Choose the Lasso tool in the toolbox, or press L.

7. On the options bar, click the Subtract From Selection button  . Lasso all the marching ants that appear on the house itself, being careful not to deselect any of the sky. Now only the sky is selected.

8. Choose Select ➤ Feather to soften the edge of the selection. Set the Feather Radius to 1 pixel, and click OK in the small dialog box that appears.

9. Open the file Sky.jpg from the CD (see Figure 3.20). Ideally, the replacement sky image you use should have larger pixel dimensions than the original image.

FIGURE 3.20
The replacement sky

TIP Keep a camera in your car and take pictures of the sky when you notice a particularly beautiful cloud formation or sunset. You can build a library of skies for use in your projects.

10. Press Ctrl+A to select all the pixels in the sky image. Then press Ctrl+C to copy the selection to the clipboard.

11. Select the house document window. The selection you made earlier should still be visible. Choose Edit ➢ Paste Into, or press Shift+Ctrl+V. The replacement sky now appears within the selection. Notice that the Layers palette shows a new layer called Layer 1, which shows a thumbnail of the replacement sky with a mask in the shape of your selection.

12. Press V to select the Move tool. Drag the sky around within the image until you find an aesthetically pleasing location for the clouds in relation to the building. Make sure not to expose the edges of the replacement sky image by moving it too far. Figure 3.21 shows the final image.

13. Close the house and sky images.

FIGURE 3.21
The house and a cloudy sky

Sharpening and Blurring

Sharpen and blur at the end of your digital darkroom work flow because they can significantly alter image data. Correct the tone, balance the color, and retouch before sharpening and blurring to minimize banding and data loss due to overmanipulation.

Sharpening and blurring are opposites—one clarifies, and the other obscures. You use both tools to your advantage in Photoshop. You sharpen images to make the edges more visually defined. We prefer images with distinct edges because they resonate with the perception of form in our minds.

Photoshop sharpens images by comparing pixels that differ in value from their neighbors and increases the contrast between them. Within the radius of this comparison, the bright areas get brighter and the darks get darker. Even though no true hard edge is really defined in the matrix of pixels, our visual systems ultimately perceive areas of higher contrast as an edge.

The amount of sharpening required varies in each image and depends on subject matter, resolution, and quality of the digital camera or scanner used to import the image into Photoshop. Every digital photograph benefits from at least a little sharpening.

WARNING You cannot effectively sharpen severely blurred images because there is not enough detail to enhance.

As the contrast between pixels is increased by sharpening, sometimes undesirable color halos appear, especially in images that have extreme levels of sharpening. Halos tend to spread around areas of overly saturated color in sharpened images. To reduce this unwanted effect, you can blur the color halos to remove noise.

TIP When the woven grid of a garment's fibers is close to the scale of the pixel grid, interference patterns, called moirés, result. You can remove a moiré pattern by blurring the color of the affected regions.

Sharpening and Removing Color Noise

You will now learn techniques to both sharpen and blur images to enhance edges and remove unwanted color noise.

1. Open the file `Basilique St Nazaire de Carcassonne.jpg` from the CD. A version of this image is included in the color section.

2. Choose Filter ➢ Sharpen ➢ Unsharp Mask to open the Unsharp Mask dialog box, as shown in Figure 3.22.

3. Change Amount to 100%, Radius to 2.0 pixels, and Threshold to 3 levels, and click OK.

NOTE For best results when using Unsharp Mask, the Amount slider should range only from 50% to 100%, Radius between 1 and 3 pixels, and Threshold between 3 and 10 levels. Although greater amount and radius values result in increased sharpening, threshold is counterintuitive with greater sharpening occurring with fewer levels.

4. Immediately choose Edit ➢ Fade Unsharp Mask, or press Shift+Ctrl+F to open the Fade dialog box (see Figure 3.23). Fade only works immediately after you perform an action. If you select another tool, Fade will not work.

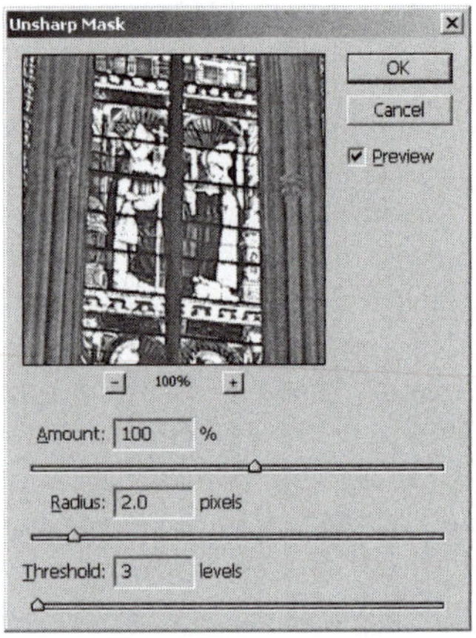

FIGURE 3.22
The Unsharp Mask
dialog box

FIGURE 3.23
Fading the last
command

5. Click the Mode pop-up and select Luminosity. Leave the Opacity slider at 100% and click OK. By fading all but this blending mode, you are effectively sharpening only the luminosity, where the detail in the image resides.

TIP   For close-up images of people, try sharpening only the Red channel in RGB color mode. This will produce the least amount of edge detail and helps keep skin smooth.

6. Even though you only sharpened the luminosity, some color halos in the stained glass have resulted from the increase in contrast. You can remove this color noise by using blur. Choose Filter ➢ Blur ➢ Gaussian Blur to open the Gaussian Blur dialog box.

TIP   Professionals always use Unsharp Mask and Gaussian Blur because they offer the most options of the available tools in Photoshop.

7. Set the Radius to 2 pixels and click OK. You want a heavy blur to obscure any color noise brought out by sharpening.

8. Press Shift+Ctrl+F to open the Fade dialog box. Choose Color from the Mode pop-up and click OK.

By fading all but this blending mode, you are effectively blurring only the color, where halos and noise reside. Figure 3.24 shows a grayscale version of this image. A version of this image is also included in the color section for a "before and after" comparison.

A technique many professional photographers use starts by converting an RGB image to Lab color mode. They sharpen the Lightness channel, which carries the luminosity detail, and blur the two color channels (a and b) before converting back to RGB. This has an effect almost identical to the technique just presented.

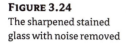

FIGURE 3.24
The sharpened stained
glass with noise removed

On the other hand, you can use a layer-based technique for more flexibility. Start by duplicating your background layer, sharpen the new layer, and convert its blending mode to luminosity. Duplicate another layer, blur it, and convert its blending mode to color. You can then adjust the amount of sharpening and blurring by adjusting the opacity of the corresponding layers.

Whichever technique you choose, it helps to record the steps you take as an action to save time. You can then apply the action with one click to sharpen your image and remove the noise all at once. Let's make an action for the first technique presented in this section.

1. Click the Actions palette to select it. Click the Create New Action button along the lower edge of the palette to open the New Action dialog box.

2. Type **Sharpen and Blur** for the name of your new action, and click Record.

3. Repeat steps 1 through 8 in the previous exercise to sharpen the luminosity and blur the color in the stained glass image.

4. Click the Stop Playing/Recording button on the lower edge of the Actions palette. That's it—your action is ready for use on other images.

5. If you want the option to set parameters in the Unsharp Mask and Gaussian Blur dialog boxes when you apply the action, toggle on the dialog box icons as shown in Figure 3.25.

FIGURE 3.25
Click the icons next to Unsharp Mask and Gaussian Blur to toggle the dialog boxes "on."

6. Choose File ➢ Revert to test your recorded action in this image.

7. Click Sharpen And Blur in the Actions palette. Click the Play Selection button along the lower edge of the Actions palette.

8. You will see both the Unsharp Mask and Gaussian Blur dialog boxes appear, giving you a chance to alter the parameters to suit whichever image you are working on. Click OK to close each dialog box. Your action successfully automated this process and reduced the number of steps you have to perform.

9. Close the file without saving when you're finished.

TIP Any time you find a series of steps tedious, record an action and reduce a lengthy series of steps to a few. You'll save tons of time in the long run.

Alternative Edge Enhancements

You may prefer to sharpen images using an alternative edge enhancement technique. Rather than rely on Unsharp Mask to determine where the edges are in your image, you can use an algorithm called Emboss to locate the hard edges.

1. Open the file Carcassonne.jpg from the CD. This is the exterior of the medieval castle that holds the stained glass you worked on before.

2. Press Ctrl+J to duplicate the Background layer. Rename the new layer Edges.

3. Choose Filter ➢ Stylize ➢ Emboss to open the Emboss dialog box, as shown in Figure 3.26.

4. Change Height to 5 pixels. The best results come from using between 3 and 5 pixels on most images. Click OK. The image in the document window appears mostly in grayscale with some strange colored highlights.

5. In the Layers palette, change the blending mode of the Edges layer to Hard Light.

The color image reappears in the document window with heavy edge enhancement.

FIGURE 3.26
The Emboss dialog box

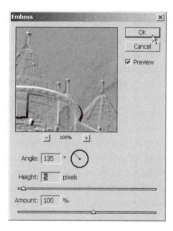

6. Lower the opacity of the Edges layer to 33% to tone down the edge enhancement effect.

7. You may notice the edges of the branches look unrealistic. Change the foreground color to middle gray (128 in all three RGB values). Paint out the branch area in middle gray to eliminate edge enhancement from this portion of the image. Figure 3.27 shows the result.

8. Close the file without saving when you're finished.

FIGURE 3.27
Embossed edges

Simulating Camera Effects

The way photographs represent reality has become part of every person's subconscious mind today. Traditional film cameras have several shortcomings that we take so much for granted today that we almost see evidence of these shortcomings as proof of the reality of an image.

Take film grain for example. The chemical development process exposes "grain" under certain lighting and aperture settings, in which the photosensitive emulsion forms a random organic pattern. In contrast, digital cameras and computer-generated imagery has no inherent grain. Consequently, digital imagery often appears "computer generated" or somehow less than real to our subconscious minds.

Cameras are designed to let light pass through their glass lenses and either expose film or a charge-coupled device (CCD) sensor, for example. Sometimes light rays reflect internally within the optical system and produce *lens flares*, or chromatic aberrations. Lens flares are sometimes used to make computer-generated imagery seem more realistic because it makes us subconsciously believe the shot was taken with a real camera. Let's take a look at how this works.

1. Open the file Building.psd from the CD. Figure 3.28 shows the original computer-generated image.

2. Press Ctrl+J and rename the duplicate layer Lens Flare.

3. Choose Filter ➢ Render ➢ Lens Flare to open the Lens Flare dialog box, as shown in Figure 3.29.

4. Click a point high up on the glazing system (shown in Figure 3.29) to locate the flare center. Drag the Brightness slider to 75%, and click the 105mm Prime lens radio button. Click OK. The lens flare appears and looks like the reflection of the sun in the glass of the building and internally within the camera lens.

FIGURE 3.28
The original computer-generated image

FIGURE 3.29
The Lens Flare dialog box

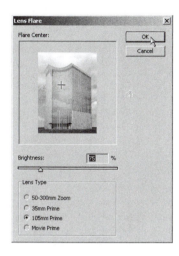

5. Press Ctrl+J and rename the duplicate layer Film Grain. Take a look at the Histogram palette and observe that this image suffers somewhat from banding. The histogram has many gaps and slender peaks.

6. Choose Filter ➢ Noise ➢ Add Noise to open the Noise dialog box.

7. Change Amount to 3%, change Distribution to Gaussian, and make sure Monochromatic is cleared. Click OK.

8. Take another look at the Histogram palette. The histogram is much smoother after applying noise. Noise evens out tonal extremes.

Figure 3.30 shows the final image after lens flare and film grain have been added. The noise may be visible on screen, but will tend to disappear when printed.

TIP   Add a small amount of noise to images that suffer from banding to improve print quality.

FIGURE 3.30
The image with lens flare
and film grain added

Summary

This chapter has exposed you to a wealth of techniques to use in your digital darkroom. You have seen the entire digital photo work flow from developing raw images through tonal adjustment, color balancing, sharpening, blurring, and simulating real-world camera effects. As always, plan to spend time practicing these techniques to build skills that you can use every day.

Chapter 4

You and Your Entourage

Entourage is a term used in traditional architectural illustration to describe elements added to a rendering that place a building in the context of its environment and relate it to human scale. Examples of entourage are people, furniture, cars, trees, plants, and flowers. This chapter will teach you how to extract and enhance image-based 2D entourage in Photoshop and then show you how to employ it in the 3D world of Autodesk VIZ.

Although it is possible to create true 3D entourage in Autodesk VIZ or to buy 3D models of cars, people, and trees, doing so may be overkill for most projects. Using 3D entourage might not produce photo-realistic results for your rendering in a reasonable time frame because it requires far greater rendering time as compared with image-based 2D entourage. However, in some instances using true 3D entourage makes sense, such as in an animation, where a moving point of view exposes the flatness of the entourage illusion.

You can use photographic entourage directly in Photoshop without ever using a 3D program. (See Chapter 6, "Elevating the Elevation," to learn how to use entourage in an elevation made from an AutoCAD drawing.) You can also use entourage in 3D scenes that are composited from image elements in Photoshop (see Chapter 7, "Illustrating Architecture").

- ◆ Extracting Entourage
- ◆ Enhancing Entourage
- ◆ Using Entourage in Autodesk VIZ

Extracting Entourage

To create your own entourage, start by taking photographs (or making scans) of the people and objects you want to use in your compositions. You must then extract the foreground "objects" from their backgrounds to use them as entourage.

In this chapter, I'll show you several extraction techniques in the tutorials that you can use to separate the foreground pixels from the image background. The first tutorial covers a person, and the second a deciduous tree. Each image involves a different challenge, and I'll show you how to use a variety of tools to accomplish your goals.

Extracting People from Photos

Arranging to take photos of people in front of a wall or a backdrop of even color and texture makes it easier to identify which parts of the image are figure and which parts are ground.

It is generally easy to arrange for people to stand in front of a neutral background while being photographed to gain the distinct honor of becoming "part of your entourage."

USING THE EXTRACT TOOL

Let's start by roughly separating figure and ground using the Extract tool.

1. Open the file WomanStanding.psd from the companion CD. This is a tonally adjusted and color-balanced photo (see Chapter 3, "Retouching Photos") showing our subject and the background from which she must be extracted (see Figure 4.1). A "before" version of this image is included in the color section.

2. To begin the extraction process, choose Filter ➤ Extract or press Alt+Ctrl+X to open the Extract dialog box (see Figure 4.2). You will separate the foreground object from the background using the tools in this dialog box. Familiarize yourself with its tools.

FIGURE 4.1
The original photo of a person to extract and use as entourage

FIGURE 4.2
The Extract dialog box

Eraser Fill   Edge Highlighter

Eyedropper
Cleanup
Edge Touchup

Zoom Hand

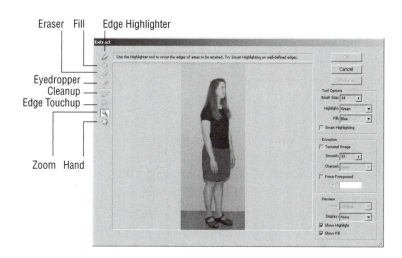

You will start by tracing around the person using the Edge Highlighter tool. Once the highlighting forms a complete enclosure, you'll use the Fill tool to designate the foreground object.

TIP Drag the resize handle in the lower-right corner of the Extract dialog box and enlarge the window to fill your screen.

3. Select the Zoom tool and click a few times to magnify the area around the person's feet.

4. Click the Edge Highlighter tool or press B to select it. Check Smart Highlighting in the Tool Options group at the right. Use Smart Highlighting so that Photoshop automatically selects an appropriate brush size when you are tracing over well-defined edges.

5. Carefully trace the edges of the woman's legs and shoes. Green highlighting will appear as you trace on the screen (see Figure 4.3). The smart highlighter feature will adjust the brush size as necessary to maintain coverage over the edge. Ideally you should aim the brush to cover half figure and half background along the edges you trace.

TIP You can optionally change the highlight color in the Tool Options group of the Extract dialog box. It is easier to work with a contrasting highlight color in relation to the image you are tracing.

6. Occasionally when tracing, you'll come upon an intersection of two edges (areas of high contrast). The smart highlighter tends to sometimes follow the wrong path. If you make a mistake, and the highlighting you are "painting" follows the wrong edge, you can correct the path by using the Eraser tool. Press E and erase any stray highlighting.

7. Press B and continue highlighting the well-defined edges of the leg and shoe area. You should also highlight the edges in between the woman's legs where you can see the background. It is important to make complete enclosures with any edges that you trace so that the enclosures can be filled in later.

FIGURE 4.3
Start dragging the Edge
Highlighter around the
edge of the woman.

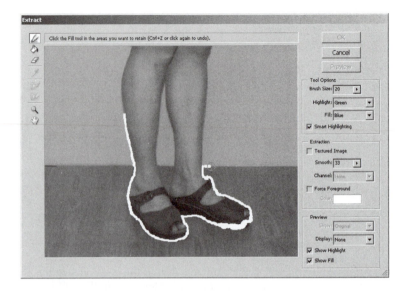

TIP You can press Ctrl+Z in the Extract dialog box to undo a single step *within the dialog box*. After
you close the dialog box, the entire Extract operation counts as one step in the History palette.

8. Hold down the spacebar to temporarily use the Hand tool. Drag the image down to pan upward
in the image. Continue tracing the edges with the Edge Highlighter tool (see Figure 4.4). For
now, you can ignore the small area inside her left hand. Instead, trace around the outer edges
of the left hand, and continue along the arm. You do not want to trace the shadow under her
skirt; follow the edge of the fabric instead.

FIGURE 4.4
Continuing to trace
the edges

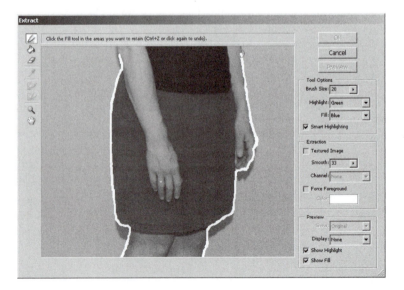

9. Pan the image down using the Hand tool. Continue tracing the well-defined edges using Smart Highlighting. Stop when you reach her hair, as the hair presents a wispy edge that should not be traced with Smart Highlighting.

10. Pan the image down by holding the spacebar until you can see the top of her head. Uncheck Smart Highlighting in the Tool Options group. Click the Brush Size pop-up and change its value to 30 pixels. You are enlarging the brush to cover more of the wispy edge.

11. Trace over the hair and stop when you reach her eyebrow and lips, as in Figure 4.5. Her face has well-defined edges, and you don't want to trace it with such a large brush.

FIGURE 4.5

Tracing wispy edges with a larger brush

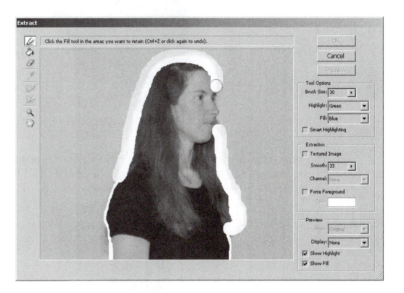

12. Check Smart Highlighting again and trace over her face to complete the highlight enclosure. Press Z to select the Zoom tool. Hold down the Alt key and click several times to zoom out until you can see her entire body in the Extract dialog box.

13. Press G to select the Fill tool and click inside her body area. The enclosure should fill with a blue color on the screen. This step is necessary to let Photoshop know what part of the image is the object you want to extract.

WARNING   If the fill covers the whole image, you have not properly traced a complete enclosure.

14. Click the Preview button to remove the background pixels outside the filled area. Do not close the dialog box yet because there is still much to do to improve the extraction.

15. Press Z and drag a small window around her left hand. Depending on how well you traced, you might see some potions of her fingers missing. In Figure 4.6, her index finger has been replaced by transparency (shown by the checkerboard pattern).

FIGURE 4.6
Portions of the extracted
figure are missing.

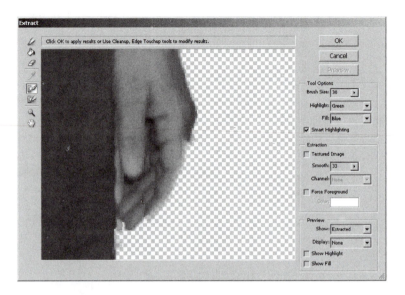

16. Select the Cleanup tool. This tool normally removes opacity from the foreground object. If you hold down the Alt key, this tool works in reverse; it adds back opacity from the background. Hold down the Alt key and paint her finger back in.

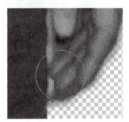

17. You may find that you have painted back in too much of her finger and that some of the background shows also. Release the Alt key and clean up these background areas as needed. You may find that by reducing the brush size you can reach into smaller areas. Press the left and right square bracket keys to reduce and enlarge the brush size, respectively.

NOTE You can leave the small area within her left hand alone for now. We will clean up the background inside her hand later in this tutorial.

18. Zoom out; you can do this by pressing Ctrl+- (that's the Ctrl key and the hyphen key) or by using the Alt key in combination with the Zoom tool. Navigate to her legs and shoes and clean up any rough edges. Alternate between holding down the Alt key to add back the background with the Cleanup tool and using the Cleanup tool normally to remove pixels as needed to define a smooth, clean edge.

19. You might notice that some of the edges are soft and blurry after cleanup. Click the Edge Touchup tool, or press T. This tool sharpens edges. Drag it along blurry edges to make them crisp.

WARNING Do not use the Edge Touchup tool on hair because you want wispy edges to remain blurry at this stage.

20. Continue working around the entire image, cleaning and touching up edges as needed. Click OK when you are satisfied with the results in the preview. The Extract dialog box closes, leaving you with just the selected portion of your image, as in Figure 4.7.

FIGURE 4.7
The extracted figure

CORRECTING ARTIFACTS

You have completed the first part of the extraction process. You have roughly extracted a figure, but you need to correct some artifacts before this figure is quality entourage.

1. The Background layer was automatically converted to a normal layer (Layer 0) because it has transparency. Rename Layer 0 to Woman Standing. Click the Create A New Layer button on the lower edge of the Layers palette and rename the new layer Backdrop. Drag the Backdrop layer below the Woman Standing layer.

2. Press D to set the default colors and then press Alt+Backspace to fill the current layer (Backdrop) with the foreground color. You now have a black backdrop behind the figure. Figure 4.8 shows artifacts that are only visible on screen when viewing the figure against a black backdrop.

FIGURE 4.8
Artifacts are easier to spot against black.

Artifacts are visible along many of the edges.

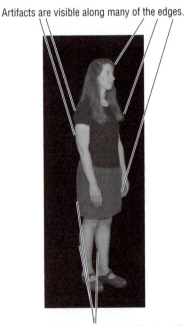

Color bleeding from the background is visible along these edges.

Saturated color from the background that bled onto the figure caused color halo artifacts to appear on many edges. Let's correct this with the Color Replacement tool.

3. Click the Woman Standing layer in the Layers palette. Select the Color Replacement tool in the toolbox. (It may be hidden under the Healing Brush.) You can also access the Color Replacement tool by pressing Shift+J multiple times to cycle through the Healing Brush, Patch, and Color Replacement tools. On the Options bar, set Mode to Color, Sampling to Continuous, Limits to Contiguous, and Tolerance to 15%, and check Anti-aliased.

4. Zoom into the head area, and concentrate on removing the artifacts in her hair and then on her face. Hold down the Alt key to change your cursor to the Eyedropper icon. Click a point on the hair on her head to sample its color. Then paint with the Color Replacement tool along the edge of her hair to replace the artifact color with the foreground color. Hold down the Alt key, sample a facial color, and then use it to replace the color halo at the edge of her face.

5. Continue around the figure, replacing the color halos along the edge (shown in Figure 4.8) with the corresponding colors that you sample by holding down the Alt key.

6. You can get a cleaner edge after using the Color Replacement tool, by following up with the Defringe tool. Choose Layer ➤ Matting ➤ Defringe. Enter a width of 2 pixels in the Defringe dialog box and click OK. Goodbye fringes!

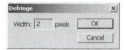

TIP When making subtle adjustments, it is often helpful to undo and redo repeatedly (press Ctrl+Z) to visualize the changes made in the document window.

7. Unless you are lucky, you probably still have some areas where the Extract tool didn't produce a perfect edge. You may be thinking that you'd like to use the Cleanup tool in the Extract dialog box, but at this point it's too late; the dialog is closed. Fortunately, you can get similar results by using the Eraser in combination with the History Brush tool. Type E to select the Eraser tool.

8. Carefully erase any edges where you still see any of the original background (see Figure 4.9). Try erasing with a reduced opacity soft brush for best results. If you put off erasing the background from inside her left hand, now is the time to remove those pixels.

FIGURE 4.9
Erasing the background

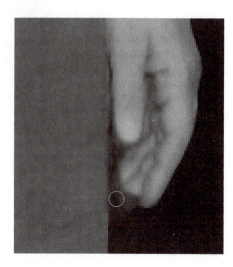

9. If you erase too much, you can rely on History to correct your mistake. Select the History Brush, and paint in any parts of the figure that you overzealously erased in the previous step. On the Options bar, set the History Brush tool to Mode Color, Opacity to 100%, and Flow to 50%.

NOTE   You can paint back in the erased figure because the source for the History Brush is set on the Open state by default. This means you can paint the original pixels back in at any time using the History Brush.

At this point you have successfully extracted the figure against a black backdrop. Check your work against a white backdrop to reveal any dark artifacts that might be present.

10. In the Layers palette, click the Backdrop layer. Press D to set the default colors, and then press Ctrl+Backspace to fill the layer with white.

11. Select the Woman Standing layer and then press E to select the Eraser. Erase any rough edges that were revealed in the last step (see Figure 4.10).

FIGURE 4.10
Erasing rough edges

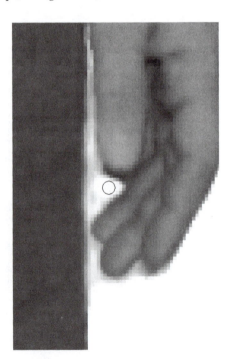

12. When the figure is finally extracted, choose Filter ➤ Sharpen ➤ Unsharp Mask. Drag the Amount slider to 100%, Radius to 2.0 pixels, and Threshold to 3 levels if these settings yielding a strong sharpening effect were not already selected. Click OK.

SAVING THE EXTRACTION AS AN ALPHA CHANNEL

Now that you have extracted the figure and sharpened the image, you might think you are done. In fact you are almost there, but a few important details remain. For entourage to work in most 3D programs, you will need to save an alpha channel. The *alpha* is a grayscale channel that shows where the figure is opaque, translucent, and/or transparent. Traditionally, white represents opaque regions, black is for transparent areas (where the figure is not), and shades of gray are translucent zones (hair, for example).

The alpha channel gets its name because it is the first extra channel in addition to the color channels (Red, Green, and Blue). If each channel stores 8 bits/pixels, an alpha channel RGB image is a 32-bit image (see Chapter 1, "The Basics"). Although you can store as many channels as desired, the alpha is the most commonly used. In Photoshop CS, an image can have a maximum of 56 channels.

Currently, the figure is represented by RGB pixels on the Woman Standing layer. There simply are no pixels in the areas of the image where the figure is not; this absence of pixels is known as transparency. We can use the Calculations tool to convert transparency to an alpha channel.

NOTE   If you extracted the figure using a technique that left pixels outside the figure (not shown in this tutorial), you would have to create the alpha channel by making a selection.

1. Choose Image ➢ Calculations to open the Calculations dialog box, as shown in Figure 4.11. In the Source 1 group, click the Layer pop-up and select Woman Standing. Just below this, click the Channel pop-up and select Transparency. Finally, select Normal from the Blending pop-up and click OK.

FIGURE 4.11
Use the Calculations dialog to make an alpha channel.

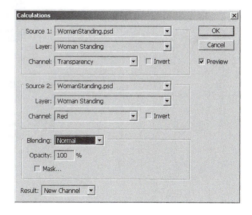

2. Click the Channels palette, and notice that the result from the previous step became a new channel called Alpha 1 and is selected. Figure 4.12 shows the result.

3. Click the RGB channel to return the normal color image to the document window.

4. Flatten the image. You can do so from the main menu (choose Layer ➢ Flatten Image) or by clicking the arrow at the top right of the Layers palette to display the palette menu (see Figure 4.13).

FIGURE 4.12
The transparency channel converted to an alpha channel

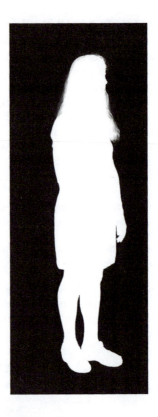

FIGURE 4.13
The Layers palette menu

5. To automatically crop pixels around the figure's outer border, choose Image ➤ Trim. Click the Top Left Pixel Color radio button, leave everything checked in the Trim Away group, and click OK.

Figure 4.14 shows the final trimmed figure as entourage, complete with alpha channel. A version of this image is also included in the color section.

FIGURE 4.14
The final version:
the woman saved
as entourage

6. The last step is to save the file in a format that supports an alpha channel. Choose File ➢ Save As. Select TIFF from the Format menu and be sure Alpha Channels is checked in the Save Options group. Save the file as WomanStanding.tif (also provided on the CD). In the TIFF Options Dialog box, select LZW in the Compression Group, and for the byte order, select the platform on which you are working. You can close the file when you're finished.

TIP The Targa (*.tga) and TIFF (*.tif) formats support alpha channels, and both are commonly used in 3D programs such as Autodesk VIZ and Discreet 3ds max. You will use the file you save here later in this chapter, in the "Entourage in Autodesk VIZ" section. Alpha channels are preserved when files are saved in TGA, PSD, PDF, PICT, PIXAR, TIFF, or RAW formats.

Extracting Objects from Photos

You can create entourage from numerous objects that you photograph. Road signs, lampposts, benches, fountains, trees, flowers, cars, and building facades are just a few examples. Small-scale objects are easier to work with if you can bring them into a studio space where you can control the background. Neutral backgrounds without much texture are best because they are easier to select and extract from.

EXTRACTING A PLUM TREE

You cannot always control the background conditions in your photographs, especially with large-scale objects. This tutorial shows how to extract a 30-foot high plum tree from its natural outdoor background. In some ways, this is more challenging than extracting a person, because of the translucency of the leaves; the intermingling of foreground and background in an outdoor setting make it more difficult. Let's dive in.

1. Open the file `PlumTree.psd` from the CD. Figure 4.15 shows the starting image; a version of this image is included in the color section.

2. Choose Filter ➢ Extract or press Alt+Ctrl+X to open the Extract dialog box. The image in Figure 4.15 is mostly shades of green on screen; choosing a highlight color other than green is therefore appropriate. In the Tool Options group at the right, select Red as the Highlight color from the drop-down menu.

FIGURE 4.15
The original plum tree photo

3. Drag the lower-right corner handle of the Extract dialog box and enlarge it to fill your screen. The size that it becomes depends on the resolution to which you have set your graphics card (see Chapter 2, "Working with Color").

Feel free to use the Zoom and Hand tools within the Extract dialog box at any time to navigate the image. These tools do not interfere with any of the other tools and work identically to the Zoom and Hand tools in the toolbox. The amount that you will have to navigate ultimately depends on the size you are able to make the dialog box; if you have less resolution, you will have to navigate more.

4. Start with a brush size of 35 (set in the Tool Options group) and use the Edge Highlighter tool (press B) to trace the outer boundary of the tree's leaves and branches. Do not worry about trying to trace interior areas of translucency yet. Also, do not use Smart Highlighting on the leaves and branches because it would be far too tedious to try to trace the edges of the myriad leaves. Instead, focus on quickly outlining the silhouette of the tree with a larger brush size first.

TIP In general, a smaller brush size is better when using the Edge Highlighter because it produces a smaller transition area between the object you are extracting and its background.

5. Check Smart Highlighting in the Tool Options group and proceed to trace the hard edges of the tree trunk itself. Intentionally draw a horizontal line at the bottom of the tree trunk where it meets the grass to create a complete highlight enclosure.

NOTE If you make any mistakes while painting with the Edge Highlighter, you have one undo (press Ctrl+Z) while in the Extract dialog box. You can also use the Eraser tool to get rid of stray highlighting; then you can go back and properly highlight the affected area.

6. Use the Fill tool (press G) and click inside the enclosure you highlighted in the previous two steps. Figure 4.16 shows the tree with proper highlight and fill. You'll find a version of this image in the color section.

There is a way to help smooth out irregularities in the highlighted areas you trace. The Textured Image feature blurs the boundary between the foreground object and its background; it is appropriate for wispy edges (such as hair) or edges with a mixing of opaque and translucent areas (such as leaves).

NOTE You can undo a preview in the Extract dialog box by pressing Ctrl+Z. This is helpful when you want to try a different smoothing setting and then preview again.

7. In the Extraction group, check Textured Image. Click the Smooth drop-down and increase its value to 33. Now that you have defined the edges (with highlight) and indicated what part of the image is the foreground object (with fill), you are ready to preview the result. Click the Preview button. Your computer may take a few seconds to process this request, and then a preview will appear as shown in Figure 4.17.

FIGURE 4.16
Extracting a tree with
Highlight and Fill

FIGURE 4.17
A preview of the initial
extraction

The initial preview is rough; parts of the background show through the tree itself. You can improve the extraction by working with the versatile Cleanup tool. When you use this tool "normally," it removes opacity from the pixels in the preview. Using it in combination with the Alt key works in reverse, adding back opacity from the background into the preview. Either way you use the Cleanup tool, it works cumulatively, so multiple passes subtract or add more pixels as you go.

NOTE   The Cleanup tool does not function like an airbrush, so holding the mouse down for a period of time does not increase its effect. Slight movement of the mouse, however, produces cleanup.

This part of the extraction process is most like an art and probably will require some practice. The process is a bit like visual sculpture, as you work to liberate the object from a matrix of background pixels.

Try to avoid using a small brush size when cleaning up internal areas, or you will be able to perceive the round brush shape in the extracted image. Make several passes with the tool and build up changes slowly.

8. Select the Cleanup tool (press C) and use it to remove pixels that do not belong to the tree. Hold down the Alt key and use the Cleanup tool in reverse to add back pixels that are missing (see Figure 4.18).

NOTE   You do not have to clean up the image perfectly at this stage. Aim to improve the rough extraction only. We'll use additional tools later to refine the image.

You can use the Edge Touchup tool following the Cleanup tool, but use Edge Touchup only along hard edges you want to sharpen. The trunk has edges that should be sharpened now.

FIGURE 4.18
Cleaning up the tree

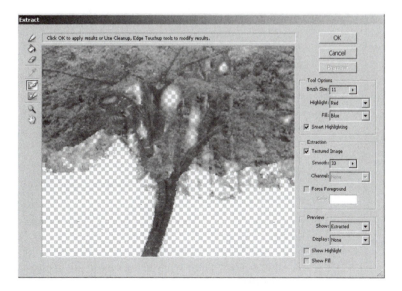

9. Select the Edge Touchup tool (press T) and drag along the edges of the main trunk. The tree bark looks harder. Click OK to accept all the changes you have made up to this point, and close the Extract dialog box. Notice how the Background layer was automatically converted to Layer 0, which now contains pixels of the foreground object surrounded by transparency.

Now that you have completed the extraction, you can do several things to improve the image before it becomes part of your entourage. Whenever you are working on a layer with transparency (such as Layer 0), create a Backdrop layer to help you see the fringes of the object.

It is wise to view your prospective entourage against both black and white backdrops alternately as you are refining the extraction. Most images have bright or dark pixels that do not belong with the foreground object; these pixels are visible only against a contrasting backdrop.

10. Create a new layer (press Shift+Ctrl+N). Give the new layer the name Backdrop. Drag this layer below Layer 0 in the Layers palette. Reset the default colors (press D). Fill the Backdrop layer with the foreground color (press Alt+Backspace). Now the backdrop layer is black. Click Layer 0 to make this the current layer for editing.

The Magic Eraser is a tool that you must be careful using. Each time you click the Magic Eraser, you have the power to erase many similar pixels in the image to transparency. It is safer (and slower) to work in Contiguous mode, where the tool will affect only similar pixels that are connected to the point you click. If you do not use the Contiguous option, the Magic Eraser will work on all similar pixels in the image at once.

11. Choose the Magic Eraser tool from the toolbox; this is under the Eraser tool, and you can also access it by pressing Shift+E multiple times to cycle through the three types of Eraser tools in Photoshop. On the Options bar, choose a Tolerance of 15, check Anti-aliased, leave Contiguous and All Layers unchecked, and leave Opacity at 100%. Finally, press the Caps Lock key.

TIP Pressing the Caps Lock key activates the *precise cursor*, which appears as cross hairs centered on the tool's *hot spot*. The hot spot is where the tool takes effect in the image. Most tools have icons whose hot spots vary in position relative to the pointer.

Each time you click the Magic Eraser, you erase many pixels in the tree image. The Magic Eraser is sensitive to the exact pixel color you select. If you think too many pixels disappear when you use this tool, undo and try again. You can also adjust Tolerance to a lower value to affect fewer pixels.

12. Now that you have a black backdrop, white fringe areas will be evident around some of the leaves. Using the Magic Eraser with the precise cursor, carefully click a white pixel. All similar pixels are erased to transparency. Repeat this step until you are satisfied that the white fringe has disappeared, all the while being careful not to erase any important parts of the foliage (see Figure 4.19).

FIGURE 4.19
Using the Magic
Eraser against a
black background

Before you are done with the Magic Eraser, take a look at the tree over a white backdrop because this will reveal the dark fringe in the tree image.

13. Select the Backdrop layer in the Layers palette. Press Ctrl+Backspace to fill the current layer with the background color. Now the Backdrop layer is white. Click Layer 0 to make this the current layer for editing.

   The dark green pixels belong to some of the evergreen trees in the background of the original image (refer to the color section).

14. Using the Magic Eraser, reduce the Tolerance to 10 on the Options bar and then click a dark green part of the fringe. Undo, and try again if necessary. Repeat this step until you are satisfied that the dark fringe has disappeared, still being careful not to erase any important parts of the foliage. Figure 4.20 shows the result. Press the Caps Lock key to toggle off Precise Cursor mode.

   Chances are, you erased a bit more than you wanted while using the Magic Eraser. One reason this may have happened is that the dark fringe is composed of dark green and brown pixels, which are similar to the plum tree's trunk and branches—therein lies the challenge. Fortunately, you can replace important parts of the tree that might have been wiped out by the Magic Eraser.

NOTE Extracting entourage often involves a give-and-take process whereby you ultimately coax the figure away from its background.

FIGURE 4.20
Using the Magic
Eraser against a
white background

15. Use the History Brush (press Y) to paint back areas on the trunk and branches that might have been magically erased in the previous step. Press Caps Lock to deactivate the precise cursor.

16. The image can also benefit from Photoshop's automatic fringe removal. Choose Layer ➢ Matting ➢ Defringe. Select 1 pixel from the Defringe dialog box and click OK.

TIP You'll find two additional commands under Layer ➢ Matting called Remove Black Matte and Remove White Matte. These commands are only appropriate when your foreground object was photographed in front of a black or a white background. Defringe yields better results for objects with multicolored backgrounds.

You can smooth the edges of the figure by clearing a feathered selection of the background. This technique slightly reduces the opacity along the edges of the figure and is appropriate for a deciduous tree if you expect to see translucency in the leaves.

NOTE Don't use this method on hard-edged objects.

17. Choose Select ➤ Color Range to open the Color Range dialog box (see Figure 4.21). Click a point outside the tree in the document window to select the background color (white), and then drag the Fuzziness slider to 50. Click OK to make a selection.

FIGURE 4.21

The Color Range dialog box

18. Choose Select ➤ Feather to open the Feather dialog box. Set Feather Radius to 1 pixel, and then click OK. This essentially creates a selection with 50% opacity along the edges of the tree and all its leaves.

19. Press Ctrl+H to hide the marching ants. Now clear the selection (press either Backspace or Delete). The edges of all the leaves are softened slightly.

WARNING Hide the selection before making subtle adjustments to a selection boundary; otherwise, the marching ants will obscure any changes. The selection remains hidden until you either deselect it or press Ctrl+H again.

20. Save your work as PlumTree2.psd.

If you are going to continue working through the following sections, leave this file open for now. Congratulations on properly extracting the plum tree from its natural outdoor background!

POST-EXTRACTION PROCESSING: MODIFYING SHAPE, COLOR, AND TONE

The extraction may have been the bulk of the work, but you must still take care of several items before the plum tree can become entourage. Let's liquify the tree to change its shape, adjust the image's hues and saturation, tweak its levels, calculate an alpha channel from transparency, flatten, trim, and finally save.

1. If you have the PlumTree.psd file open from the last section, you can continue here. If not, open the PlumTree2.psd file from the companion CD.

2. Choose Filter ➤ Liquify or press Shift+Ctrl+X to open the Liquify dialog box, as shown in Figure 4.22. Press W to select the Forward Warp tool (the finger icon). Set Brush Size to 250 in the Tool Options group. Click over the lower part of the tree trunk, as shown in Figure 4.22, and drag to the right to make the shape of the trunk vertical. The trunk will flow over as if liquid, and the bend in the tree is eliminated. Click OK to close the dialog box.

FIGURE 4.22
Liquifying the tree

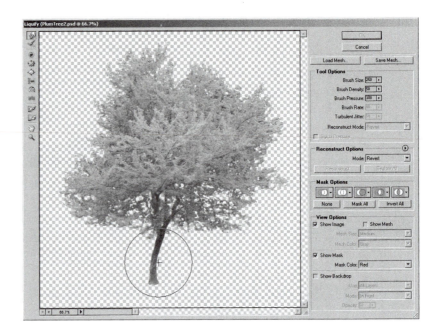

NOTE   Liquify has a great depth of features that go beyond the scope of this book. See Photoshop Help to learn more about this powerful command.

Adjustment layers affect all the layers below them in the Layers palette. Therefore, turn off the Backdrop layer before adjusting.

3. Turn off the Backdrop layer (click its eye icon in the Layers palette). Apply a Hue/Saturation adjustment layer. (Click the Create New Fill Or Adjustment Layer button along the bottom edge of the Layers palette, and choose Hue/Saturation from the menu that appears.)

4. In the Hue/Saturation dialog box, drag the Saturation slider to –10 to tone down the bright colors a bit. Experiment with the Hue slider by dragging it back and forth. You can make yellow leaves by dragging the Hue slider to –20. For a vibrant summer look, drag the Hue slider to +10 and click OK.

5. Next apply a Levels adjustment layer; click the Adjustment Layer button in the Layers palette and choose Levels from the menu. In the Levels dialog box, tweak the levels so that a complete tonal range is represented in the image. Drag the shadow input marker to the right until it meets the left edge of the histogram, as in Figure 4.23. Similarly, drag the highlight input slider toward the right until it likewise meets the right edge of the histogram and click OK.

FIGURE 4.23
Altering tone in the
Levels dialog box

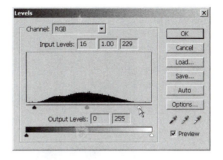

SAVING THE EXTRACTION AS AN ALPHA CHANNEL

Now that you are nearing the end of the tutorial, it is time to create an alpha channel so that you can use the tree as entourage in 3D programs. (You will use the alpha channel in the "Entourage in Autodesk VIZ" section later in this chapter.)

Use the Calculations dialog box to save the image's transparent areas as an alpha channel, as I described earlier. For specific instructions on how to do that for this particular image, follow these steps:

1. Choose Image ➢ Calculations to open the Calculations dialog box. Select Transparency from the Channel drop-down in the Source 1 group. If you leave everything else with the default settings as shown in Figure 4.24, you can click OK to create the alpha channel.

FIGURE 4.24
Calculating an
alpha channel from
transparency

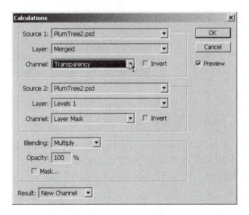

2. Figure 4.25 shows the grayscale alpha channel image that was generated in the previous step. This image will tell 3D programs where to make the entourage object opaque (white), translucent (shades of gray), or transparent (black). To return the color image, click the Channels palette and click the RGB channel.

FIGURE 4.25
The alpha channel image

3. To automatically crop the image, choose Image ➢ Trim. In the Trim dialog box, click the Transparent Pixels radio button and click OK.

4. Rename Layer 0 to PlumTree so that it will be identified properly when you drag this layer into other Photoshop projects.

5. If you plan to use this image in your own work, now is a good time to save it as a native Photoshop file so that its adjustment layers and channels are preserved for future editing. Save the file as `PlumTreeEntourage.psd`. If you're going to continue working through the following section, you can leave this file open for now.

TIP You can use this tree in an autumn scene by tweaking the Hue/Saturation adjustment layer in the Photoshop file to make yellow or orange leaves.

To prepare the entourage for 3D programs, it is best to save in a flattened format that supports alpha channels to save memory in the 3D program.

6. Return to the Layers palette and turn the Backdrop layer back on. Then flatten the image (choose Layers ➢ Flatten Image, or click the Layers palette menu and choose Flatten Image).

7. Save the image as PlumTreeEntourage.tif. Be sure to leave Alpha Channels checked in the Save As dialog box. In the TIFF Options dialog box, select LZW in the Compression Group, and for the byte order, select the platform on which you are working. Close this file after saving.

Figure 4.26 shows the final image. A version of this image is included in the color section.

FIGURE 4.26
The plum tree saved for use as entourage

Enhancing Entourage

As you use entourage in Photoshop projects, you'll discover many options for enhancing these image objects. For example, you can transform an entourage layer, adjusting its size to match the scale of a building elevation. You can drop a shadow and then distort it to add interest. You can obtain extra mileage from repetitive entourage elements, such as trees, by skewing each one differently or by mirroring each duplicate so that the eye doesn't perceive an obvious copy-and-paste job. You can use photographic entourage in an abstract way, to give a sense of human scale without diverting attention from the main subject of your composition. This section will show you how to start building your own entourage library, which can become an important asset in your future projects.

Adding People to an Elevation

If you have the `PlumTreeEntourage.psd` file still open from the previous exercise, you can continue here; if not, open that file from the CD before following these steps.

1. Open the files `BuildingElevation.tif` and `WomanFront.psd` from the companion CD. Figure 4.27 shows the elevation (see Chapter 6) without any entourage as yet.

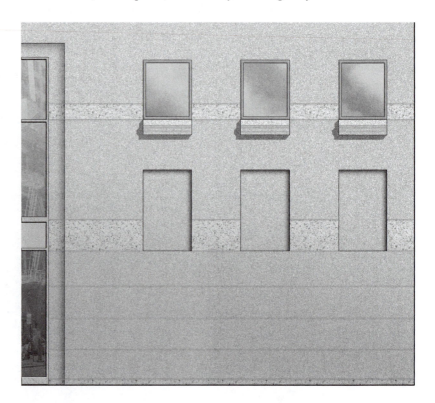

You can drag and drop an entourage layer from one image to another in Photoshop. Entourage layers that have the foreground object surrounded by transparency work best because the entourage will not obscure the document you paste it into.

2. Click the title bar of the `WomanFront.psd` document window. The layers of this document appear in the Layers palette. Drag the WomanFront layer from the palette and drop it anywhere inside the `BuildingElevation.tif` document window, as shown in Figure 4.28.

To make the woman smaller with respect to the building, we'll transform the WomanFront layer. You can both scale and move this layer using the Transform command.

FIGURE 4.28
Drag-and-drop
entourage

Drag this layer from the Layers palette...

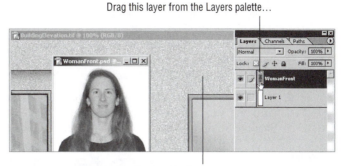

...and drop it onto the elevation here.

3. Choose the Move tool (press V). Then press Ctrl+T to switch into Transform mode, or choose Edit ➢ Transform ➢ Scale. Click the Maintain Aspect Ratio button. (The icon looks like two chain links.) This mode ensures that width and height values remain equal when you scale the layer; otherwise, distortion occurs.

Click inside the Width text box, and then press and hold the Down arrow key to decrease the numeric values quickly. Release the Down arrow key when the values in the W and H text boxes reach 20%.

4. Place your mouse inside the entourage's transform bounding box (the cursor is shown inside in Figure 4.29), and drag the figure down to the ground line.

FIGURE 4.29
Transforming the
entourage

The bottom of the woman's toes snap just above the ground line; Photoshop automatically aligns layers based on their edges. Because this elevation is an orthographic projection, the woman's shoes look a little strange; they were taken with a camera and are in perspective. To hide this mismatch, press the Down arrow key three times to move her slightly lower. Now her toes are cropped, and the figure looks better in the elevation because the perspective cues are less pronounced. Click the Commit button on the Options bar to complete the Transform command.

5. You can add depth to the elevation by dropping a shadow behind the figure using a layer style. Click the Add A Layer Style button on the lower edge of the Layers palette, and choose Drop Shadow from the menu to open the Layer Style dialog box (see Figure 4.30).

FIGURE 4.30
Dropping a shadow with style

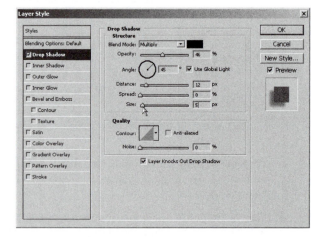

6. The circular Angle graph in the Structure group represents the angle of illumination; however, shadows are 180° out of phase with Photoshop's global light because shadows are ultimately cast by the light source. To move the direction of the shadow below and to the left of the figure, drag the line in the Angle graph to 45°.

7. To make the shadow appear farther from the person, increase the Distance slider to 12 pixels. To soften the shadow, increase the Size slider to 5 pixels. Tone down the darkness of the shadow by decreasing the Opacity slider to 46%, just above the Angle graph. Click OK to close the Layer Style dialog box.

TIP Another way to control a slider is to click inside its text box and then press the Up arrow or Down arrow key, instead of dragging the sliders with the mouse. Each press of these keys changes the values slowly and doesn't require that you input numeric values on the keyboard.

Adding Trees to an Elevation

Keep all the documents open that we've been using the preceding sections. Next, we'll drag and drop the tree entourage into the elevation image, move the tree relative to the building, and adjust the layer stacking order to control the visibility of entourage in the composition. And I'll even show you how to add a tree to your scene without showing a tree at all!

1. Click the title bar of the `PlumTreeEntourage.psd` document window. This file uses Hue/Saturation and Levels adjustment layers (see the previous section for the rationale), as shown in Figure 4.31. You will have to create a Composite layer above the adjustment layers if you want to take the adjusted entourage with you into the elevation.

FIGURE 4.31

The layers in
`PlumTreeEntourage.psd`

2. Click the Levels 1 layer to select the top layer in the palette. Then press Shift+Ctrl+N to create a new layer. Rename the new layer Tree. Press Alt+Shift+Ctrl+E to stamp all the visible layers onto the Tree layer.

3. With the `PlumTreeEntourage.psd` file selected, drag the Tree layer into the `BuildingElevation.tif` document window. The adjusted tree entourage appears in front of the building. Switch to the Move tool if it is not already selected by pressing V. Drag the tree to the lower-left corner of the elevation, as shown in Figure 4.32.

FIGURE 4.32

Plant a tree

4. Adjust the opacity of the tree layer to 85% to account for more translucency through the deciduous leaves; this also allows a bit more of the building to show through the canopy.

When you start to have multiple layers of entourage, you can arrange the layers on top of each other, much as you arrange cutout photos in a montage.

5. Select the WomanFront layer in the Layers palette. Choose Layer ➢ Arrange ➢ Bring Forward, or press Ctrl+]. You can also drag layers around in the palette. The top layer will be on top of the montage.

The tree could also benefit from a drop shadow. However, to make more realistic shadows, it is helpful to liberate the shadow from the layer style that generated it, by converting it from a layer style to a layer. Then, you can transform the shadow independently of the tree for more advanced effects.

6. Select the Tree layer in the Layers palette. Click the Add A Layer Style button and choose Drop Shadow from the menu. In the Layer Style dialog box, change Opacity to 50%, Distance to 0 pixels, and Size to 1 pixel for a slight blurring of the shadow edge. Click OK. The shadow is directly under the tree because you set Distance to 0 pixels.

7. Right-click the Drop Shadow icon under the Tree layer in the Layers palette. A context menu appears showing choices relevant to layer styles. Select Create Layer. In the warning dialog box, click OK.

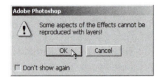

8. The Drop Shadow layer style is gone; a new layer appears called Tree's Drop Shadow. Select this layer and reduce its opacity to 50%. Drag the shadow down and to the left, as if it were cast by the sun overhead at a 45° angle.

9. Press Ctrl+T to activate the Transform command. Right-click inside the transform bounding box and select Distort from the context menu. Drag the upper handles as shown in Figure 4.33 to distort the shadow. Click the Commit button on the Options bar when you are satisfied.

TIP Distorted shadows appear more realistic when they are cast by objects with wispy or translucent edges. Try to avoid shadows that are obvious cutouts. When the eye recognizes the exact same pattern, it seems more like an illusion.

An option you have with elevations is to show more abstract trees by illustrating only their shadows. Although less realistic, this technique imparts a sense of scale to an elevation, while obscuring less of the building facade. You can also use another trick to get more mileage out of the same piece of entourage—mirror and distort. The eye is less able to perceive the same pattern when it is flipped around and warped.

10. Right-click the Tree's Drop Shadow layer and choose Duplicate Layer from the menu that appears. Name the new layer Shadow2.

FIGURE 4.33
Distorting a Drop
Shadow layer

11. Choose Edit ➤ Transform ➤ Flip Horizontal. Press Ctrl+T, right-click inside the transform bounding box, and select Distort from the context menu. Drag the transform handles to warp the image slightly. Finally, position the new shadow more or less as shown on the right in Figure 4.34.

12. You can close all the open files without saving.

FIGURE 4.34
Revealing the shadow
of another tree

Building an Entourage Library

After you create some quality entourage and realize how much time can go into preparing each object, you will want to find ways to reuse your assets in future projects. It is helpful to create a library of entourage in a single Photoshop file where you can quickly see each piece and evaluate it for its appropriateness. Often the entourage that you can use in a given project is determined by the camera angle and the lighting conditions of your composition. Instead of trying to come up with descriptive names for each piece, it is faster to locate pieces visually within your library.

In the Chapter 4 folder on the companion CD, I've provided a starter library for you. I recommend that you keep adding to this library with entourage that you make. You can then drag and drop pieces from the library into your projects as needed.

Open the file `EntourageLibrary.psd` from the companion CD, and save it to a convenient location on your hard disk. This file contains three pieces of entourage, each on its own layer with a transparent background. Figure 4.35 shows the beginnings of your library. You are welcome to use these images in your projects.

FIGURE 4.35
Beginning your entourage library

As you get new pieces to add to your library, increase Canvas Size (choose Image ➤ Canvas Size) if necessary so that there is more room, and drag in a new piece. Make sure that each piece you add has already been extracted so that you're always ready to drag and drop from the library when needed.

You can also purchase ready-made photographic entourage on the Internet. When you consider how much time it takes to photograph and extract entourage yourself, it may make sense to buy it instead, especially if you are facing a deadline. On the other hand, you can reap a huge savings if you plan ahead and make entourage to your own specifications.

WARNING   Anyone well acquainted with computer graphics can spot specific pieces of entourage that seem to get used over and over again by beginners. Chances are, any free entourage you can find on the Web has been used countless times by others looking for an easy way to dress up their renderings. Your best bet is to either make or buy quality entourage. Your renderings will appear more professional.

Check out these websites for more information on buying professional quality entourage:

www.archvision.com

www.marlinstudios.com

www.imagecels.com

Entourage in Autodesk VIZ

Using entourage in a 3D program is simple in concept, but often difficult in practice. We will look at the procedure for setting up entourage in Autodesk VIZ 2005. The steps are similar in other versions of VIZ and 3ds max. The concepts you learn here will apply in other 3D programs, although the steps may be different, depending on the features of the software.

The main idea is that you take the photographic entourage you create in Photoshop and use it in a *material* that you design in VIZ. This material defines the surface qualities of a 3D object and uses both the color pixels and alpha channel of the entourage file. You map this material to the surface of plane geometry to create the illusion of a 2D cutout in a 3D scene.

Creating Entourage Geometry

The first order of business is to make a flat object onto which you'll later map a material. Although any flat geometry will do, an object that has the correct orientation and pivot point location for ease of manipulating the object in a 3D scene is better. Follow these steps:

1. Launch Autodesk VIZ 2005. Choose Customize ➤ Units Setup to open the Units Setup dialog box (see Figure 4.36). Click the US Standard radio button; select Feet w/Fractional Inches in the drop-down, select 1/8 in the precision drop-down, and click the Feet radio button to set Default Units. Click OK to close the Units Setup dialog box.

FIGURE 4.36
The Units Setup
dialog box

NOTE You can use metric units if you prefer. This tutorial will use feet and inches. You should use the system that you are most comfortable with.

Make a box object that has the overall volume of the entourage you are planning to create—in this case we'll be making a person. You will use this box as a visual template to guide you in creating flat plane geometry that you will later map to the entourage material you will be designing in this tutorial.

2. Press Alt+W if necessary to maximize the current viewport. Press T to switch to the Top viewport.

3. Click the Create tab of the Command Panel, click the Geometry button, select Standard Primitives from the drop-down, and click the Box tool in the Object Type rollout.

4. Drag out a box in the Top viewport, and adjust its parameters in the Command Panel to have a length and width of 2´ each (the approximate width of a typical human body), and set the height to match the height of the person—in this case, set it to 5´8˝.

Before you make the plane object that you will ultimately map your entourage material to, you need to know the proportions of the image you will be using. You want to match the aspect ratio of the plane geometry to the image file so that no distortions occur. If the plane is wider than the image, the figure will stretch and appear wider than it is in real life.

5. Choose File ➤ View Image File to open the View File dialog box, as shown in Figure 4.37. Navigate to the folder on your hard drive where you stored WomanStanding.tif from earlier in this chapter. (You can also find this file on the CD.) Single-click WomanStanding.tif in the View File dialog box so you can see the statistics data at the bottom before opening this file. Make a note that this image measures 345×1415 pixels.

It is a good idea to preview the image you will use for entourage to make sure it contains an alpha channel.

6. Double-click WomanStanding.tif in the View File dialog box. The Rendered Frame Window (RFW) opens, displaying the selected image (see Figure 4.38). Click the Display Alpha Channel button in the RFW. The grayscale alpha channel displays in the RFW. Close the RFW.

FIGURE 4.37
Viewing the image in VIZ

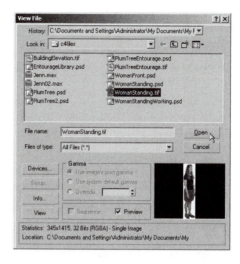

FIGURE 4.38
The Rendered Frame
Window

7. Press F to switch to the Front viewport. Press G to toggle the grid on. Click the Plane button in the Object Type rollout. Drag out a plane next to the box. Don't worry about its exact size or placement yet.

We need to temporarily change to generic units to match the size of the plane to the pixel dimensions of the image.

8. Choose Customize ➤ Units Setup to open the Units Setup dialog box. Click the Generic Units radio button and then click OK. Changing units does not scale objects; it merely changes the system of measurement. Using generic units may be less confusing than feet and inches in the next step.

9. Click the Modify tab of the Command Panel. Change Length to 1415 and Width to 345. These generic values match the pixel dimensions of the image.

10. Click the Select And Uniform Scale tool on the main toolbar. Drag the Scale gizmo down to reduce the size of the plane. Keep dragging until the plane's height roughly matches the height of the box. Right-click, choose Move from the Transform quad, and move the plane so that its lower edge rests on the major line of the grid (see Figure 4.39). Finally, erase the box, now that it has fulfilled its job as your visual template (click to select it and press Delete).

FIGURE 4.39
Scaling the plane to match the box

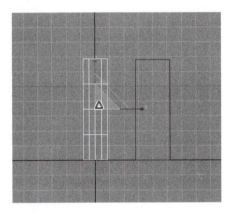

11. Select the plane again. Click the Hierarchy tab of the Command Panel, and click the Pivot Category button if it's not already selected. In the Adjust Transform rollout, click the Scale button in the Reset group. Now the object's transform scale is readjusted to 100% at the plane's current size.

Now that you have created the plane to match the pixel dimensions of the image using generic units, you can set the units back to feet and inches.

12. Change the units to US Standard, just as you did in step 1.

By default, the plane primitive's pivot point is located at the center of the object. However, you will find entourage more useful if you move the pivot down to the ground. You can then place entourage planes on floor surfaces in VIZ and rest the figure's feet firmly on the ground.

13. Still on the Hierarchy tab of the Command Panel, click the Affect Pivot Only button in the Move/Rotate/Scale group in the Adjust Pivot rollout.

14. Click the Select And Move tool. Right-click the Z spinner in the Transform type-ins at the bottom of the user interface. This moves the pivot to the ground. Toggle the Affect Pivot Only button off. Title the object WomanStanding01 in the Name text box at the top of the Hierarchy tab of the Command Panel.

Designing an Entourage Material

The geometry is complete. Now it is time to focus on designing the material that will later be mapped onto this object. This material will incorporate both a diffuse color map and an opacity map using different channels of the same image file. Follow these steps:

1. Press M to open the Material Editor. The upper-left sample slot is selected by default. Click the Material button to change its type, as shown in Figure 4.40.

FIGURE 4.40

The Material Editor

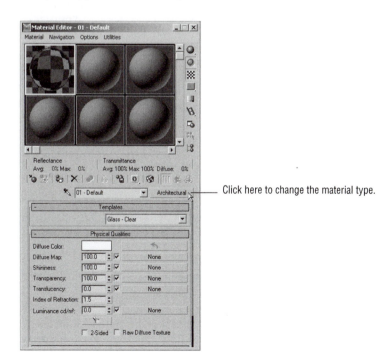

Click here to change the material type.

2. The Material/Map Browser opens, displaying materials. Select Standard from the list and click OK to close the dialog box. All the parameters change in the Material Editor to correspond to the Standard material.

3. In the Blinn Basic Parameters rollout, click the blank button next to the Diffuse color swatch.

4. The Material/Map Browser opens again, but this time it displays maps. Choose Bitmap from the extensive list and click OK. The Select Bitmap Image File dialog box opens automatically in this standard file browser. Select WomanStanding.tif and click Open. The Material Editor's rollouts change to those of the bitmap. Click the Go To Parent button to return to the top of the material hierarchy.

Now that you have the diffuse color map, the next task is to copy it to create an opacity map. The opacity map determines the boundaries of the object and gets its data from the image's alpha channel.

5. Drag the M icon (meaning mapped) from the Diffuse Color channel to the Opacity channel, as shown in Figure 4.41. The Copy (Instance) Map dialog box opens. Click the Copy radio button and then click OK. Because the Opacity map must take data from the image's alpha channel, it is necessarily different from the diffuse map, so a unique copy is needed.

FIGURE 4.41
Copy the diffuse map to the opacity Map.

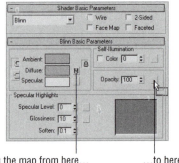

Drag the map from here…   …to here.

Right now you have an identical copy of the diffuse map in the Opacity channel. You still must change the output of the opacity map to read the alpha channel of the image; otherwise, it reads the RGB values by default to determine opacity.

6. Click the M button next to the Opacity channel to enter a deeper level of the material hierarchy. The Bitmap controls appear in the Material Editor. Scroll down and locate the Bitmap Parameters rollout. Click the Alpha radio button in the Mono Channel Output group. Click the Go To Parent button to return to the top level of the material hierarchy.

7. Make sure the WomanStanding geometry is still selected, and then click the Assign Material To Selection button.

8. To see the bitmap on the object, the viewport shading must be set to Smooth and Highlights. To change from wire-frame shading, right-click the viewport name in the upper-left corner, and select Smooth + Highlights from the list.

9. You still can't see the entourage on the object until you click the Show Map In Viewport button. Click this button to display the entourage in the viewport. You might also need to check Self-Illumination in order to see the figure in your viewport.

TIP If the entourage looks too bright in renderings, try decreasing the RGB Level parameter in the Output rollout of the Diffuse Color bitmap. You shouldn't illuminate entourage images with 3D lights because the entourage was already lit in the photograph.

The final version of the entourage is shown in Figure 4.42. The Autodesk VIZ 2005 file WomanStanding.max is provided on the CD for your reference. You must place this file in the same folder as WomanStanding.tif before opening it.

FIGURE 4.42
The entourage mapped
to an object in a 3D scene

Summary

In this chapter, you have seen how to photograph, extract, enhance, and use entourage in Photoshop and VIZ. Using entourage gives your compositions a sense of scale and context; it can elevate the impression your audience takes home from the mundane to the spectacular. In the next chapter you will learn how to use Photoshop and AutoCAD together to create stunning plans.

Chapter 5

Presenting Plans

Designers in all professions use plans as their single most common form of graphical communication. If you are an architect, an engineer, a contractor, an industrial designer, or a real estate developer or are in any other profession that uses measured drawings every day, chances are, the ability to read plans has become part of your subconscious mind.

It is easy to assume that showing plans to your clients should communicate your design intent to them as clearly as you understand it. However, it can be helpful to step back a moment and realize that not everyone is trained to read plans. Understanding orthogonal (or orthographic) projection line drawings (which are really what plans are) is not necessarily an intuitive skill. Remember that we never actually experience "plans" as humans physically inhabiting spaces—instead, plans are abstractions.

Photoshop is a wonderful tool for making plans legible to almost everyone. By adding tonality, color, pattern, and shadow, plans are transformed into beautiful images that your clients can immediately understand. By enhancing CAD drawings, Photoshop can help you effectively communicate your design intent and thereby improve your organization's marketing potential. This chapter's topics include:

◆ Preparing Plans in AutoCAD

◆ Transferring Multilayer Drawings to Photoshop

◆ Using Patterns

◆ Layer Style Techniques

◆ Laying Out Plans on a Sheet

Preparing Plans in AutoCAD

The process of preparing plans for Photoshop begins in a CAD program. I will be using AutoCAD 2005 in the tutorials in this chapter. However, all the CAD sample files on this book's companion CD are saved in AutoCAD 2000's drawing (.dwg) format, so you can use an earlier version of AutoCAD or another CAD program that can read this format. Although the steps won't exactly match the procedure given here if you are using another program, the essence is the same.

Cleaning Drawings

The data of CAD drawings must be in a suitable form before it can be used successfully in Photoshop. It is important to follow a few basic guidelines when preparing CAD drawings for use in Photoshop:

◆ Follow "clean" drafting practices so that end points of entities snap together.

◆ Verify that entities are on the correct layers.

◆ Give the drawing's layers meaningful and descriptive names.

◆ Purge any unused layers and blocks (because blocks can trap layers).

◆ Cut away and erase any nonessential areas of the drawing that won't be used in Photoshop.

◆ Erase any filled areas, symbols, title blocks, or dimensions that you don't want to appear.

◆ Simplify the drawing as much as possible to maximize readability.

Here's some practice in opening a simple drawing and doing some minor cleaning in CAD.

1. Open the file `Cottage.dwg` from the companion CD. Figure 5.1 shows the Cottage First Floor plan.

    Only one area in the cottage drawing needs cleaning before it is ready to be brought into Photoshop.

2. Zoom into the area on the lower left, where the wall meets the first French door (press Z and then press Enter). Then click two points to define a zoom window around the area of interest (see Figure 5.2).

    Although the wall looked fine when you were zoomed out, the entities do not actually meet up close. You had to zoom in closer to perceive this problem.

FIGURE 5.1

The cottage CAD drawing

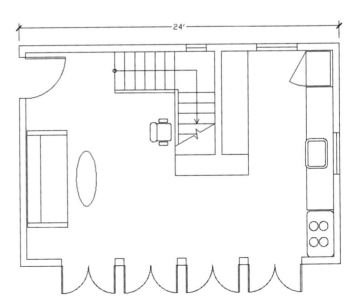

FIGURE 5.2
Zoomed in. Notice the
area where the end
points of the lines do
not meet.

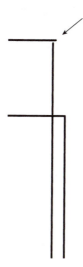

3. Fillet the two lines that do not meet together with a zero radius; type **FILLET,** press Enter, **R,** and press Enter to select the radius option. Type **0** and press Enter to set a zero fillet radius. Finally, click each of the two lines to join them in a perfect corner (see Figure 5.3).

WARNING If you do not follow "clean" drafting practices in CAD, your job in Photoshop will be much harder. It is best to spend some time in CAD cleaning legacy drawings before working on them in Photoshop.

4. If you are going to continue working through the following sections, you can leave this file open for now.

FIGURE 5.3
Fillet these two lines to
join their end points.

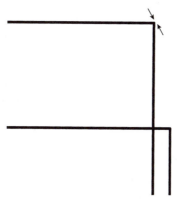

Setting Up an Image Printer Driver in AutoCAD

AutoCAD is fundamentally a vector program, meaning it stores entities as mathematical objects using a spatial coordinate system. Lines are stored as end points that are located by their (x,y,z) coordinates in space. To convert this vector data to pixels, you need to set up an image printer driver. After you "print" the drawing, the entities from CAD end up as black pixels on a white background in a raster image.

The follow procedure doesn't actually print on a real device; we are merely setting up a virtual "printer" to export raster data from AutoCAD. These steps only need to be performed once. After you configure the image printer driver, you can use it as often as you'd like to export images from AutoCAD.

1. In AutoCAD, choose Tools ➤ Wizards ➤ Add Plotter to start the Add Plotter Wizard. On the Introduction screen, click Next to open the Begin screen.

2. Leave the My Computer radio button selected and click Next to open the Plotter Model screen, as shown in Figure 5.4. Click Raster File Formats in the Manufacturers list, and then click the TIFF Version 6 (Uncompressed) option in the Models list.

FIGURE 5.4

The Plotter Model screen in the Add Plotter Wizard

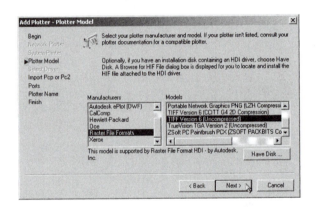

NOTE This is the same wizard you use to set up a plot device such as an inkjet printer.

3. Click Next to open the Import PCP Or PC2 screen. Click Next again to open the Ports screen. Leave Plot To File selected, and click Next again to open the Plotter Name screen. In the Plotter Name text box, type **ImagePrinter,** and then click Next to open the Finish screen.

WARNING The name *ImagePrinter* is used in the AutoLISP file on the accompanying CD. Please use this name so that the program functions properly later in this chapter.

4. Click the Edit Plotter Configuration button to open the Plotter Configuration Editor dialog box, as shown in Figure 5.5. Click the Device And Document Settings tab, and then click Filter Paper Sizes under the User-Defined Paper Sizes & Calibration node in the driver hierarchy.

   Next, let's get rid of all the default "paper sizes," which in the case of this virtual image printer driver are actually pixel sizes. You'll then create your own custom size that is larger than any of the presets.

FIGURE 5.5

The Plotter Configuration Editor dialog box

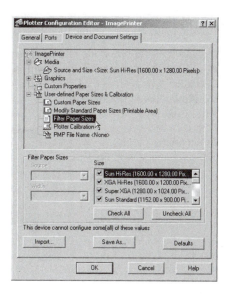

5. Click the Uncheck All button in the Filter Paper Sizes group, click the Custom Paper Sizes node in the driver hierarchy, and then click the Add button in the Custom Paper Sizes group to start the Custom Paper Size Wizard.

6. On the Begin screen of the Custom Paper Sizer Wizard, leave the Start From Scratch radio button selected and click Next to open Media Bounds screen, as shown in Figure 5.6. For both the width and height parameters, type **2000**. Leave the Units drop-down set to Pixels.

7. Click Next to open the Paper Size Name screen. In the text box, type **ImageSize** and click Next. Finally, click Finish to close this wizard. ImageSize appears in the Plotter Configuration Editor now.

WARNING   The name *ImageSize* is referenced in the AutoLISP program used later in this chapter. It is important that you use this name exactly.

FIGURE 5.6

Setting media bounds

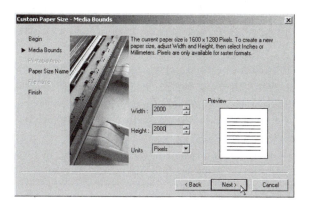

Limit the color depth that your ImagePrinter driver uses to create images to black and white pixels only. This will make smaller image files and save hard drive space. To do so, follow these steps:

1. Expand the Graphics node in the driver hierarchy and click the Vector Graphics node. In the Resolution And Color Depths group, click the Monochrome radio button, and then choose 2 Shades Of Gray from the Color Depth drop-down, as shown in Figure 5.7. Click OK to close the Plotter Configuration Editor.

FIGURE 5.7
Limiting the color depth of the output

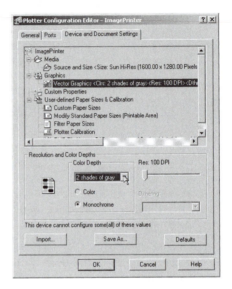

2. Finally, click the Finish button in the Add Plotter wizard to create the `ImagePrinter.pc3` file on your hard drive.

ACCESSING PLOTTER DRIVERS

You can use AutoCAD's PLOTTERMANAGER command to open Windows Explorer to the folder where your plotter drivers are stored. In AutoCAD 2004 and 2005, these are typically stored under the following:

```
C:\Documents and Settings\Administrator\Application Data\Autodesk\AutoCAD 2005\
R16.1\enu\Plotters
```

This path assumes you are logged in as the administrator. You need to adjust this if you are logged in under another account, by substituting your login name for Administrator in the path.

It is possible to set AutoCAD to store its print drivers in the location of your choosing. Use the OPTIONS command, click the Files tab, and expand the Printer Support File node. Here you can set the Printer Configuration Search Path.

When you create a custom paper size, it is stored in a Plotter Model Parameters file (.pmp). By default, these files are stored in a PMP Files subfolder under the Plotters path mentioned earlier.

Creating a Plot Style Table for Images

When you convert vector line work, ideally you want the lines to show up as single-pixel–width lines in the image. Thin, unbroken lines provide the most flexibility in Photoshop, where you will be learning techniques for enhancing this type of image later in this chapter.

NOTE For many architects, it's important to vary line weight and thickness. I believe it's better to add line weight intentionally in Photoshop using the stroke effect, rather than exporting thicker lines from AutoCAD.

Plot style tables control the line width in AutoCAD output. Here's how to create a custom color-dependent plot style to use in creating output with your new ImagePrinter:

1. On the Command line in AutoCAD, type **OPTIONS** and press Enter to open the Options dialog box. Click the Plot And Publish tab (see Figure 5.8).

FIGURE 5.8

The Options dialog box

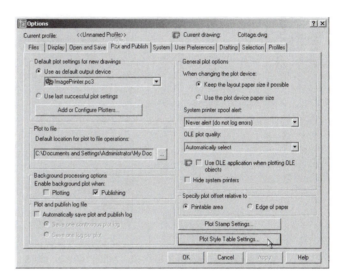

2. Click the Plot Style Table Settings button in the lower-right corner of the Options dialog box to open the Plot Style Table Settings dialog box, as shown in Figure 5.9. Make sure the Use Color Dependent Plot Styles radio button is selected, and then click the Add Or Edit Plot Style Tables button to open Windows Explorer.

TIP Some organizations follow specific CAD standards; you can set AutoCAD to use named plot styles after you use the ImagePrinter if necessary.

3. Figure 5.10 shows Windows Explorer open to the folder where AutoCAD's plot style tables are stored. Double click Add-A-Plot Style Table Wizard to start the Add Plot Style Table Wizard.

FIGURE 5.9
The Plot Style Table
Settings dialog

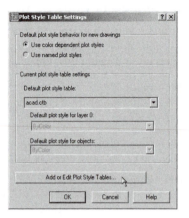

FIGURE 5.10
The Plot Styles window

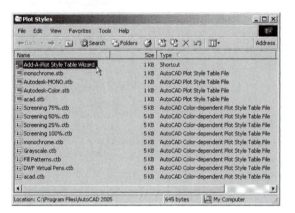

TIP You can also access the Plot Styles folder by using the STYLESMANAGER command in AutoCAD.

4. Read the introductory message and then click Next. Make sure the Start From Scratch radio button is selected on the Begin screen and click Next. Choose Color Dependent Plot Style Table, and click Next to open the File Name screen.

5. Type the name **Images** in the text box, and click Next again. Click the Plot Style Table Editor button to open the Plot Style Table Editor dialog box, as shown in Figure 5.11.

6. Click the Form View tab if it is not already selected. Drag out a selection window in the Plot Styles list box that shows the color numbers. Keep dragging until the list automatically scrolls and all 255 colors are selected.

FIGURE 5.11

The Plot Style Table
Editor dialog box

Start here and drag a window all the way to the bottom.

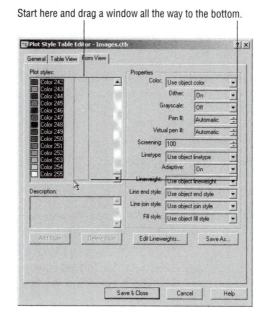

7. In the Properties group, click the Color drop-down and select the Black option. Click the Lineweight drop-down and select 0.0000 mm. (This is the thinnest possible lineweight.) Click Save & Close. A file called Images.ctb was automatically created in the Plot Styles folder on your hard drive.

8. Click Finish to close the Add Plot Style Table Wizard. Click OK twice more to close the two remaining open dialog boxes. You have finally completed the arduous setup procedure!

Now you have configured the ImagePrinter as a raster printer driver that you can use to convert vector line work in AutoCAD to the pixels of an image that you'll be able to manipulate with Photoshop.

Scale and Resolution

CAD drawings are made in *real-world scale*, meaning they are drawn to actual size. Thus, drawing in CAD is easy because you don't have to worry about scale until it comes time to lay out the drawings on a sheet of paper. You choose a specific *graphic scale* (such as 1/8″ = 1′-0″) in a layout to fit the measured drawing on a sheet of paper.

When you convert drawings to images, the scale must relate to image resolution in a specific way in order to maintain the graphic scale on the printed page. For example, 1/8″ scale means that 1/8″ on paper represents 1′ in the real world. Another way of saying this is that 1″ on paper is equivalent to 8′ in the real world. If you stay in the same units, that's like saying 1″ on paper equals 96″ (8 feet × 12 inches / foot) in the real world. In other words, AutoCAD must scale down your drawing 96 times to print it in 1/8″ scale on paper.

If you use the ImagePrinter in AutoCAD to convert 1 square inch of vector space to 1 pixel, there is a direct equivalence between the units of graphic scale and resolution. Therefore, set the resolution in Photoshop to 96 pixels per inch (ppi) to represent 1/8″ scale in the image. The following list shows this relationship.

Graphic Scale:	1/8″ on paper	=	1′-0″ in the real world
	1″	=	8′
	1″	=	96″
ImagePrinter in AutoCAD:	1″	=	1 pixel
Resolution in Photoshop:	1″ on paper	=	96 pixels

All this talk about scale and resolution can be confusing, so let's walk through a practical example.

1. If you have the `Cottage.dwg` file open in AutoCAD from an earlier section, you can continue here; if not, open this file from the companion CD.

   Look back at Figure 5.1. The wall on the top was drawn exactly 24 feet in length in AutoCAD, as the dimension indicates. In 1/8″ scale, this line should be exactly 3″ long on paper. Let's try converting this data from vector to raster with the ImagePrinter and see if we can maintain the graphic scale inside Photoshop.

2. In AutoCAD, choose File ➢ Plot, or press Ctrl+P. Click OK if a warning dialog box appears indicating a missing driver; you'll select the correct driver in a moment. The Plot dialog box opens, as shown in Figure 5.12. Click the Name drop-down under Printer/Plotter, select ImagePrinter.pc3, and click OK in the Paper Size Not Found dialog box if it appears.

FIGURE 5.12
Plotting the Image

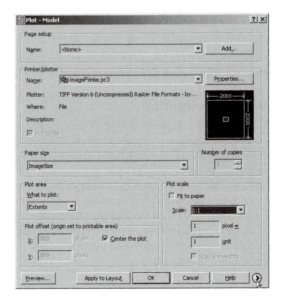

Click the drop-down in the Paper Size group and select ImageSize. (This is the 2000×2000 pixel custom size you made earlier.) In the Plot Area group, choose the Extents option for What To Plot. Check Center The Plot in the Plot Offset group and select 1:1 for the scale option (1 pixel = 1 unit). Next, click the right arrow button to see more options.

3. The Plot dialog box expands to show more options. Choose Images.ctb from the Plot Style Table drop-down. If a dialog box appears asking if you want to assign this plot style table to all layouts, click Yes. Make sure Plot With Plot Styles is checked in the Plot Options group and click OK to open the Browse For Plot File dialog box.

4. Navigate to a folder on your hard drive where you are saving project files, and title the new file `Cottage1-1.tif` to indicate that it is plotted at 1:1 with the ImagePrinter. Leave AutoCAD open.

5. Launch Photoshop, and open `Cottage1-1.tif`. Double-click the Zoom tool in the toolbox to go to 100% magnification. Press Ctrl+R or choose View ➤ Rulers to turn on the rulers.

   You can use guides to visually connect the edges of the building and the rulers. You can also move the origin point of the rulers to coincide with the corner of the building. This way, you can accurately measure the length of the top wall.

6. Drag a guide out from the vertical ruler on the left edge of the document window, and align it with the left edge of the building. Repeat this process, and align the second guide with the right edge of the building. Then drag out the origin marker in the upper-left corner of the rulers, and drop it on the building corner, as shown in Figure 5.13.

   Right now the top wall measures 4″ on the ruler. We need to change the image resolution to match the image up to a 1/8″ graphic scale.

7. Choose Image ➤ Image Size to open the Image Size dialog box, as shown in Figure 5.14. By default, the image appears with a resolution of 72 pixels/inch. Make sure that Resample Image is unchecked because you do not want to change the number of pixels in the image.

FIGURE 5.13
Setting up the rulers

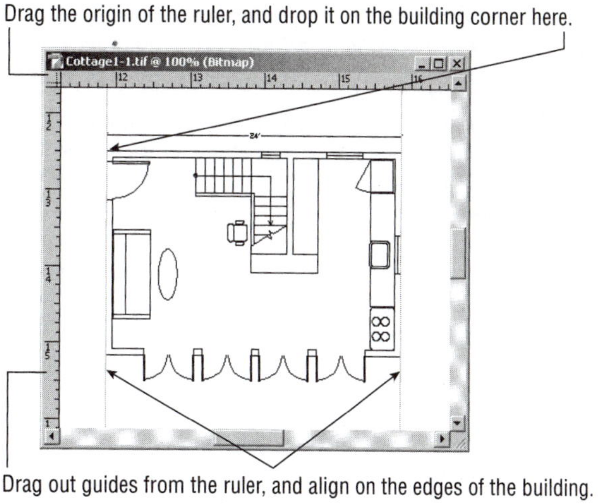

Drag the origin of the ruler, and drop it on the building corner here.

Drag out guides from the ruler, and align on the edges of the building.

FIGURE 5.14
Image size and
resolution

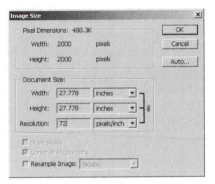

THE HISTORY OF "SCREEN RESOLUTION"

There is actually no such thing as standard screen resolution, but this concept has been kicking around since 1984 and has influenced countless millions! Back when Apple introduced its first Macintosh computer, it sported a monitor that actually had 72 pixels per inch on its 9″ screen. Now it was a lucky coincidence that text fonts are traditionally measured in point sizes that are fractions of 1/72″. For example, a 12-point font was 12/72″ in predigital typography. So Apple's great marketing scheme was *what you see is what you get* (WYSIWYG) because the size of the text on the monitor was the same absolute size the text was when it was printed. This has never been true since because the size of pixels varies on every monitor. *Monitors are measured in pixels, not resolution*; most actually have resolutions anywhere from 60–150 pixels per inch of viewable screen area.

To complicate things, Microsoft later used 96 pixels as its measure of the *logical inch* in Windows. The logical inch is just an arbitrary measurement that the operating systems uses to calculate font size on screen, but has no bearing on the actual text size because every monitor is different.

Because of this legacy, most web designers use either 72 or 96 ppi when designing for the screen. The irony is that these measurements are arbitrary, and images and text are actually displayed in different sizes on every monitor.

We are using a resolution of 96 ppi because it matches the image that was plotted at 1:1 with 1/8″ graphic scale. It is purely a coincidence that 96 ppi is also the measurement of the logical inch in Windows (also known as screen resolution).

8. In the Image Size dialog box, change Resolution from 72 to 96 pixels/inch. Click OK. Figure 5.15 shows the resulting relationship between the printed size (in the ruler) and the building. The 24′ wall now correctly measures 3″ on the printed page. The image is now precisely in 1/8″ scale.

NOTE Rule to remember: When you print at 1:1 (meaning 1 inch = 1 pixel) in AutoCAD, setting the resolution to 96 pixels/inch in Photoshop produces a 1/8″ scale image.

FIGURE 5.15

The image adjusted to 1/8˝ scale

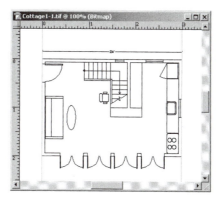

Once you understand this relationship between scale and resolution, you can produce any graphic scale by doubling or halving the factors involved. Let's plot again to understand how this works.

9. Switch back to AutoCAD and issue the Plot command again.(Press the spacebar to repeat the last command issued in step 2.) Change the plot scale to 4 pixels = 1 unit (see Figure 5.16). Click OK, and then save the plot file as `Cottage4-1.tif` on your hard drive.

10. Switch back to Photoshop and open the file `Cottage4-1.tif`. Drag guides out from the vertical ruler, and align them with the sides of the building as you did in step 6. You may need to zoom in the image to see the sides of the building. Move the ruler origin to the corner of the building as you did before. Choose Image ➤ Image Size and set the resolution to 96 pixels/inch. Figure 5.17 shows the image in 1/2˝ scale. The top wall now measures 12˝ across, as it should in 1/2˝ scale.

FIGURE 5.16

Plotting at 4:1

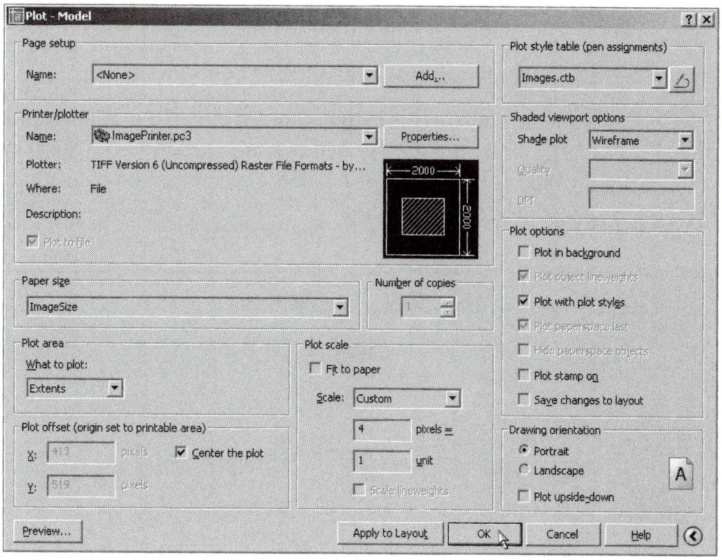

FIGURE 5.17
The image plotted
in 1/2″ scale

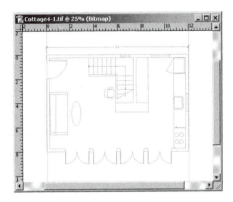

The image is now in 1/2″ scale because you printed it at 4:1 in step 9. To understand why this is so, let's think through the logic of scale. Starting with 1:1 (1 pixel = 1 unit), double the first factor to 2:1, thereby doubling the graphic scale from 1/8″ to 1/4″. Double the factor again, moving from 2:1 to 4:1. This effectively doubles the graphic scale once again, taking you from 1/4″ scale to 1/2″ scale. Table 5.1 lists the most common scale factors.

TIP Doubling the printed resolution in AutoCAD *doubles* the graphic scale.

You can work through scales in this fashion, doubling or halving as necessary to arrive at your desired scale. In step 10 you set the resolution to 96 pixels/inch. Doubling or halving the resolution in Photoshop likewise affects scale, but in reverse compared with doing so in AutoCAD.

11. Choose Image ≻ Image Size and double the resolution to 192 pixels/inch (this is 96 × 2). The top wall measures 6″ across, proving that you are now in 1/4″ scale.

TIP Doubling the resolution in Photoshop *halves* the graphic scale and printed size.

12. Close all open files in AutoCAD and Photoshop.

Scale can be a confusing issue. To make things as simple as possible, I recommend always starting with the rule to remember and working from there, doubling or halving factors in AutoCAD and/or Photoshop as needed. A combination of factors yields the graphic scale, resolution, and printed size you want.

TABLE 5.1: Common Scale Factors

SCALE	RATIO
12″	1′-0″ : 1
6″	1′-0″ : 2
3″	1′-0″ : 4

TABLE 5.1:   Common Scale Factors *(CONTINUED)*

SCALE	RATIO
1.5″	1′-0″ : 8
1″	1′-0″ : 12
3/4″	1′-0″ : 16
1/2″	1′-0″ : 24
3/16″	1′-0″ : 64
1/8″	1′-0″ : 96
3/32″	1′-0″ : 128
1/16″	1′-0″ : 192
1″	10′ : 120
1″	20′ : 240
1″	50′ : 600
1″	100′ : 1200

Transferring Multilayer Drawings to Photoshop

You have already seen how to transfer drawings from AutoCAD to Photoshop and maintain the graphic scale in the image. Drawings transferred in this way appear on a single layer in Photoshop. However, typical CAD drawings contain many layers, and more creative possibilities open up if you can access these as individual image layers in Photoshop.

It is possible to transfer the layers from an AutoCAD drawing to a Photoshop image by printing each layer one at a time and then integrating the image files in Photoshop. Fortunately for you, I have written a program (included on the companion CD) that automates part of this process, saving you many hours of tedium.

The program runs in AutoCAD and automates plotting by making each layer an image file. It is called lay2img (layer to image) and is written in Autodesk's subset of the ancient list processing language (developed in the 1950s) called AutoLISP. Programming in AutoLISP is beyond the scope of this book, although you will learn how to edit a few simple parameters in the program to suit your needs.

After you load and use lay2img to print each layer as an image file, I'll show you a technique in ImageReady (Photoshop's sister product) to automate the integration of the image files into layers within a single document. Finally, we'll use the Magic Eraser tool to composite the layers transparently together in a working Photoshop file.

Let's begin by opening a new drawing file of a kitchen project.

1. Launch AutoCAD if it is not already running and open the file Kitchen.dwg from the companion CD. Figure 5.18 shows the cleaned-up drawing (see the "Cleaning Drawings" section earlier in this chapter) that is ready to be transferred to Photoshop.

FIGURE 5.18
The kitchen CAD drawing

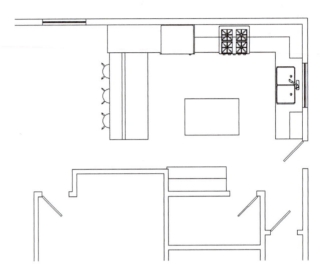

2. Press Ctrl+P to open the Plot dialog box. Click OK if a warning dialog box appears indicating a missing driver; you'll select the correct driver in a moment. Just as you have done before, select ImagePrinter.pc3 in the Printer/Plotter group, ImageSize in the Paper Size group, and Images.ctb as the Plot Style Table. Set Plot Scale to 4 pixels = 1 unit as shown in Figure 5.16, earlier in this chapter. Click the Preview button to display an image similar to Figure 5.18. Press Esc twice to cancel the preview and close the Plot dialog box.

It is always wise to preview a plot manually before automating plot output. If you need to make any adjustments, it is better to be aware of them before you output all the layers to image files.

Because our preview showed no obvious problems, we are ready to load the program and edit it as necessary to match our current plot settings.

3. Choose Tools ➢ AutoLISP ➢ Visual LISP Editor. A new process launches with its own task button on the Windows Taskbar. Within the Visual LISP for AutoCAD window, choose File ➢ Open File, navigate to the companion CD, and select the file lay2img.lsp. Figure 5.19 shows the Visual LISP Editor that is built into AutoCAD with the program file open. There is a version of this image in the color section.

Each parameter is color coded and commented with descriptive information. Change the Plotted pixels = drawing units parameters to "4=1", to match the settings you used in step 2.

TIP You can customize the plot parameters in the lay2img program to suit the needs of your own projects.

FIGURE 5.19

The Visual LISP Editor with the program open

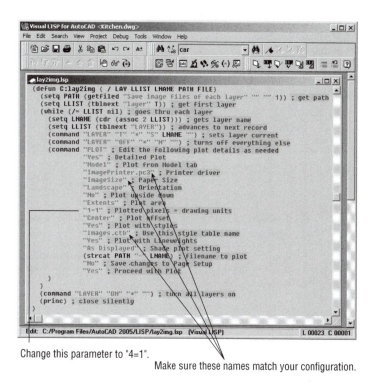

Change this parameter to "4=1".

Make sure these names match your configuration.

4. In the Visual LISP for AutoCAD window, choose File ➢ Save to record the changes you made to the source code. Next, load the program into AutoCAD by choosing Tools ➢ Load Text In Editor, or press Ctrl+Alt+E.

WARNING You cannot load the text in the Visual LISP Editor into AutoCAD unless the program window is selected and active.

5. Click the AutoCAD button on the Windows Taskbar or click anywhere in the AutoCAD window to switch back to AutoCAD. On the Command line, type **lay2img** and press Enter to open the Save image files of each layer dialog box , which asks you to choose a path and a filename to save the image files of each layer. Make a subfolder on your hard drive called Images, type the filename **Kitchen,** and click Save.

The automated process begins, and an image is plotted for each layer in the drawing. Figure 5.20 shows the newly created image files in the Images subfolder. There is one image file for each layer in the CAD drawing. The filenames are preceded by the name you typed in step 5, but the layer name from AutoCAD completes the filename after the dash. For example, one of the generated files is called Kitchen-A-wall.tif; Kitchen was the name you typed, and A-wall was the layer name. The program concatenates this descriptive text automatically in the filename.

FIGURE 5.20

The image files for each layer

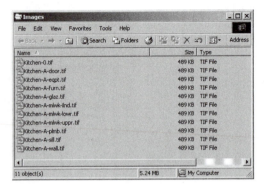

6. Close AutoCAD without saving the file. The Visual LISP Editor automatically closes because it depends on AutoCAD.

7. Launch Photoshop if it is not already running, and then switch to ImageReady. To open Image-Ready, click the Edit In ImageReady icon at the bottom of Photoshop's toolbox, or press Shift+Ctrl+M. ImageReady may take a few moments to load, so be patient.

NOTE ImageReady is included with Photoshop and is designed specifically for editing images destined for screen—especially for the Web. Many specialized commands in ImageReady are not part of Photoshop and vice-versa.

We can take advantage of ImageReady's Import Folder As Frames command to automatically integrate all the files in a folder into the layers of a single document.

8. From the ImageReady menu, choose File ➢ Import ➢ Folder As Frames to open the Browse For Folder dialog box. Navigate to the Images folder where you saved your output from AutoCAD in step 5, and click OK. It may take a while for ImageReady to process your request (approximately 1 minute).

9. To edit the document in Photoshop, press Shift+Ctrl+M in ImageReady or click the Edit In Photoshop icon, the bottom button in ImageReady's toolbar. It will take a few moments for the data to transfer into Photoshop. When the document appears in Photoshop, close ImageReady to save memory. You only used ImageReady to take advantage of its specialized import command (Folder As Frames).

10. In Photoshop, save the document as Kitchen.psd. Take a look at the Layers palette as shown in Figure 5.21. Each of the image files has been converted to layers, and their filenames have become layer names.

Next, we need to remember to set the resolution in Photoshop as an increment of 96 to maintain the graphic scale. Because we printed the drawing at 4:1 in AutoCAD, a resolution of 96 pixels/inch in Photoshop would bring the image to 1/2″ scale (see the preceding section).

11. Choose Image ➢ Image Size. Make sure Resample Image is unchecked, and set the resolution to 192 pixels/inch (96∗2). Click OK. By doubling the resolution, we are halving the graphic scale, thus bringing the image ultimately to 1/4″ scale.

FIGURE 5.21

Image files converted
to layers

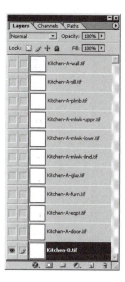

NOTE Make a mental note that we are working in 1/4″ scale in this Kitchen project in Photoshop; we will need this information when we design a scale bar, in the "Laying Out Plans on a Sheet" section later in this chapter.

12. Nothing is on the Kitchen-0.tif layer except white pixels (because there was nothing on Layer 0 in the CAD file), so let's convert this layer to the Background. Select Layer 0, and choose Layer ➤ New ➤ Background From Layer. Now you have a white background.

   The last thing to prepare this file for work in Photoshop is to use the Magic Eraser tool on all the remaining layers. You can set the Magic Eraser to erase all the white pixels, leaving only the black pixels on each layer that contains line work.

13. Press Shift+E until the Magic Eraser appears in the toolbox (it is under the Eraser And Background Eraser tools). On the Options bar, set Tolerance to 1, uncheck Contiguous and Use All Layers if they are checked, and set Opacity to 100%. In the Layers palette, click the Kitchen-A-door.tif layer to turn it on. Rename the layer Kitchen-A-door for clarity, because the .tif file extension is not needed for layer names. Click anywhere within the document window where there are white pixels to erase them all from the layer; be careful not to click on top of any line work (black pixels), or you'd be erasing them.

14. Repeat this process on each layer: turn on the layer, rename it (stripping the .tif file extension), and then erase all the white pixels using the Magic Eraser. Figure 5.22 shows the Layers palette after this process is complete.

   The layer thumbnails show transparency where the white pixels have been erased. Now all the layers are visible in the document window.

15. All that remains is some final cleanup. Choose Image ➤ Trim. Select the Top Left Pixel Color radio button in the Trim dialog box and click OK. The image is automatically cropped to the borders of the line work.

FIGURE 5.22
The layers after using the
Magic Eraser tool

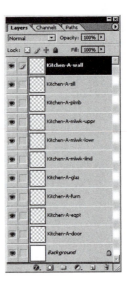

16. To reorient the image to match the way the drawing looked in AutoCAD, choose Image ➢ Rotate Canvas ➢ 90° CCW (counter-clockwise). Press Ctrl+R to turn off the rulers if necessary. Figure 5.23 shows the completed Kitchen drawing that has been transferred into Photoshop as an image.

17. Press Ctrl+S to save the file. You can close this file for now; you will return to it after the next section.

FIGURE 5.23
The kitchen image

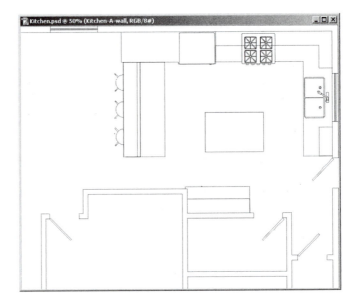

Each of the layers from AutoCAD has been transferred to Photoshop layers. The image maintains a precise $1/4" = 1'-0"$ graphic scale. The document is now prepared for enhancement in Photoshop. Before we dive in to the section on layer style techniques, you'll do a little prep work by creating some useful patterns.

Using Patterns

Patterns are one of the primary tools for enhancing CAD drawings. In Photoshop, a *pattern* is an image that is repeated in its application. Patterns are tiled; they are formed from a repetition of smaller image elements called tiles. (A *tile* is a single unit of pattern repetition.) An image is said to be *tilable* when the edges between tiles are not especially apparent in a pattern.

Real-world material samples are photographed or scanned into the computer. In this section, you will experiment with creating and applying a basic pattern directly from a scan. Later, I'll show you how to use the Pattern Maker tool to generate tilable patterns. After we create some patterns, we'll organize them into a custom pattern library that can be reused in future projects. Finally, you'll learn to use several tools to apply patterns from the pattern libraries.

Creating and Applying a Basic Pattern

Defining any image as a pattern is easy. Follow these steps, and then apply the basic pattern to a blank document.

1. Open a scan of a small sample of a walnut, the file `Walnut.jpg` from the companion CD.

2. You can easily define this image as a pattern. Choose Edit ➢ Define Pattern to open the Pattern Name dialog box.

In the Name box, type **Walnut** and click OK. The pattern is added to the current pattern library. Do not close the Walnut image yet.

Now that you have defined your first pattern, let's see what it looks like when it is applied in a new blank image.

3. Choose File ➢ New to open the New dialog box. Choose 640×480 from the Preset drop-down and click OK.

4. The basic way to apply a pattern is with the Paint Bucket tool. Choose the tool (press G), and choose Pattern from the Fill drop-down on the Options bar. Click the arrow button next to the pattern swatch to open the Pattern Picker drop-down. This displays the current pattern library. Double-click the Walnut pattern at the bottom of the picker to make it active.

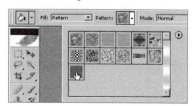

5. Click anywhere inside the Untitled document window. The pattern automatically tiles to fill the image with the Walnut pattern. Figure 5.24 shows how this pattern is not tilable because the seams between tiles are clearly evident.

FIGURE 5.24
Our first pattern application: seams between tiles are evident.

6. Close the Untitled document without saving; it was used only to illustrate a pattern that does not tile properly. Keep `Walnut.jpg` open.

Generating Tilable Patterns

Next, let's use the Pattern Maker tool to generate patterns whose seams are smoothed out. These patterns will appear more as a continuous material, rather than as a series of repeated images. Ideally, you can achieve tilable results that are not perceived as being composed of smaller image elements. Follow these steps:

1. Click the Walnut document window that you opened earlier. This will be the basis of a new tilable pattern that you will generate with the Pattern Maker. You must copy the contents of this document to the Windows Clipboard. Press Ctrl+A to select all, and then press Ctrl+C to copy the selection to the Clipboard.

2. Create a new blank document to contain the new pattern; press Ctrl+N. For this pattern, type **WalnutPattern** in the Name text box, change Width and Height to 300 pixels each, set Resolution to 72 pixels/inch, set Color Mode to RGB 8 bit, and set Background Contents to White. Click OK to create a new document window.

3. Choose Filter ➢ Pattern Maker or press Alt+Shift+Ctrl+X to open the Pattern Maker dialog box. Check Use Clipboard As Sample in the Tile Generation group. Click the Use Image Size button just below this to match the tiled size to the WalnutPattern document window. Click the Generate button to tell the Pattern Maker to attempt to tile this image. Figure 5.25 shows the first attempt.

FIGURE 5.25

Using the Pattern
Maker tool

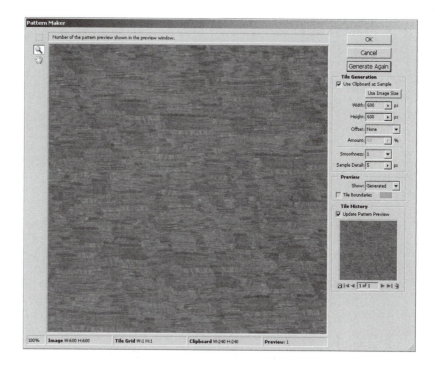

NOTE The Pattern Maker command is available only for 8-bit images in RGB, CMYK, Lab, and Gray-scale color modes.

Each time you generate a tile, a thumbnail goes into the Tile History, and the Pattern Maker dialog box remains open. The Smoothness and Sample Detail controls affect pattern generation. You will usually need to generate tiles several times before you are satisfied with the overall pattern, but this is usually worth the effort so you can compare the results in the Tile History before deciding.

4. Change the Smoothness drop-down to 3, drag the Sample Detail slider to 10, and click the Generate Again button. You will have to wait while Photoshop processes the new tile.

5. Change Smoothness to 1, and set Sample Detail to 20. Click Generate Again. The second tile seems better in this example because the seams are the least visible while enough detail remains in the image overall.

6. Click OK to close the dialog box and apply your new pattern to the document window. Leave the WalnutPattern window open for now (see Figure 5.26).

FIGURE 5.26
The tilable walnut pat-
tern: compare this with
Figure 5.24.

Creating a Custom Pattern Library

Now that you have generated a tilable pattern, you can save it in a custom pattern library. I recommend either creating a new pattern library for each project or, if you have loads of patterns, categorizing them into an organizational structure that makes sense for the type of work you are doing.

For example, you might make pattern libraries for stone, wood, carpet, brick, and other real-world
materials. In this example, we will create a single pattern library and populate it with a few patterns
needed for the Kitchen project in the next section. You will begin by cleaning out the default library
of all its patterns so you can start fresh with your own custom patterns.

1. Choose the Paint Bucket tool (press G), and select Pattern in the Fill drop-down on the Options
   bar. Click the drop-down menu to open the Pattern Picker. Right-click a pattern and choose
   Delete Pattern from the context menu. Repeat this process, and delete every single pattern in
   the default library.

NOTE   You will be restoring the patterns you delete from the default pattern library later; these patterns will not be lost. Clearing these out, though, lets you create a new pattern library that contains
only your custom-defined patterns.

2. Click the WalnutPattern window to activate it. Choose Edit ➤ Define Pattern to open the Pattern
   Name dialog box. In the Name box, type **Walnut** and click OK to add this pattern to the empty
   library.

NOTE   This time you are saving a tilable version of the Walnut pattern to the library.

3. Open the files BlueCarpet.jpg, CeramicTile.jpg, and Mahogany.jpg from the companion
   CD (see Figure 5.27). These tilable images are ready to go into your pattern library.

FIGURE 5.27
Adding materials to your pattern library

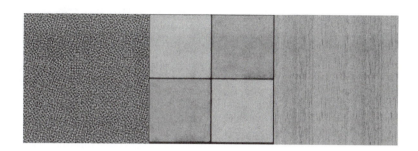

4. Now you're ready to add these materials to the current pattern library. Click the BlueCarpet.jpg document window. Choose Edit ➤ Define Pattern to open the Pattern Name dialog box. In the Name box, remove the dot and the file extension (leaving the name `BlueCarpet`), and click OK.

5. Repeat step 4 twice more, and add CeramicTile and Mahogany to the library. Close all the document windows without saving.

6. Now that you have added all the patterns to the library, you can save the library for future use: Choose the Paint Bucket tool (press G), and select Pattern in the Fill drop-down on the Options bar. Click the drop-down menu to open the Pattern Picker. Click the right-facing arrow to open the Pattern menu. Select Save Patterns to open the Save dialog box (see Figure 5.28). Type the filename **My Patterns** and click the Save button. You now have a separate pattern library that includes *only* the patterns you defined.

NOTE By default, Photoshop saves patterns in `C:\Program Files\Adobe\Photoshop CS\ Presets\Patterns`. Pattern libraries have a `.pat` file extension in Windows.

FIGURE 5.28
Saving the pattern library

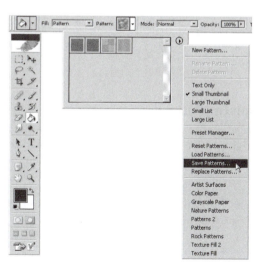

7. From the Pattern menu, choose Reset Patterns. This option restores the patterns you erased in step 1 to their factory-fresh state. Click OK when asked "Replace current patterns with the default patterns?"

8. Close Photoshop and then launch it again. Photoshop builds a new Pattern menu at launch time. My Patterns appears in the Pattern menu; select it and click OK.

NOTE   You can load the custom pattern library from a file without relaunching Photoshop, but the new library's name won't appear in the Pattern menu until relaunch.

You can create as many custom pattern libraries as you want, and their names will appear in the Pattern menu.

9. Open the Pattern Picker and take a look at your custom pattern library containing the four patterns you'll use in the Kitchen project (see Figure 5.29).

FIGURE 5.29
Your custom pattern library

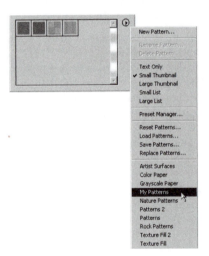

Applying Patterns

You can apply patterns in many ways, and now that you know about the possibilities, you can choose the right tool for the job. The Paint Bucket tool is good for completely filling a pattern into a selection. The Pattern Stamp tool is helpful when you don't want the pattern to completely fill an area, but prefer soft edges or incomplete coverage. The Pattern Fill layer offers more control with pattern selection and scale controls that retain editability.

Let's try out these three methods (see Figure 5.30). To experiment, use a new blank document with a white background.

FIGURE 5.30

Applying patterns with different tools: top left, a Paint Bucket pattern; right, the Pattern Stamp tool; bottom left, a Pattern Fill layer

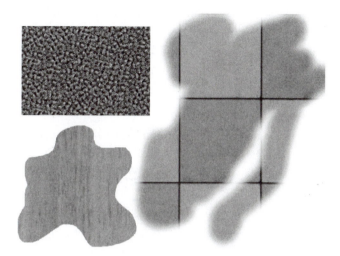

The simplest way to apply a pattern is to fill a selection using the Paint Bucket tool:

1. Select the Rectangular Marquee tool (press M) and drag out a small selection.

2. Select the Paint Bucket tool (press G) and select Pattern from the Fill drop-down.

3. Open the Pattern Picker and double-click BlueCarpet.

4. Click inside your selection to fill it with the pattern. Press Ctrl+D to deselect.

You have more control applying patterns with the Pattern Stamp tool because you can paint in the pattern:

1. Press Shift+S to select the Pattern Stamp tool. (It is under the Clone Stamp tool in the toolbox.)

2. On the Options bar, select a 100 px soft brush, choose the CeramicTile pattern, and check Aligned.

3. Paint the pattern into the blank document. The edges of the pattern can be as soft as you like because you are using a brush.

You can also apply patterns using a fill layer. This gives you the advantage of being able to change the scale of the pattern, and you can revisit the fill layer later and even change the pattern itself:

1. Select the Lasso (press L) and draw a curvy selection, which will become the fill layer's mask.

2. Apply a Pattern Fill layer; click the Create New Fill Or Adjustment Layer button at the bottom of the Layers palette and choose Pattern from the menu to open the Layer Style dialog box.

3. Select the CeramicTile pattern in the Pattern Fill dialog box. Change the Scale slider to 30% and click OK.

4. In the Layers palette, double-click the Pattern Fill 1 layer's thumbnail. In the Pattern Fill dialog box, select the Mahogany pattern and change the Scale slider to 200%.

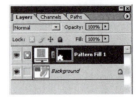

Layer Style Techniques

Although you can usually accomplish the same goal in many ways in Photoshop, layer style techniques provide you the most flexibility because they retain editability in the Layers palette. Therefore, you don't have to get the effect you are looking for 100 percent perfect the first time around; you can try something and adjust it later. As you enhance drawings, you will learn to treasure the freedom and power of layer style techniques.

You will build two projects in these tutorials: a small floor plan and a large-scale site map. The techniques presented in the course of both tutorials will expose you to the wide range of possibilities for enhancing plans with Photoshop.

The Kitchen Project

This small floor plan project illustrates the way a new kitchen appears to a hypothetical client. The spacing and relationship of the major work zones, fixtures, and appliances in the kitchen are immediately understood in the enhanced image. Color and texture add additional levels of information that are not present in the original CAD drawing.

Before you get started, take a look at the color section for the before and after images of this project. We pick up here where we left off earlier in the chapter.

1. Open the file Kitchen.psd that you saved earlier. This file is also available on the companion CD in case you are jumping in here (see Figure 5.23).

2. Switch to 50% or 100% magnification; press Ctrl++ or Ctrl+- (that's the Ctrl key with the "plus" or "minus" key) to zoom in or out so the image fills your screen as much as possible. The line work looks best when the magnification is either halved or doubled from the actual pixel size (12.5%, 25%, 50%, 100%, 200%, and so on). Intermediate magnifications (16.7%, 33.3%, 66.7%) suffer from partial resampling that causes some of the line work to appear to be missing.

TIP   I recommend checking Zoom Resizes Windows under Edit ➤ Preferences ➤ General. The size of the document window that you can fit on your screen without the scroll bars appearing depends on the resolution setting of your graphics card.

Filling an enclosed area is also the first step in preparing to use layer style effects. Let's fill the walls and island with black to make them stand out. Technically, you don't have to fill with black; any color will do, including white. You control where the layer style effects appear based on the placement of pixels on the layer to which they are bound. Layers styles do not appear in transparent areas (where there are no pixels).

3. In the Layers palette, select the Kitchen-A-wall layer. Select the Paint Bucket tool in the toolbox, and select Foreground from the Fill drop-down on the Options bar. Press D to set the default colors so that black is in the foreground. Click inside each one of the walls with the tip of the Paint Bucket cursor to fill them in with black, as shown in Figure 5.31.

TIP   You might find selecting easier with the precise cursor. Press Caps Lock to toggle into Precise Cursor mode featuring the crosshair cursor. You can press Caps Lock again to toggle out of the mode. Each tool once again has its own characteristic cursor icon.

4. Select the Kitchen-A-mlwk-ilnd (meaning "architectural-millwork-island") layer. Using the Paint Bucket, click inside the island to fill it with black.

APPLYING LAYER STYLES

You can apply multiple effects within the Layer Style dialog box in a series of steps. The following steps overlay a grayscale pattern and scale it down to suit the size of the kitchen island.

1. With the Kitchen-A-mlwk-ilnd layer still selected, click the Add A Layer Style button (at the bottom of the Layers palette) and select Pattern Overlay from the menu. In the Layer Style dialog box, open the Pattern Picker and click the triangle button. Select the Texture Fill library from the menu (see Figure 5.32). Click OK when the small warning dialog box appears.

FIGURE 5.31
Filling the walls
with black

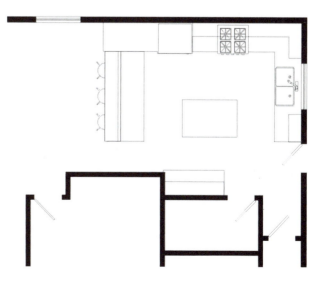

FIGURE 5.32
Changing pattern
libraries within
pattern overlay

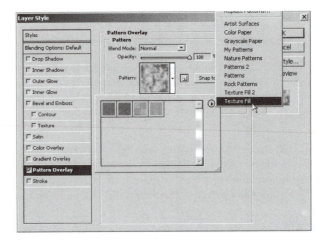

We'll spend the next few steps in the Layer Style dialog box.

2. In the Pattern Picker, select the Concrete texture; hold your mouse still over the textures and wait for the Tool Tips to appear and identify the textures by name. Concrete is the first swatch in the second row; double-click the swatch, or click it and then click outside the Pattern Picker to close it.

3. In the Pattern area, drag the Scale slider to 50% to decrease the size of the pattern showing on the kitchen island in real time. If the dialog box is covering the kitchen island, you'll need to drag the dialog box out of the way to see the preview of the effect.

TIP You can use the Color Overlay effect to colorize a grayscale pattern. You can get extra mileage out of this type of pattern library because grayscale patterns can generate textures of every color.

4. Click Color Overlay in the left panel; the controls on the right side of the dialog box change accordingly. If you just checked the Color Overlay box, the controls may not have changed. You also need to make sure that Color Overlay is the active effect (it is highlighted when active) by clicking its name. Change Blend Mode to Overlay so that the pattern you overlayed in the preceding step will show through.

5. Click the color swatch to open the Color Picker. Select a red hue that is half-saturated and half-bright. Either click a point in the center of the color ramp, or type **0** for Hue, **50%** for Saturation, and **50%** for Brightness in the H, S, and B text boxes. Click OK to close the Color Picker. To tone down the color overlay a bit, drag the Opacity slider to 75%.

Drop shadows add an illusion of depth to an otherwise two-dimensional floor plan. Because you are essentially faking shadows in Photoshop (rather than casting them with light sources as in a 3D program), be aware of how shadows appear in the real world. Shadows should be softer and farther from tall objects; short objects should have harder-edged shadows that remain closer to the object doing the casting.

6. Click Drop Shadow in the left panel to display new controls on the right side of the Layer Style dialog box. Change Angle to 45°. To create a soft shadow that adds an appropriate amount of

depth to the island, drag the Distance slider to 10 pixels, set Spread to 4%, and set Size to 13 pixels. To reduce the darkness of the shadow, drag the Opacity slider down to 55% (see Figure 5.33). Click OK to close the Layer Style dialog box. Figure 5.33 also shows the completed kitchen island.

NOTE The actual values you use in Layer Style Effects depend on the absolute pixel size of the image in which you are working. Therefore, the actual percentages or numbers of pixels that you use for the controls in one project may not transfer directly to another project. However, you can scale the Layer Style Effects globally by choosing Layer ➢ Layer Style ➢ Scale Effects.

FIGURE 5.33

(top) The drop shadow effect; (bottom) the kitchen island with the pattern overlay, the color overlay, and drop shadow effects

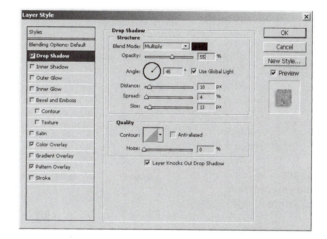

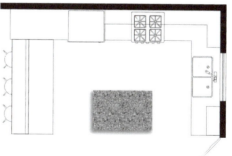

7. In the Layers palette, expand the triangle next to the Kitchen-A-mlwk-ilnd layer name. Each effect you applied is accessible with an effect icon. You can also toggle the visibility of each effect with the corresponding eye icon. You can jump to a specific page within the Layer Style dialog box; double-click the effect icon next to Color Overlay to open the Layer Style dialog box with the Color Overlay options. Now that you have seen how this works, press Esc to cancel.

APPLYING PATTERNS

Sometimes you want to create more than one pattern on a line-work layer. You can do so by applying layer styles to new layers instead of to line-work layers:

1. Turn off the Kitchen-A-mlwk-uppr layer that contains the upper cabinets. Create a new layer by pressing Shift+Ctrl+N and type the name **Walnut** in the New Layer dialog box. Choose Red from the Color drop-down (to help differentiate the new layer from the other line-work layers) and click OK.

2. Select the Paint Bucket tool if it is not already selected. Make sure All Layers is checked on the Options bar; this feature allows the Paint Bucket to identify a boundary from all visible layers while depositing its pixel paint on the current layer (Walnut). Click the outer part of the bar countertop to fill this area with black. Click again on the desk at the bottom of the kitchen, as shown in Figure 5.34.

FIGURE 5.34
Filling the bar counter
and desk with black

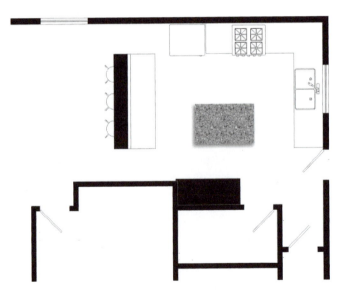

3. Apply a Pattern Overlay effect to the Walnut layer; on the bottom of the Layers palette, click the Add A Layer Style button and select Pattern Overlay from the menu. In the Layer Style dialog box, open the Pattern Picker and click the triangle button. Select My Patterns from the menu (created in the last section). Click OK when the small warning dialog box appears. Select the Walnut pattern from the Pattern Picker. Click OK to close the Layer Style dialog box.

4. In the Layers palette, drag the Drop Shadow effect you've already built from the Kitchen-A-mlwk-ilnd layer to the Walnut layer. Figure 5.35 shows where to start dragging and where to drop the effect so that it becomes part of the Walnut layer.

TIP   Save time by reusing Layer Style Effects!

FIGURE 5.35
Drag and drop Layer
Style Effects

…and drop the effect just below the destination layer name.

Drag the effect from its icon here…

APPLYING GRAIN IN TWO DIRECTIONS

Now you will create another material-based layer and fill it with a pattern from your custom library. Let's apply a vertical grain mahogany pattern to the counter surrounding the sink and a horizontal grain mahogany surrounding the stove. To apply two different patterns, we need a transition line on the line-work layer.

1. Create a new layer (press Shift+Ctrl+N). In the New Layer dialog box, type **Mahogany Vertical Grain,** give the layer a red color, and click OK. Fill the right side of the bar countertop with black. Apply a Pattern Overlay layer style. Choose Mahogany from the Pattern Picker and click OK to close the Layer Style dialog box. Figure 5.36 shows the results so far.

FIGURE 5.36
The mahogany and
walnut patterns applied

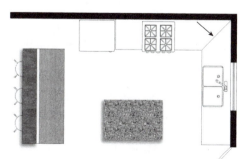

2. Select the Kitchen-A-mlwk-lowr layer. Select the Line tool in the toolbox; on the Options bar, select Fill Pixels mode, set Width to 1 pixel, and uncheck Anti-aliased. Hold down the Shift key and draw a line at a 45° angle across the countertop as indicated in Figure 5.36.

3. Click the Mahogany Vertical Grain layer, and use the Paint Bucket to fill in black in the area surrounding the sink. The pattern appears immediately because any black pixels on this layer have the Pattern Overlay effect already applied.

4. Create a new layer called Mahogany Horizontal Grain. (Press Shift+Ctrl+N, name the layer, give it an orange color to differentiate it, and click OK in the New Layer dialog box.) Select the Magic Wand tool (press W). On the Options bar, set Tolerance to 1, uncheck Anti-aliased, and check Contiguous and Use All Layers. Click inside the counter area surrounding the stove. Click the Add Layer Mask button at the bottom of the Layers palette to turn the selection into a mask (see Figure 5.37).

FIGURE 5.37

Adding a layer mask from the Magic Wand selection

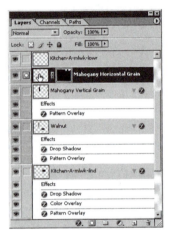

5. Click the thumbnail of the Mahogany Horizontal grain layer to activate it. Select the Paint Bucket tool (press G); change the Fill drop-down to Pattern and select the Mahogany pattern from the Pattern Picker. On the Options bar, uncheck All Layers, and then click anywhere in the document window to fill the layer with the pattern.

6. Unlink the mask from its layer: click the link icon between the layer thumbnail and the mask thumbnail in the Layers palette. Transform the layer (press Ctrl+T). In the Set Rotation text box on the Options bar, type **90**. Finally, drag the pattern over to the right so that it fills the masked area, and click the Commit button on the Options bar. Figure 5.38 shows the result.

FILLING WITH FLAT COLOR AND GRADIENTS

Now that you have filled in the countertops with patterns, some remaining areas, such as the stove and the barstool legs, need some basic flat color. And let's use gradient overlays to color in the refrigerator and sink.

1. Create a new layer called Flat Color; give this layer a yellow color in the Layers palette. With the Paint Bucket tool selected, change the Fill drop-down to Foreground, set Tolerance to 1,

uncheck Anti-aliased, and check Contiguous and All Layers on the Options bar. Fill the dividing space between the walnut bar and the mahogany countertop with black.

2. Click the foreground color swatch in the toolbox and select a medium gray from the Color Picker. Fill the doors in with medium gray.

3. Zoom in closer to the stove. Fill in the body of the stove with medium gray. Fill the background of the stove's burners with a darker gray and the knobs on the front of the stove with black. Fill the edge of the sink and the faucet itself with light gray; however, do not fill the sinks themselves yet.

WARNING   Sometimes fill spills out of enclosed areas and floods a larger space. If this happens, you have to undo. The reason fill escapes an enclosure can be as simple as a single missing pixel in the boundary. The fix is easy; track down the break in the boundary, and repair it with pixels using the Pencil tool. Be careful to repair a broken boundary on the same layer as the boundary line work.

For a more flexible approach, apply flat colors using a layer style; that way you can change the color more easily in the future if you change your mind.

4. Toggle off the visibility of the Drop Shadow effect on the Walnut layer. (We need to do this before we can fill the barstools, because the shadow interferes with the barstool boundary.)

5. Create a new layer called Barstools. (Press Shift+Ctrl+N, name the layer, and give it a green color.) Press D to set the default colors, and select the Paint Bucket tool from the toolbox. Fill each barstool seat with black.

FIGURE 5.38
Rotating the masked pattern to create horizontal grain

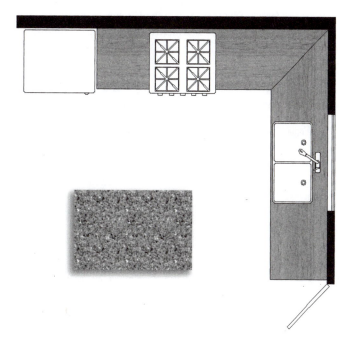

6. Apply a Color Overlay layer style to the Barstools layer. In the Layer Style dialog box click the color swatch and select a beige color. Click OK to close the Color Picker.

7. To give the stools more interesting variation, click Satin in the left pane of the Layer Style dialog box. In the Satin controls (see Figure 5.39), set Distance to 9 pixels and set Size to 32 pixels before clicking OK.

FIGURE 5.39
The Satin effect

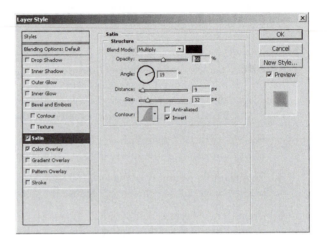

8. You can fill small areas directly with the Pencil tool one pixel at a time; let's fill in the barstool legs in this way. Select the Kitchen-A-furn layer where the barstool line work resides. Using the Pencil tool, draw in the barstool legs in medium gray with black tips, one pixel at a time (see Figure 5.40). Zoom in as close as necessary to see the pixels. Be careful not to color outside the lines!

FIGURE 5.40
Flat color applied to the bar wall, stove, and stool legs

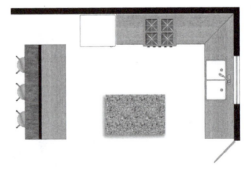

NOTE Don't worry if the line work looks ragged up close; it will appear smooth when you zoom out and perceive the entire composition.

9. Create a new layer called Refrigerator and make it blue in the New Layer dialog box. Use the Paint Bucket to fill the refrigerator in with black.

10. Apply a Gradient Overlay effect to the Refrigerator layer. In the Layer Style dialog box (see Figure 5.41), select the Black To White gradient from the Gradient Picker. Check Reverse and set Angle to 125°. Increase the Scale slider to the right end at 150% to create a more gradual transition from black to white. Click OK.

FIGURE 5.41

The Gradient Overlay effect

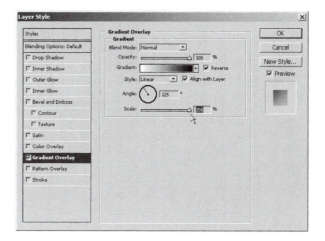

11. Create a new layer called Sinks and make it blue in the New Layer dialog box. Use the Paint Bucket tool to fill the two sinks with black. Apply a Gradient Overlay effect. In the Layer Style dialog box, check Reverse, select the reflected style (essentially two linear gradients reflected in the middle), set Scale to 150%, and click OK. Figure 5.42 shows the gradients you applied to the refrigerator and sinks.

FIGURE 5.42

The refrigerator and sinks with gradients

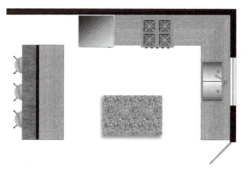

12. Click on the Kitchen-A-mlwk-uppr layer. Apply a Stroke effect (see Figure 5.43). In the Layer Style dialog box, set Size to 1 pixel, set the Position drop-down to Outside if it not already, and click OK. This process outlines the existing line work with 1 red pixel on either side of the line, to indicate the line of the upper cabinets that are above the plan cutline.

FIGURE 5.43
The Stroke effect

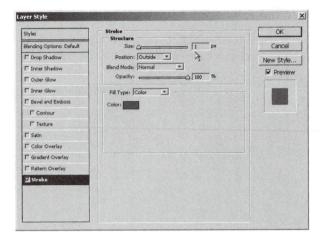

A full-height cabinet is adjacent to the refrigerator. Now that the stroke is visible, you can see the boundary for this cabinet. Let's use both color overlay and inner shadow effects to help render this object.

13. Create a new layer called Cabinet and make it violet. Use the Paint Bucket to fill black into the cabinet's boundary surrounding the refrigerator. Apply a Color Overlay effect. In the Layer Style dialog box, click the color swatch in the Color group to open the Color Picker. Notice that your cursor is an eyedropper and that the Color Picker is open so that you can also sample colors from the document window. Instead of selecting a color from the Color Picker, click one of the mahogany countertops to select a light brown hue, and then click OK to close the Color Picker.

14. Click Inner Shadow in the left pane of the Layer Style dialog box (see Figure 5.44). Set the Opacity slider to 52%, set Distance and Choke to 0, set Size to 81 pixels, and then click OK to close the dialog box.

FIGURE 5.44
The Inner Shadow effect

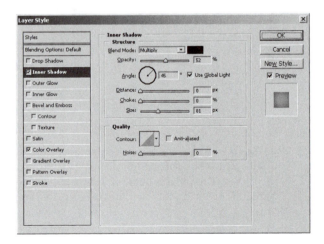

ALIGNING PATTERNS

We need to add a transition line where floor materials meet. This transition was not shown in the CAD drawing, but it's easy enough to add a straight line in Photoshop and then apply two floor materials:

1. Select the Kitchen-A-wall layer in the Layers palette. Select the Line tool in the toolbox; on the Options bar, set Fill Pixels mode, set Width to 1 pixel, and uncheck Anti-alias. Hold down the Shift key and draw a horizontal line across the middle of the threshold, as shown in Figure 5.45.

FIGURE 5.45
Draw a 1-pixel-wide transition line here.

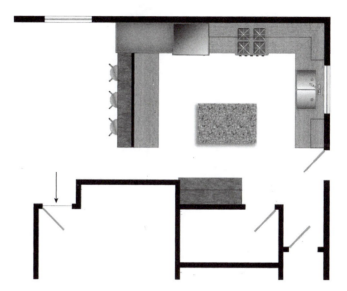

2. Create a new layer called Carpet and make it gray in the New Layer dialog box. Use the Paint Bucket and click a point inside the small room below the new transition line to fill this room with black.

3. Apply a Pattern Overlay effect to the Carpet layer. In the Layer Style dialog box, open the Pattern Picker and select the BlueCarpet pattern. Close the Pattern Picker, set the Scale slider to 50%, and click OK.

4. Before you can create the remaining floor pattern, you have to temporarily turn off any effects that interfere with the boundary. In the Layers palette, toggle off the Drop Shadow effect belonging to the Kitchen-A-mlwk-ilnd layer.

    Let's add the tile floor using another Pattern Overlay effect. In this case, we can cover two boundaries using one layer, registering the tile grid with an object in the kitchen.

5. Create a new layer called Ceramic Tile and make it gray in the New Layer dialog box. Use the Paint Bucket and click the floor space in the middle of the kitchen to fill it with black. Notice the small white space at the bottom of the plan; click inside this space to fill it with black also.

NOTE   Although it might not be realistic for the kitchen tile to extend into a separate room, notice how two non-contiguous areas can be filled with the same pattern on one layer.

6. Apply a Pattern Overlay effect to the Ceramic Tile layer. In the Layer Style dialog box, select the CeramicTile pattern from the Pattern Picker. Set the Scale slider to 38%. While you have the Layer Style dialog box open, bring your mouse over the document window; notice that it appears with the Move cursor. Drag the pattern so that the tile grid registers with the corner of the bar counter, as shown in Figure 5.46. Click OK in the Layer Style dialog box.

FIGURE 5.46
Registering tile pattern grid: drag the tile grid and align it with this corner both vertically and horizontally.

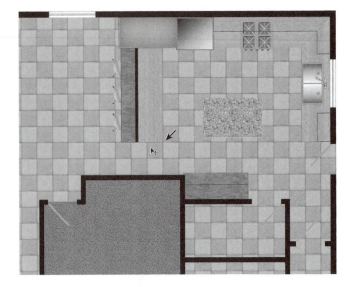

FINISHING TOUCHES

When you're done filling and styling the layers of a plan, you need to turn any effects back on that you turned off temporarily when you were filling boundaries. You might have to rearrange layer order to be sure you see effects that overlap other layers. In addition, you might need to copy Layer Style Effects—such as drop shadows—to other layers for more realism. And once you finish enhancing the plan, it is helpful to save a composite layer that shows all your work to date.

Follow these steps to complete the final checks for our kitchen plan.

1. Toggle on the Drop Shadow effects in the Walnut and Kitchen-A-mlwk-ilnd layers. Notice that you can't see these shadows; they are obscured by the Ceramic Tile layer because it is at the top of the Layers palette.

2. Drag the Ceramic Tile layer to the bottom of the Layers palette and drop it just above the Background layer. Drag the Drop Shadow effect from the Walnut layer and drop it on the Mahogany Vertical Grain layer; this copies the effect to the destination layer. Copy additional Drop Shadow effects onto the Barstools and A-door layers.

3. Create a new layer at the top of the Layers palette and call it Composite in the New Layer dialog box. Press Alt+Shift+Ctrl+E to stamp all the visible layers onto the current one.

4. Save your work as Kitchen2.psd (see Figure 5.47). You can close this file for now. You'll be opening it once more in this chapter in the "Laying Out Plans on a Sheet" section.

FIGURE 5.47
The enhanced kitchen

The Hollyhock Project

This project is a large-scale site map that illustrates the layout of an entire facility. It shows the relationship of the buildings to the overall site and how they are connected with curving footpaths. You will be creating the map that is given to visitors as they arrive at Hollyhock.

NOTE   Hollyhock is Canada's leading educational retreat center (www.hollyhock.ca). The facilities are in a natural setting where the rainforest meets a sandy beach on a beautiful island in British Columbia. The map you will develop in this project is the map I made for Hollyhock, which they give to their guests upon arrival.

Before you get started with this tutorial, take a look at the color section for before and after images of this project. You'll begin with the original CAD layers already transferred to layers in Photoshop. (See "Transferring Multilayer Drawings to Photoshop" earlier in this chapter.)

WARNING   This tutorial is more generalized and is at a higher level than the preceding kitchen tutorial. If you haven't already done so, work through the kitchen tutorial first to understand the mechanics of Layer Style Effects.

1. Open the file Hollyhock.psd from the companion CD. The layers you see in this Photoshop file come directly from the AutoCAD layers. (Hollyhock.dwg is also provided on the companion CD for your reference.)

   CAD layers work differently than Photoshop layers in terms of how they are used. CAD layers contain the line work itself and delineate boundaries. In Photoshop, you will be using layers to overlay patterns, colors, and other Layer Style Effects that fit within and fill these boundaries.

   Generally, the procedure for enhancement begins with identifying the boundaries of your area of interest and selecting or creating a layer to use. You then fill the area of interest with black and apply Layer Style Effects.

2. Select the Hollyhock-Waterline layer and toggle it on and off to see where it is in the image (lower edge). Using the Paint Bucket, fill the ocean with black. To the Hollyhock-Waterline layer, apply the following Layer Style Effects:

Pattern Overlay   Use the Rough pattern from the Patterns 2 library at 100% scale.

Gradient Overlay   Use the linear black-to-white gradient at an angle of 87° and a scale of 150%. Change Opacity to 70%, and set the Blend mode to Overlay.

Color Overlay   Select a light blue-green hue with HSB values of 180,50,65. Change the Blend mode to Overlay.

Bevel and Emboss   Use smooth inner bevel directed down with 40% depth, 9 px size, and 16 px soften.

The pattern imparts a rough texture; gradient adds darkness to the depths; color is overlaid to lighten; and bevel smoothes the transition between ocean and shore (see Figure 5.48).

Temporarily applying a stroke helps you visualize the boundaries of line work because it allows you to change the color. After you fill the layer, discard the stroke effect.

3. Select the Hollyhock-Property layer and apply the Stroke effect, using 1 pixel inside position settings in the Layer Style dialog box. The property lines highlight in red. Use the Paint Bucket and fill all the vacant spaces in the property shown in Figure 5.49. Then drag the Stroke effect to the Trash icon at the bottom of the Layers palette. (You can click the triangle next to the layer name to expand the layer hierarchy and reveal the Stroke effect.)

FIGURE 5.48
Applying Layer Style
Effects to the ocean

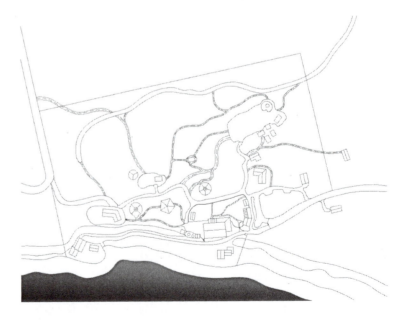

FIGURE 5.49
Filling the property
with black

4. Play around with effects until you are satisfied with the layer's appearance. Use the following effects as guidelines for the Hollyhock-Property layer:

   Pattern Overlay Use the Stucco 2 pattern from the Texture Fill 2 library with a scale of 99%.

   Color Overlay Select a forest green with HSB values of 100,50,50. Set the Blend mode to Overlay.

   Bevel and Emboss Use a Smooth Inner Bevel directed down with 100% Depth, 3 px Size, and 8 px Soften.

   Inner Shadow Set Opacity to 50%, set Distance to 5 px, set Choke to 0%, and set Size to 5 px.

   I used a grayscale pattern here and overlaid it with a green hue. A bevel makes the edges of the fill more distinct, and the inner shadow adds depth to the forest.

TIP Setting a scale of 99% in the Pattern Picker is qualitatively different from a setting of 100%. Photoshop blurs patterns at all scales other than 50%, 100%, and 200%. Therefore, setting a scale of 99% looks blurrier than a setting of 100% even though the pattern appears almost the same size.

5. Work on each of the four road layers in turn, starting with Hollyhock-RoadA. Fill the layer and then creatively apply Layer Style Effects to enhance each layer's appearance. The road layers are segregated to illustrate their uses. RoadA is a paved road for vehicle traffic. RoadB is a gravel right-of-way. RoadC is a cart path, and RoadD is a foot path. You will have to turn off the Trails layer temporarily because it obscures RoadD.

NOTE If you are not feeling particularly creative, the completed tutorial is provided on the CD for your reference as Hollyhock2.psd. You can open this file and investigate how effects were applied to the road layers.

6. To draw more attention to the footpaths, accent them using a stroked line. First, work on the dashed line on the Hollyhock-Trails layer: The line going down the center of the already patterned RoadD layer was already given its dashed line type in AutoCAD. All you have to do is stroke the layer to change the color of the line and widen it slightly.

TIP   It is best to control line type from AutoCAD; dashed, hidden, center, and phantom lines as seen on architectural plans are examples of line type. Set the line type in your AutoCAD layers (and set the scale with LTSCALE) before bringing image layers into Photoshop.

Stroke the Hollyhock-Trails layer. Choose crimson red for the stroke color. Setting the size to 4 pixels in a centered position will do nicely. Figure 5.50 shows the results from work on the road network.

FIGURE 5.50
The road network
enhanced

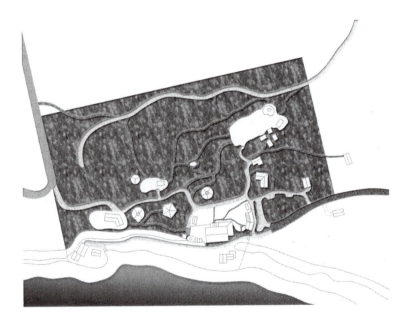

The buildings on the Hollyhock grounds fall into four categories: accommodations, session houses, major structures, and minor structures. Let's color code each type of building and use effects to make them appear almost three-dimensional. Once you develop a layer style, some structures can use the same style with just a change to their color coding.

7. Select the Hollyhock-Session Houses layer. Temporarily add a single pixel inside stroke effect like you did in step 3 to help you identify which structures are session houses. Fill the session houses with black. Then apply the following Layer Style Effects:

Color Overlay   Select an orange with HSB values of 50,85,80.

Bevel and Emboss   Choose Inner Bevel Style, Chisel Soft Technique, Direction Up, Size 20 px, Soften 7 px.

Drop Shadow   Set the angle to −125°, set Distance to 11px, and set Size to 6 px.

This process gives the session houses orange color coding with color overlay, making them look as if they have sloped roof surfaces with bevel and emboss and giving the structures depth with the Drop Shadow effect. Notice that we changed the global sun angle in this step, which affects all the shadows in the document. An angle of –125° indicates that the sun will come from the lower-left portion of the image. Turn off the Stroke effect.

8. Select the Hollyhock-Accommodations layer. Apply an inside red stroke as usual to reveal the locations of these structures on screen. Using the Paint Bucket, fill the selected structures, as shown in Figure 5.51.

FIGURE 5.51
Fill the selected accommodation structures with black.

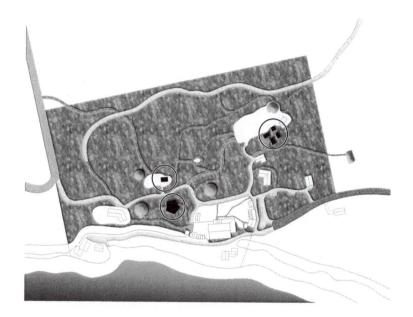

9. Copy the entire layer style from Hollyhock-Session Houses to the Hollyhock-Accommodations layer. (Drag and drop the word *Effects* from one layer to the other in the Layers palette.) Double-click the Color Overlay effect under Hollyhock-Accommodations and change the color to blue with a Hue value of 245 in the Color Picker.

Notice that many of the accommodation structures have pitched roofs. Instead of using the Bevel And Emboss effect, some hand coloring is in order to maintain the sharp ridgelines. You will have to think about where the sun is in order to plan your hand-painted color scheme; lighter shades of blue will be used where the surfaces are in full light, and darker shades of blue will be painted on surfaces that are partial shadow.

10. Temporarily turn off the Drop Shadow effect belonging to the Hollyhock-Accommodations layer because it obscures the boundaries of the roof line work. Create a new layer called Accommodations-Hand Colored. Click the Swatches palette, and hold your mouse over the swatches until you can read their Tool Tips. Click Pastel Blue to set it as the foreground color. Select the Paint Bucket tool and click the roof surfaces indicated in Figure 5.52.

FIGURE 5.52
Hand painting
illuminated roof
surfaces: make these
pastel blue.

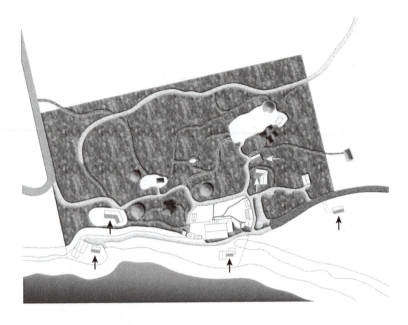

WARNING Drop Shadow and Outer Glow effects extend beyond their fill boundaries. As such, these effects create pixels that overlap other layers or can themselves be covered by other layers. You might need to temporarily toggle off these effects while selecting or filling adjacent boundaries. Arranging the stacking order of layers can reveal a drop shadow or an outer glow that is covered by another layer.

Painting roof surfaces is quite subjective; you simply want to convey the idea that the hues get darker the more the roofs are in shadow, given that the sun is coming from the lower-left corner of the image. Although we know there would naturally be tonal variation in the real world, to simplify matters you can color each flat roof facet with a solid color. This simplification gives the map a pleasing cartoonish feeling that actually makes it easier to read.

11. Use the Swatches palette to help you select various shades of blue. Using the Paint Bucket, drop solid colors into the boundaries of the roof facets shown in Figure 5.53. Feel free to choose your own colors or color surfaces.

The rest of this project repeats the techniques you have already been using in this tutorial. Rather than simply follow more steps, it will help you to build skills if you participate in the completion of the project based upon the techniques you have learned in this chapter.

Go ahead and complete the Hollyhock map as you see fit, creatively applying Layer Style Effects to the remaining layers, creating new layers, and hand painting wherever you deem appropriate. I recommend using red color-coding for the major structures and purple for the minor structures. You can refer to the color section for inspiration as to one way the completed project might look; feel free to change the effects to reflect your own personal aesthetic taste. Figure 5.54 shows the completed project with text added to identify the site's facilities.

FIGURE 5.53
Hand painting darker
surfaces

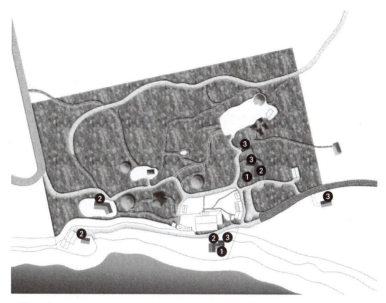

❶ Light blue
❷ Pure blue
❸ Dark blue

FIGURE 5.54
The completed
Hollyhock project

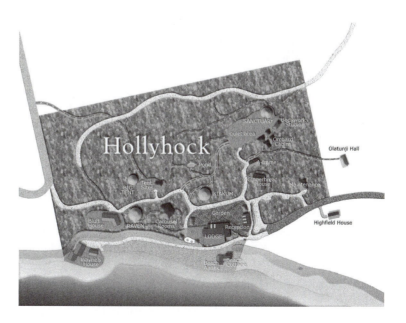

Save your own project and then open the file `Hollyhock2.psd` from the companion CD. Investigate which Layer Style Effects were applied to the remaining layers. Completed project files such as this are a great learning resource and reference for your creative inspiration.

Laying Out Plans on a Sheet

Laying out your final project image on a sheet is the last consideration when preparing your project to be printed. Although Photoshop isn't a page layout program as such, some basic layout tasks are possible. Page layout programs such as QuarkXPress and Adobe InDesign are specifically designed to position multiple images and text for printing on actual pages, whereas layout in Photoshop must occur within the boundaries of the image itself. Therefore, to lay out a project in Photoshop you increase the canvas size to give you some maneuvering room and then move layout objects around within a single document to create the final composition.

In these steps, you will enhance the kitchen project's sheet layout by adding a logo and a title, placing a graphic scale bar at the proper size on the sheet, and fading the edges of the project image for a soft border effect. We'll open a logo artwork file and add it to the default shape library so that you can insert the logo in the project as a custom shape.

When you are laying out a project on a sheet, you want the freedom to move the artwork around in the final composition. The myriad layers that you used to create the project overly complicate the situation and are no longer relevant to the task at hand. Therefore, it is much easier to simplify by starting a new file that contains only the composite image of your project.

1. Open the file `Kitchen2.psd` from the companion CD, or open the project file you completed earlier in this chapter (see Figure 5.47).

2. Select the Composite layer at the top of the Layers palette and press Ctrl+A to select all. Copy the entire image to the Clipboard (press Ctrl+C). Next, to create a new image with the same dimensions as the Clipboard, press Ctrl+N and then press Enter or Return to accept the defaults in the New dialog box. Finally, press Ctrl+V to paste the image from the Clipboard into the new document.

3. Close `Kitchen2.psd` without saving. This saves memory as the project source document is no longer needed.

4. Increasing the canvas size is the way to add a border around the image, and the background color is used by default in the Canvas Size dialog box. Click the background color swatch in the toolbox to open the Color Picker. Select an off-white color with HSB values of 50,10,100. Then, choose Image ➢ Canvas Size to open the Canvas Size dialog box. Check Relative, and set the measurement drop-downs to inches if they are not already. Type **2** in both Width and Height text boxes and click OK.

5. Press X to switch the foreground and background colors so that off-white is in the foreground. Use the Paint Bucket tool to fill off-white into the small spaces surrounding the glazing in the windows. This makes the windows blend more with the canvas color.

6. Open the file `Logo.psd` from the companion CD. Figure 5.55 shows this grayscale artwork.

FIGURE 5.55
The logo artwork

7. Select the Magic Wand tool in the toolbox or press W. On the Options bar, set Tolerance to 1 and uncheck Anti-aliased if it is checked. Click anywhere inside the black portion of the logo. Because this particular design is all connected, the entire logo shape is selected on the first click. Other logo designs might require more elaborate procedures to get only the logo pixels selected.

8. You must convert the selection to a path before the logo is defined as a custom shape. Click the Paths palette. At the bottom of the Paths palette, click the Make Work Paths From Selection button. Choose Edit ➢ Define Custom Shape to open the Shape Name dialog box. Type **Logo** and click OK. This custom shape is added to the default library.

9. Close Logo.psd without saving, and click the open project window to select it. Set the foreground color to bright red. (HSB values are 0,100,100.) Select the Custom Shape tool in the toolbox. (It is under the Line tool.) On the Options bar, click Shape Layers mode, open the Shape Picker, scroll down to the bottom, and click the Logo icon.

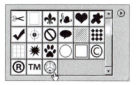

10. In the lower-left corner of the image, drag out the logo, holding down Shift to match its aspect ratio with that of the original. See Figure 5.56 for sizing and placement for the logo custom shape.

FIGURE 5.56
The logo size and place-
ment on a sheet

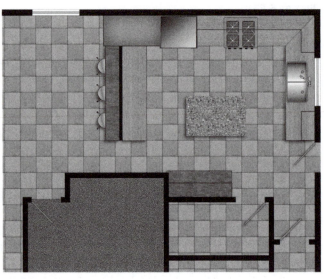

11. Add the sheet title next to the company logo. First, press D to set the default colors. Then press T to select the Text tool, and on the Options bar choose Verdana font at 20 pt size. Type **Kitchen Project** and click the Commit button. Press V, and move the text adjacent to the logo.

    Because this image is actually to scale (see the "Scale and Resolution" section earlier in this chapter), we can indicate 1/4″ scale and include a graphical scale bar on the sheet. You will approach this task by drawing a scale bar in a blank document, saving it as a custom shape, and finally inserting the symbol into the project sheet. We'll use guides to help draw the scale bar with accuracy.

    NOTE Alternatively, you can create the scale bar in AutoCAD and bring it into Photoshop with the drawing layers.

12. Create a new document by pressing Ctrl+N. In the New dialog box, set the size to 4″ × 4″ at 72 dpi in grayscale mode with a white background.

13. Press Ctrl+R to activate the rulers in the blank document. Drag out guides from the vertical ruler every 1/2″. Drag out three guides from the horizontal ruler and leave 1/8″ spaces between them (see Figure 5.57). The exact placement of the horizontal guides does not matter— only that they have equal spacing.

FIGURE 5.57
Drag out guides to create
the scale bar.

14. Select the Rectangle tool in the toolbox. (It is under the Custom Shape tool.) On the Options bar, select Paths mode, and then click Add To Path Area (+).

15. Drag out a long and narrow rectangle that fills one cell of the guide grid on the left edge. Drag out another that fills two units, offset below. Drag out a third rectangle filling four grid cells, as shown in Figure 5.58.

FIGURE 5.58
Drawing the three rect-
angles of the scale bar

16. Choose Edit ➢ Define Custom Shape to open the Shape Name dialog box. Type **Scale Bar** and click OK. Close the document window without saving.

17. Select the project window, and click Shape Layers mode and Custom Shape on the Options bar. Open the Shape Picker, and select Scale Bar.

18. Hold down Shift and start dragging out the Scale Bar on a whole inch mark on the ruler in the project sheet. Release the mouse when the first hash mark measures 1/4″ on the ruler. Figure 5.59 shows the scale bar correctly sized. The first hash mark must equal 1/4″ at this scale.

19. Add the text shown in Figure 5.60 to complete the scale bar. Link the text layers with the shape layer (click the link icons in the Layers palette) and move these layers to the lower-right edge of the sheet.

    The last task is to create soft edges where the plan abruptly ends, along its bottom and left sides. These soft edges downplay the continuation of the building beyond the kitchen. We can use the Gradient tool to fade these edges to transparency.

TIP Soft edges are a great way to gently direct the viewer's interest to the subject area of a floor plan (in this case, the kitchen). You can avoid using sharp cutlines in favor of this gentler approach.

FIGURE 5.59
Creating a scale bar at the correct size for 1/4″ scale

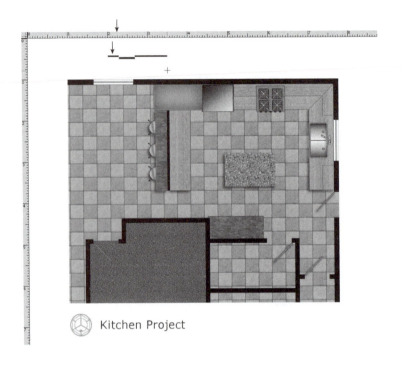

FIGURE 5.60
Adding numbers above and text below the scale bar and positioning it on the sheet

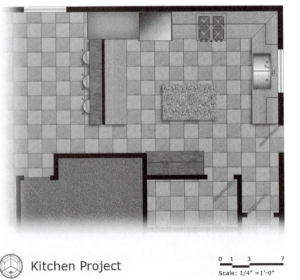

20. Select Layer 1 (containing your project image) in the Layers palette and rename it Composite. Select the Gradient tool in the toolbox. (It is under the Paint Bucket.) Open the Gradient Picker and select Foreground To Transparent.

21. On the Options bar, click the Linear Gradient button (first on the left) and check Transparency. Hold down the Alt key and click the off-white canvas color to place it in the foreground color swatch in the toolbox.

22. You have to repeatedly apply the Gradient tool to progressively fade the edges: Hold down the Shift key and drag a line approximately 2 inches in length across the edge of the project image from left to right. Do this five to ten times until the edge of the composite layer fades away. Repeat this process by dragging a vertical gradient along the lower edge from bottom to top to fade the edge to transparency. Figure 5.61 shows the final sheet. There is also a version of this image in the color section.

23. Save your work as `Kitchen3.psd`. This file is also provided on the companion CD for your reference.

Congratulations on completing the kitchen plan!

FIGURE 5.61
The completed
kitchen plan

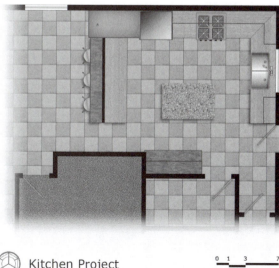

 Kitchen Project

Scale: 1/4" =1'-0"

Summary

You have been exposed to a large toolkit of techniques for enhancing plans in this chapter. Using Photoshop, we've transformed rather mundane line drawings in CAD into exciting and readable plans that can be understood by a much wider audience. In the next chapter, you will learn a related set of tips and tricks for transforming elevations into veritable works of art.

Enhancing CAD Drawings in Color

This full-color gallery demonstrates the wide variety of techniques this book teaches you. Collected as a source of inspiration as well as instruction, it includes examples demonstrating the synergistic power of using Photoshop, ImageReady, AutoCAD, and VIZ together to present imagery to your clients. What you see here is just a glimpse of the impressive work you'll be able to produce after going through the step-by-step tutorials in this book.

Proper tonal range balances the light and shadow in an image, and more detail can be discerned. **TOP:** The original image's detail is hidden in the darkest and lightest areas. **BOTTOM:** Adjusting shadows and highlights, controlling exposure with layers, and dodging and burning by painting and blending brings out detail and balances the tonal range of the image (see Chapter 3).

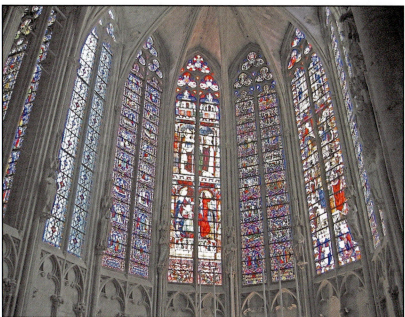

The stained glass in this basilica deserves the sharpest focus you can give it. Blur is a complement to Sharpen used in Chapter 3 to obscure the color noise of this digital image. **TOP:** The original digital photo. **BOTTOM:** After sharpening the luminosity and blurring the color, the edges of the stained glass are well defined, and the color is more clear.

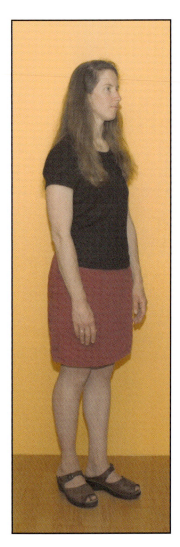  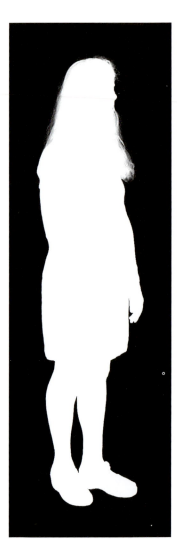

Extracting images of real people from photographs is a great way to add interest to your plans and projects. **LEFT:** This ordinary digital photo was taken against a solid background. **MIDDLE:** Extracted as entourage, the woman can be inserted into any elevation, compositing project, or 3D scene. **RIGHT:** The alpha channel was generated from transparency using the Calculations tool after extraction and is used in Autodesk VIZ as an opacity map (see Chapter 4).

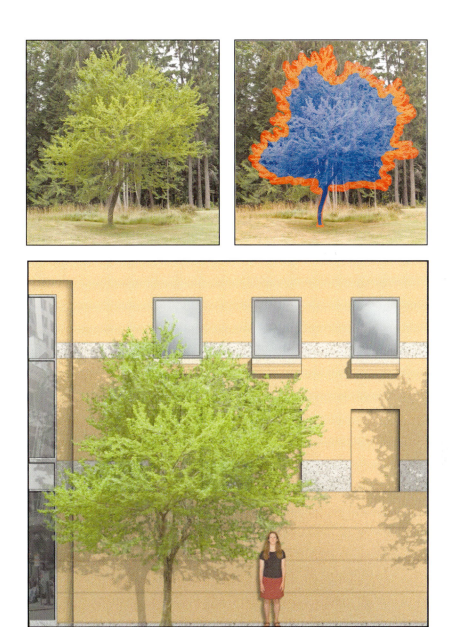

TOP LEFT: Original photo of plum tree with natural background. **TOP RIGHT:** Highlight and fill during extraction of the tree from its background. **BOTTOM:** Completed foliage and human entourage placed in elevation image. You'll find tutorials showing how to extract the woman and the tree in Chapter 4.

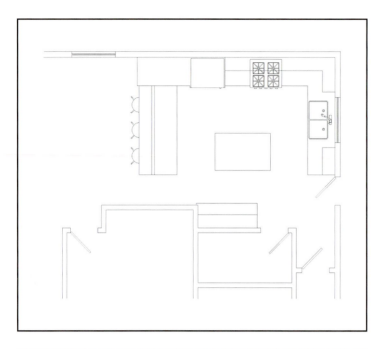

Kitchen Project

Scale: 1/4" =1'-0"

TOP: The kitchen line drawing shown in AutoCAD. **BOTTOM:** The completed Kitchen Plan project from Chapter 5 enhanced with color, patterns, strokes, gradients, and shadow.

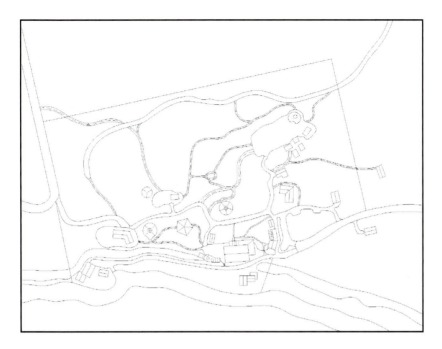

© 2004 Scott Onstott

TOP: Original AutoCAD drawing converted to a bitmap image with the raster print driver. The spline curves were carefully drawn to enclose boundaries in AutoCAD. **BOTTOM:** The completed Hollyhock project from Chapter 6. Layer styles are the primary tool used to enhance this image.

```
(defun C:lay2img ( / LAY LLIST LNAME PATH FILE)
  (setq PATH (getfiled "Save image files of each layer" "" "" 1)) ; get path
  (setq LLIST (tblnext "layer" T)) ; get first layer
  (while (/= LLIST nil) ; goes thru each layer
    (setq LNAME (cdr (assoc 2 LLIST))) ; gets layer name
    (setq LLIST (tblnext "LAYER")) ; advances to next record
    (command "LAYER" "T" "*" "S" LNAME "") ; sets layer current
    (command "LAYER" "OFF" "*" "N" "") ; turns off everything else
    (command "PLOT" ; Edit the following plot details as needed
      "Yes" ; Detailed Plot
      "Model" ; Plot from Model tab
      "ImagePrinter.pc3" ; Printer driver
      "ImageSize" ; Paper Size
      "Landscape" ; Orientation
      "No" ; Plot upside down
      "Extents" ; Plot area
      "1=1" ; Plotted pixels = drawing units
      "Center" ; Plot offset
      "Yes" ; Plot with styles
      "Images.ctb" ; Use this style table name
      "Yes" ; Plot with Lineweights
      "As Displayed" ; Shade plot setting
      (strcat PATH "-" LNAME) ; filename to plot
      "No" ; Save changes to Page Setup
      "Yes" ; Proceed with Plot
    )
  )
  (command "LAYER" "ON" "*" "") ; turn all layers on
  (princ) ; close silently
)
```

RenderMatte0.4.ms - MAXScript
File Edit Search Help

```
Utility RenderMatte "Render Matte" (
  --define ui
    group "Choose Output Path First" (
      Button pathgo "Get Path"
    )
    group "Render Each Object" (
      Button nowgo "Start Rendering"
      label about00 "This could take a while..."
    )
    group "What It Does" (
      label about01 "Renders each object to TGA"
      label about02 "whilst all else is matted"
      label about03 "http://ScottOnstott.com"
    )
  --define actions
    --Get Path button
    on pathgo pressed do (
      --get selected path as string
      global new_path = getSavePath()
    )
    --Start Rendering button
    on nowgo pressed do (
      --get all objects in an array
      scene_nodes = geometry as array
      --loop through all objects
      for i in scene_nodes do (
        --select the ith object in the scene
        select i
        --select inverse
        actionMan.executeAction 0 "40044"
        --turn undo recording on so that we can restore the original material later
        undo on (
          --assign material to selection
          $.material = MatteShadow opaqueAlpha:false affectAlpha:false receiveShadows:false
          backgroundColor = color 0 0 0
        ) -- end undo control
        --set Targa format to 32 bits/pixel, compressed, not split, store alpha
        targa.itgaio.setColorDepth(32)
        targa.itgaio.setCompressed(true)
        targa.itgaio.setAlphaSplit(false)
        targa.itgaio.setPreMultAlpha(true)
        --render as tga to chosen path
        render outputFile:(new_path + "\\" + i.name + ".tga") vfb:off
        --undo the matte material application
        max undo
      )--end for
      --select none
      actionMan.executeAction 0 "40043"
      --notify user of completion
      messageBox "Done" title:"Render Matte"
    )--end on
)--end utility
```

TOP: This AutoLISP program for AutoCAD from Chapter 5 prints each line-work layer as a raster image. **BOTTOM:** This MAXScript for Autodesk VIZ from Chapter 7 renders each 3D object as an alpha channel image.

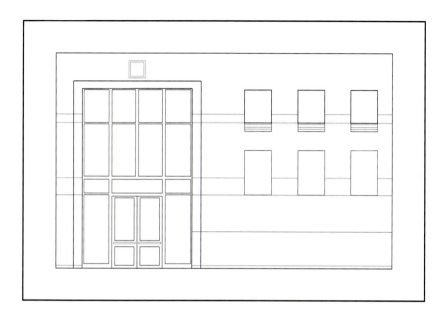

TOP: Original elevation drawing with line weights shown in AutoCAD. **BOTTOM:** Completed elevation project from Chapter 6. Layer styles, textures, reveals, shading, shadows, reflection, refraction, and entourage were added in Photoshop to enhance the composition.

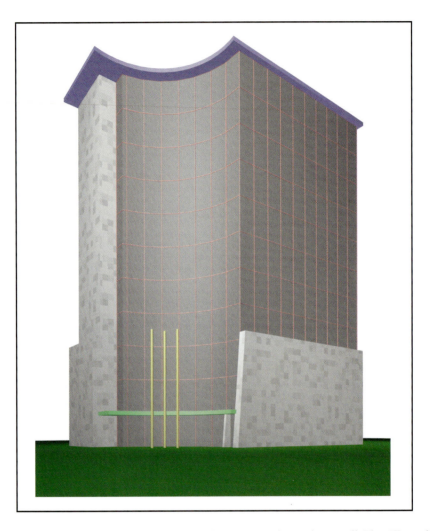

A basic high rise doesn't motivate your clients the way an enhanced one will. This 3D model was created and rendered in Autodesk VIZ using simple geometry, materials, and lighting.

The finished compositing project from Chapter 7 shows the impressive transformation of the 3D model using real-time image-editing techniques in Photoshop.

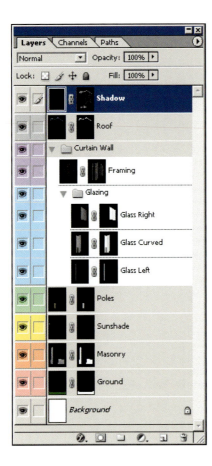

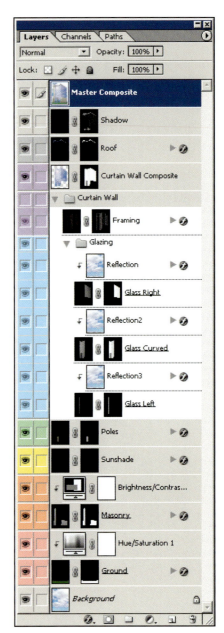

LEFT: Compositing layers shown before enhancement in Photoshop. Each object in the 3D scene was converted to an image layer with alpha channel–based layer mask.

RIGHT: Layers shown after enhancement with adjustment layers, clipping groups, layer styles, and stamped composite layers.

TOP: This 3D model shown in the Autodesk VIZ viewport is the basis of an illustration done in Photoshop (see next page). **BOTTOM:** 3D model with shadows scan line rendered in VIZ. Only color materials and basic lighting are required to set up the model for the illustration project.

TOP: Based on a 3D model (see previous page), the illustration project in Chapter 8 is masked and painted in Photoshop. **BOTTOM:** This duotone illustration with artistic filtering gives a looser, less-defined type of illustration.

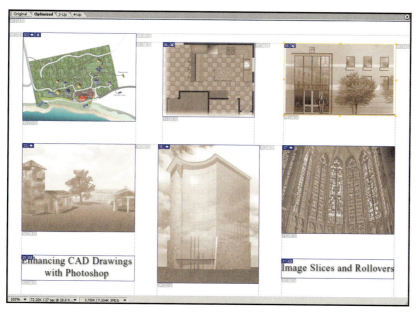

TOP: Original graphic from Chapter 9 to be shown to clients as an optimized web page with rollovers. **BOTTOM:** Slices and rollovers are applied in ImageReady.

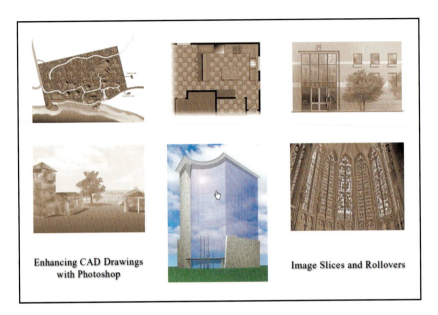

Enhancing CAD Drawings
with Photoshop

Image Slices and Rollovers

TOP: Rollover functioning in browser. The thumbnails appear in sepia tone before the mouse instantly changes them to color when it rolls over them. **BOTTOM:** Your intellectual property is protected in Chapter 9 by a visible watermark (shape layer logo) applied to copyrighted artwork.

Chapter 6

Elevating the Elevation

Elevations are often used to give clients and the general public a first impression of what a structure looks like. Although not as realistic as a perspective drawing or a 3D rendering, elevations convey the essential qualities of proportion and scale.

By enhancing elevations with Photoshop, you increase their effectiveness as a means of graphical communication and thereby transfer greater design understanding to a wide audience. Usually no extra work is required to produce the elevation drawings themselves. Because they are a required element of a design development drawing set, you probably have to draw them anyway.

You can save a lot of time by enhancing elevations with Photoshop as compared with making photo-realistic 3D renderings in a program such as Autodesk VIZ. Another timesaving alternative is compositing image layers in Photoshop from a simple 3D model made in VIZ (see Chapter 7, "Creative Compositing").

In this chapter you will be exposed to many elevation enhancement techniques, including the following:

◆ Converting AutoCAD Drawings

◆ Simulating Texture

◆ Casting Shadows

◆ Faking Reflection and Refraction

◆ Adding Entourage

Converting AutoCAD Drawings

AutoCAD elevations are line drawings that often include line thickness (called line weight in AutoCAD) as another graphical dimension. Traditionally, elevations convey the outlines of a structure's major features, and line weight emphasizes depth and the relative importance of the objects shown.

Elevation layers in AutoCAD are usually numbered sequentially (Elev-1, Elev-2, and so on), thus identifying their line thickness; for example, progressive layer numbers might refer to thinner lines. In contrast, plan layers refer to the building systems to which the lines belong (for example, the layer A-wall represents an architectural wall).

Line thickness information is not needed when you convert AutoCAD drawings, because you will be illustrating the elevation's depth with more expressive tools available in Photoshop: texture, shadow, and reflection. Therefore, there is usually no benefit in preserving the layer structure with elevations when converting CAD drawings to images as you did in the previous chapter.

In the following steps, you will convert the entire elevation drawing from the CD as a single image. Later in this chapter, you'll see how you can reimport additional information from CAD once your Photoshop project is underway.

1. Launch AutoCAD and open the file Elevation.dwg from the Chapter 6 folder on the companion CD (see Figure 6.1).

FIGURE 6.1
Elevation line drawing in AutoCAD

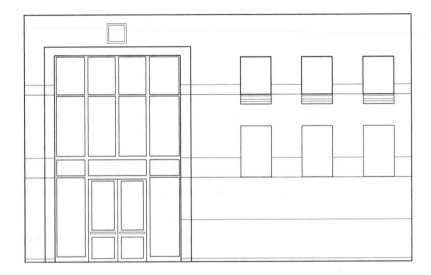

NOTE   I'm using AutoCAD 2005 in this book, but the .dwg files on the CD are stored in AutoCAD 2000 format for backward compatibility.

2. One the Command line, type **LAYER** and press Enter. The Layer Properties Manager dialog box (see Figure 6.2) shows how this drawing's layers are organized: numerical layer names range from Elev-1 through Elev-7 (plus layer 0), and each layer has a different line-weight setting. Click the Cancel button; this step was for your information only.

FIGURE 6.2
The Layer Properties Manager dialog box

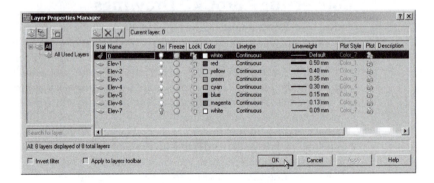

TIP The sample elevation CAD drawing has already been cleaned. See Chapter 5, "Presenting Plans," if you are referring to this tutorial but working on your own elevation drawing.

To convert this AutoCAD file to an image, you will use the printer driver, plot style table, and custom paper size that were set up in Chapter 5. If you haven't performed these steps, skip ahead to step 5 and open an already-converted image from the CD.

3. Choose File ➤ Plot or press Ctrl+P to open the Plot dialog box, as shown in Figure 6.3. Click OK if you see a warning dialog about a driver and plot device.

FIGURE 6.3

Plotting with the Image-Printer in AutoCAD

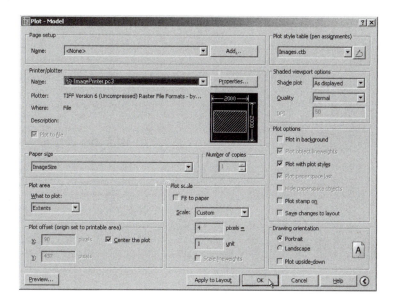

4. Select ImagePrinter.pc3 from the Name drop-down list box in the Printer/Plotter group. Next, select ImageSize from the Paper Size drop-down list box. Click the More Options arrow button if necessary, and choose Images.ctb from the Plot Style Table drop-down list box. In the Plot Area group, select Extents from What To Plot drop-down list box; check Center The Plot. Change the plot scale to 4 pixels = 1 unit. Click the Portrait radio button in the Drawing Orientation group. Click OK, and save the image file as Elevation-Model.tif in the Browse for Plot File dialog box that appears.

5. Close AutoCAD without saving the file, and then launch Photoshop. In Photoshop, open the file Elevation-Model.tif that you saved in the preceding step. If you skipped that step, you can open this file from the companion CD.

6. The AutoCAD ImagePrinter outputs a bitmap image (white and black pixels only, see Chapter 1, "The Basics"). Because you can't convert directly from bitmap to RGB color mode, you must convert this image first to grayscale and then to RGB. Choose Image ➤ Mode ➤ Grayscale to open the Grayscale dialog box. Set a size ratio of 1 and click OK. Next, choose Image ➤ Mode ➤ RGB Color to change color modes.

TIP Switch to 50% or 100% magnification; press Ctrl++ or Ctrl+- to zoom in or out so that the image fills your screen as much as possible. The line work looks best when the magnification is either halved or doubled from the actual pixel size (12.5%, 25%, 50%, 100%, 200%, and so on). Intermediate magnifications (16.7%, 33.3%, 66.7%) suffer from partial resampling that causes some of the line work to appear to be missing.

7. An uneven border surrounds the elevation because the rectangular building was plotted on a square image size in AutoCAD. Automatically crop the excess border with the Trim command: choose Image ➤ Trim to open the Trim dialog box. Click the Top Left Pixel Color radio button and click OK.

8. Now that the image is trimmed to the edges of the actual line work, we can add an even border back to the image using the Canvas Size dialog box. Type D to ensure that the default colors are set. Choose Image ➤ Canvas Size to open the Canvas Size dialog box, as shown in Figure 6.4. Check Relative in the New Size group, and then change the measurement drop-down list boxes to inches if they're not already. Type **5** in both Width and Height text boxes and click OK. The background color was automatically used to color the added canvas (white in this case).

FIGURE 6.4
Increasing the
canvas size

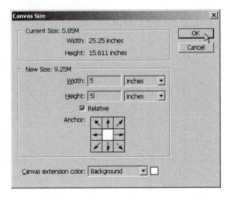

9. From the toolbox, select the Magic Eraser tool (it is under the Eraser). On the Options bar, set Tolerance to 1, and uncheck all the other options. Click a white portion of the image to convert the white pixels to transparency. The background layer is automatically renamed to Layer 0 because it must show transparency; in the Layers palette; rename Layer 0 to Linework.

10. Now that the white pixels have been eliminated, the line work can be layered on top of a new background layer. Create a new layer by clicking the Create A New Layer button in the Layers palette. Drag the new layer (Layer 1) below Linework, changing the layer order.

11. Click the background color swatch in the toolbox to open the Color Picker. Set the HSB values to 200,15,100 to select a pale sky-blue color, and click OK to close the Color Picker. Press Ctrl+Backspace to fill Layer 1 with the background color. Finally, choose Layer ➤ New ➤ Background From Layer; Layer 1 becomes Background.

12. Save the file as Elevation.psd. The file is ready for enhancement in Photoshop. If you're going to continue working through the following sections, you can leave this file open for now.

Simulating Texture

Perhaps the most important transformation made to a line drawing in Photoshop is simulating texture, because it gives the image realistic-looking surfaces. Let's start by filling areas with flat color and then texturize them by filtering with visual noise. In addition, you can add scans or photos of real materials to your pattern library and then apply them to the elevation. Later in this section you will learn how to cut reveals (gaps) into the stonework, patterning a surface with proportional lines.

1. If you have Elevation.psd open from the previous exercise, you can continue here; if not, open that file from the Chapter 6 folder on the companion CD before continuing.

   The Swatches palette can be a great aid if your project calls for a specific color scheme because you can see all the colors you'll be using for quick visual reference. Rather than try to remember the specific HSB or RGB values for particular colors, you can save them as swatches and sample them throughout the project. You will add two such swatches representing the major field and accent colors of cut stone used on the building facade.

2. Click the foreground color swatch in the toolbox to open the Color Picker. Set the HSB values to 40,40,90, and click OK to close the Color Picker. Position your mouse over a blank portion of the Swatches palette (at the bottom), and notice that your cursor changes to a Paint Bucket. Click to add a new swatch; type **Field Stone** into the Color Swatch Name dialog box and click OK. A new swatch is added at the bottom of the palette.

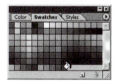

TIP   You can save custom swatch libraries on the hard drive as .aco files, share them with others, and reuse them in multiple projects. Use the Swatches palette menu to manage these files.

3. Click the foreground color swatch in the toolbox to again open the Color Picker. Set the HSB values to 35,25,100, and click OK to close the Color Picker. Click again inside a blank portion of the Swatches palette to add another swatch. Type the name **Accent Stone** and click OK to close the Color Swatch Name dialog box.

   Because all your line work resides on a single layer, you'll want to preserve this layer and not add any fill or layer style effects to it. You will need to create a new layer for each texture you will be applying.

4. Select the Linework layer at the top of the Layers palette, and then press Shift+Ctrl+N. Type **Field Stone** in the New Layer dialog box, make the layer Red, and click OK.

5. Click the Field Stone color swatch in the Swatches palette. Select the Paint Bucket tool from the toolbox (it may be hidden under the Gradient tool). On the Options bar, set the Fill drop-down to Foreground, set Tolerance to 1, uncheck Anti-aliased, check Contiguous, and check Use All Layers.

NOTE You'll use these same settings for the Paint Bucket throughout this chapter unless otherwise noted.

6. Fill the fieldstone flat color into appropriate locations in the elevation: Using the Paint Bucket, click inside each boundary to fill the locations shown in Figure 6.5 with the fieldstone color.

FIGURE 6.5
Fill flat color into the fieldstone boundaries (the darker areas of this image).

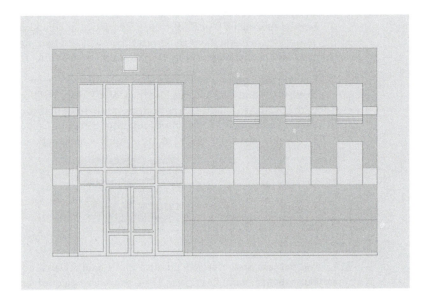

7. You can texturize the fill added in the last step because it's on a separate layer. Adding visual noise is a great way to simulate texture: Choose Filter ➢ Noise ➢ Add Noise to open the Add Noise dialog box. Set Amount to 10% and click the Gaussian radio button (for more variety). Check Monochromatic so that the noise affects intensity but not hue and click OK. The solid color has become stone!

You will create a more realistic texture with the pattern overlay effect (see Chapter 5). However, before applying it, let's open a scan of a real piece of granite and add it to the pattern library.

8. Open the file Granite.jpg (see Figure 6.6) from the companion CD. This tilable image is in grayscale.

9. With the Paint Bucket tool selected, change the Fill drop-down list box to Pattern on the Options bar. Open the Pattern Picker and click the triangle button to open the Pattern menu; select My Patterns to load your custom library. Click OK to the message "Replace current patterns with the patterns from My Patterns.pat?"

FIGURE 6.6
A sample of granite

WARNING If you haven't created a custom pattern library (see Chapter 5), choose Reset Patterns from the Pattern menu. You can add the Granite pattern to the default library instead.

10. With the Granite document window selected, choose Edit ➤ Define Pattern to open the Pattern Name dialog box. Type Granite in the Pattern Name dialog box and click OK to add this to the current pattern library. Close Granite.jpg without saving.

In contrast to filling boundaries with a specific color, layer style effects require only that pixels be placed on a new layer to indicate where these effects are made visible. (The pixels can be any color, but they should be black for consistency.)

11. Press D to set the default colors (black in the foreground). Turn off the Field Stone layer visibility. Create a new layer called Accent Stone, and give the layer an orange color. Select the Paint Bucket and change the Fill drop-down list box to Foreground on the Options bar. Click inside each boundary to fill the locations with black, as shown in Figure 6.7.

FIGURE 6.7
Fill black into the accent stone boundaries.

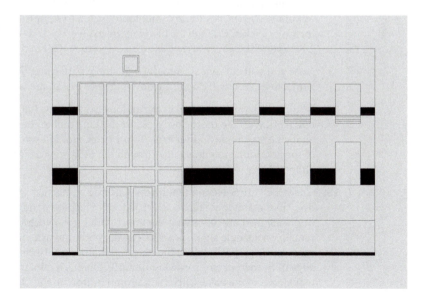

12. Because the Granite pattern you added in step 10 was in grayscale, you have the added flexi-
    bility of being able to overlay color on top of the pattern with layer style effects: Apply a Pat-
    tern Overlay effect (see Figure 6.8) to the Accent Stone layer. In the Layer Style dialog box,
    open the Pattern Picker and select the Granite swatch. Click outside the picker to close it, and
    then drag the Scale slider to 50%. Do not close the dialog box yet.

FIGURE 6.8
Pattern Overlay

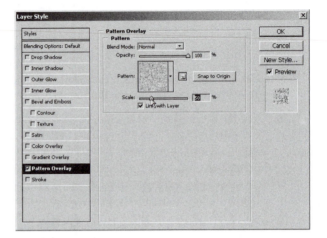

13. Click Color Overlay in the left pane of the Layer Style dialog box. Click the color swatch in the
    Color group to open the Color Picker. Instead of selecting a color, hover your mouse over the
    Swatches palette. (You might have to drag the Color Picker and/or Layer Style dialog boxes
    out of the way.) Click the Accent Stone swatch to sample its color, and then click OK to close
    the Color Picker. Change the blend mode to Overlay and drag the Opacity slider to 70%. Click
    OK to close the Layer Style dialog box, and turn the Field Stone layer back on.

    Now you will cut reveals into the fieldstone, patterning the surface with evenly spaced hori-
    zontal lines. You will do this by drawing lines in a shape layer and applying layer style effects.

14. Double-click the Zoom tool in the toolbox to switch to 100% magnification so that you can see
    line work with the most clarity. Select the Line tool in the toolbox. On the Options bar, click
    Shape Layers mode and set Weight to 1 pixel. Hold down the Shift key and trace a line on top
    of the horizontal line that cuts through the fieldstone, as shown in Figure 6.9. Rename the
    Shape 1 layer to Reveals.

15. Select the Path Selection tool (press A). Drag a selection window around the entire line you
    drew in the previous step to select all four of its path handles. Press Ctrl+C and then Ctrl+V to
    duplicate the path. (Copying the linear path on the vector mask allows duplicate reveals to
    remain on a single shape layer.) Drag the path upward and then hold down the Shift key to
    constrain it vertically; drop the new path halfway between its original location and the lower
    edge of the accent stone (see Figure 6.10). Do this again, making another copy of the line half-
    way down to the base. Click the Commit button on the Options bar.

FIGURE 6.9

Trace a line as a shape layer on top of the horizontal line work from CAD.

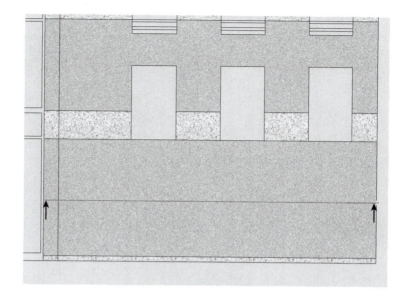

FIGURE 6.10

Copy the path twice.

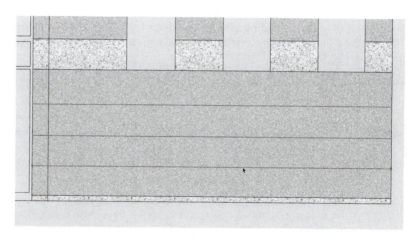

16. Apply a Stroke effect to the Reveals shape layer. In the Layer Style dialog box, click the color swatch in the Fill Type group. When the Color Picker opens, drag your mouse over the field-stone in the document window. The active color changes in real time in the Color Picker. Release the mouse button when a dark-brown hue appears in the picker, and then close it by clicking OK. Apply the following parameters in the Layer Style dialog box:

Color Overlay   Set Size to 2 px and Position to Center.

Drop Shadow   Use a 45° angle, 3 px distance, 0% spread, and 5 px size.

Close the Layer Style dialog box, zoom out to 50% and take a look (see Figure 6.11).

FIGURE 6.11
Reveals added and
emphasized

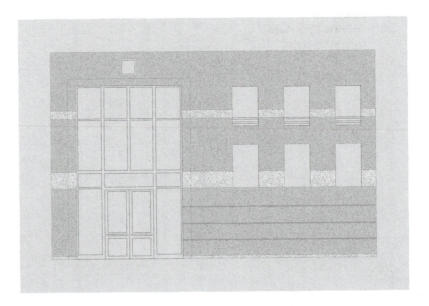

Varying the shading across the stonework will make it look more realistic. You can accomplish this by adding a Dodge And Burn layer (see Chapter 3, "Digital Darkroom Skills"). In addition let's mask everything but the stonework to keep the changes neatly contained.

17. Turn off the Linework layer temporarily. Create a new layer called Dodge And Burn and make the layer yellow. Make sure the layer is on top of the stone layer in the Layers palette. Change the blend mode to Hard Light and the opacity to 50%.

18. Press W to select the Magic Wand tool. On the Options bar, set Tolerance to 0, uncheck Anti-aliased, check Contiguous, and check Use All Layers. Click inside the blue portion of the image. Press Shift+Ctrl+I to invert the selection; now only the stonework is selected. Click Add A Layer Mask in the Layers palette. (It's not strictly necessary to add a mask, but it is good practice to mask off the area of interest for safety.)

19. Click the Dodge And Burn layer *thumbnail* to select the layer itself (not the mask). Press B to select the Brush tool. Select a soft large brush on the Options bar; a 700 pixel soft brush will do in this case. (You can type a value or use the square bracket keys in conjunction with Shift to change the size and hardness of the brush.) Paint a few black brushstrokes diagonally across the base of the elevation; it darkens as it's *burned*. Press X to exchange the colors in the toolbox (so that white is in the foreground). Paint another brushstroke across the upper-right corner of the facade; it lightens as it's *dodged* (see Figure 6.12).

20. Turn down the opacity of the Dodge And Burn layer to 35% to tone down the overall effect. Turn the Linework layer back on.

FIGURE 6.12
Dodging and burning

21. Next, we'll add metallic texture to the large window framing system in the elevation. Create a new layer called Framing System, and make the layer green. Press D to set the default colors, and select the Paint Bucket tool in the toolbox. Click inside the border of the framing system line work to fill it with black. Apply the following layer style effects:

    Color Overlay   Select a medium-gray color.

    Bevel And Emboss   Select Inner Bevel Style, Chisel Hard Technique, 300% Depth, Up Direction, 3 px Size, and 0 px Soften.

    Contour   Open the Contour Picker and select the Cove - Shallow Profile, 25% Range.

    Texture   Choose BlueCarpet from the Pattern Picker, 50% Scale, and +10% Depth.

    Color Overlay gives the metal a gray hue, Bevel gives dimensionality to the framing system, Contour helps shape the bevel, and Texture adds low relief to the surface. Figure 6.13 shows the result.

    The doors and door handles are made in much the same way as the framing system. You can get a head start by copying and pasting the effects from one layer to another. Then you will make a few changes, customizing the set of effects to differentiate the doors.

22. Create a new layer called Doors, and make this layer green also (because it is closely associated with the framing system). Drag the Effects from the Framing System layer to the Doors layer in the Layers palette. Using the Paint Bucket tool, click inside each of the door panels (the rails and stiles bounding the doors) and then inside each of the door handles.

FIGURE 6.13
The metallic framing
system made with layer
style effects

23. Double-click the word *Effects* under the Doors layer to open the Layer Style dialog box. Click the Bevel And Emboss effect and change Size to 1 pixel. Click Color Overlay in the left pane, and click the color swatch to open the Color Picker; change the color to a light gray. Click OK to close the Color Picker, and click OK again to close the Layer Style dialog box.

24. Save the file as `Elevation2.psd`. If you're going to continue working through the following sections, you can leave this file open for now.

Casting Shadows

Casting shadows is the primary way to create the illusion of depth in an elevation. You can cast shadows in many ways, and you will be exposed to several techniques in this section.

Three niches are just above ground level in the elevation. We'll apply the Inner Shadow effect to make these appear recessed into the facade. We'll also create the illusion of a frame projecting out from the facade surface, for the ornament above the glazing system where the building address belongs, through creative use of shadows. Inner shadows make surfaces recede, and drop shadows make them appear to float above. In addition, you'll use a layer set to contain the multiple layers generated in this technique.

1. If you have `Elevation2.psd` open from the previous exercise, you can continue here; if not, open that file from the companion CD before continuing.

2. Create a new layer called Niches, and give the layer a blue color. Sample the Field Stone swatch in the Swatches palette. Select the Paint Bucket and fill each of the niches with the flat color. Choose Filter ➢ Noise ➢ Add Noise and apply 10% Gaussian Monochromatic noise. In the Layers palette, apply an Inner Shadow layer style effect with the following parameters: 50% Opacity, 15 px Distance, 0% Choke, and 10 px Size. Figure 6.14 shows the niches with inner shadows.

3. Click the Create A New Set button at the bottom of the Layers palette. Rename Set 1 to Ornament.

FIGURE 6.14
Creating niches with
inner shadows

4. Create a new layer called Inner; notice that it automatically appears in the Ornament set. Using the Paint Bucket, click inside the inner boundary of the ornament (see Figure 6.15). Press Ctrl+F to reapply the last-used filter (Noise); the inner layer gains texture. Apply an Inner Shadow effect to the Inner layer with 50% Opacity, 5 px Distance, and 5 px Size.

5. Create a new layer called Outer. Sample the Accent Stone color in the Swatches palette. Use the Paint Bucket to fill the outer boundary of the ornament. Press Ctrl+F to apply the Noise filter again. Apply the following layer style effects:

Drop Shadow   75% Opacity, 5 px Distance, 0% Spread, and 5 px Size.

Bevel And Emboss   Select Inner Bevel Style, Chisel Hard Technique, 70% Depth, Up Direction, 5 px Size, and 0 px Soften.

FIGURE 6.15
Creating the inner part of
the ornament: fill the
boundary with field-
stone color.

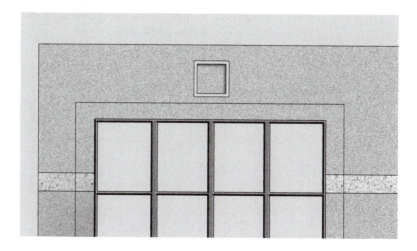

6. Press D to set the default colors, and then press T to select the Horizontal Type tool. On the Options bar, choose Garamond, 42 pt, and Center Justified. (Choose another font if you don't have this one on your system.) Click the middle of the ornament, type **271**, and click the Commit button. Drag and drop the Effects from the Outer layer to the 271 Type layer. In the Layers palette, close the Ornament Layer Set. Figure 6.16 shows the completed ornament.

FIGURE 6.16
Completing the ornament

The window boxes just below the three separate windows are yet to be filled into the elevation. Before casting shadows from the window boxes, texture the window boxes by adding fill to existing layers. The way to do this depends on how the existing layers were made, and adapting your procedure to the existing setup is an important skill to learn.

TIP In real projects you will often have to change the content of existing layers simply because you won't think of everything at the beginning of your project or be perfectly organized throughout. Therefore, it's important to know how to adjust work you've already performed.

7. Select the Accent Stone layer. Using the Paint Bucket tool, fill black into the boundaries, as shown in Figure 6.17. Because this layer is controlled by layer style effects, filling in black is all you have to do here. In many ways, using layer style effects is preferable to other techniques because of how easy it is to edit them.

FIGURE 6.17
Adding more accent stone: Filling black into these areas applies the granite pattern.

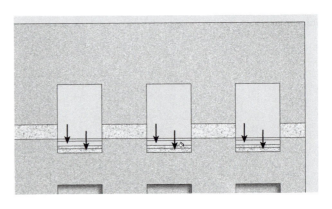

8. Select the Field Stone layer. Sample the Field Stone color in the Swatches palette. Fill this color into the boundaries shown in Figure 6.18. Notice that there is no texture in the newly filled areas, just flat color. This layer does not use layer styles and requires more work to edit; you will have to make a selection before adding texture to the areas you filled. Press W to select the Magic Wand tool; on the Options bar click the Add To Selection button. Click inside each of the boundaries you just filled. Press Ctrl+F to apply Noise to the selection. Finally, press Ctrl+D to deselect.

FIGURE 6.18
Editing the Field
Stone layer

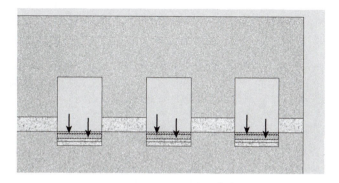

The window boxes have a complex profile that can't be represented by a simple drop or inner shadow effect that follows the outer edge of a filled boundary. Therefore, you will cast custom shadows by drawing them manually. When drawing custom shadows, pay special attention to the angle of global illumination in the image so that you cast shadows in the proper direction. Keeping the angle of illumination in mind (up and to the right), you will draw custom shadows down and to the left with the Pen tool.

9. For your information, choose Layers ➤ Layer Style ➤ Global Light. Notice that the global illumination is coming at a 45° angle, at an altitude of 30° above (in front of the facade). Adjust your parameters to match these if yours are different. You can set these parameters in the Global Light dialog box and in several places within the Layer Style dialog box. Press Esc to cancel.

10. Click the Ornament layer set at the top of the Layers palette. Select the Pen tool in the toolbox. On the Options bar, click the Shape Layers button and then click the Geometry Options arrow; check Rubber Band in the Pen Options drop-down list box. Open the Styles Picker. Double-click the Default Style (none) thumbnail because you don't want to use the layer style effects from previous steps.

11. Zoom into 300% magnification near the leftmost window box. Draw the rough shadow outline as shown in Figure 6.19. Hold down the Shift key as you draw to constrain the lines you draw in 45° increments.

FIGURE 6.19
Drawing a shadow with
the Pen tool

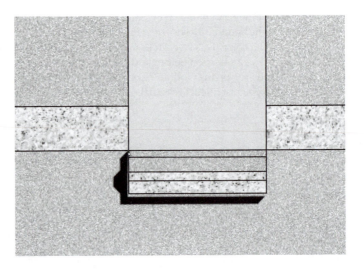

12. Choose the Direct Selection tool in the toolbox (under the Path Selection tool). Drag a window around a corner handle and move it to the edges of the window box, as shown in Figure 6.20. Repeat and move the other handle to cover the other corner. Rename the Shape 1 layer to Window Box Shadow. Change the opacity of this layer to 50% to lighten the shadow.

FIGURE 6.20
Adjusting a shadow
path: drag these handles
to the edges of the
window box.

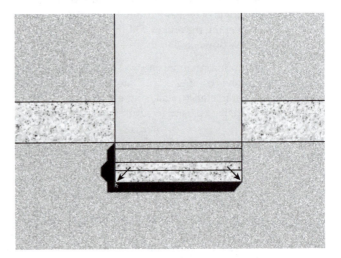

TIP You can use the arrow keys to nudge handles one pixel at a time.

13. The shape layer has a path on its vector mask that you will duplicate to make additional shadows: select the Path Selection tool (press Shift+A). Click the shadow's path, press Ctrl+C, and then press Ctrl+V to duplicate the path on this shape layer. Drag the path to the right and then

hold down the Shift key to constrain it horizontally. Drop the duplicate shadow on the middle window box. Repeat this process, make another duplicate shadow, and move it over to the third window box. Click the vector mask thumbnail on the Window Box Shadow layer to deselect it; Figure 6.21 shows the result.

FIGURE 6.21
Duplicating
shadow paths

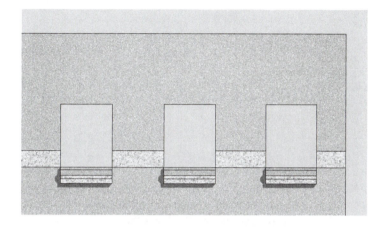

You have just seen how a shape layer represents a shadow by revealing black through its vector mask. It is also possible to use a shape layer to cast a shadow using a layer style effect (Drop Shadow or Inner Shadow).

In this last technique, the layer style effect casts the shadow; you want the shape layer itself to be invisible. Shape layers cannot be filled with transparency. However, you can make a shape layer invisible by using a white color in Darken blending mode. You'll see how this works by creating a shadow that makes the entire framing system appear inset into the facade.

14. Zoom out to 100% magnification. Select the Rectangle tool in the toolbox (under the Line tool). Click the color swatch on the Options bar, and choose pure white in the Color Picker. As you drag out a rectangle that covers the entry area (see Figure 6.22), a new shape layer is created called Shape 1. Rename Shape 1 to Entry Shadow, and set the opacity of this layer to 75%, allowing you to see through.

    Chances are, you didn't draw the rectangle directly on top of the line work because you were zoomed out. Line it up and then make the shape layer disappear.

15. Zoom in closely to one corner of the white rectangle. Select the Direct Selection tool (press Shift+A). Drag a selection window around the corner handle and use the arrow keys to nudge the handle on top of the line work below. Repeat this process on each of the four vertices, precisely lining up the handles of the rectangular path with the line work. Change the opacity of the Entry Shadow layer to 100%, and change its blending mode to Darken. Click its vector mask to deselect it. The rectangle completely disappears because the white shape does not darken the image.

FIGURE 6.22
Drawing a white shape
layer: drag out a rectangle
on top of the existing
line work.

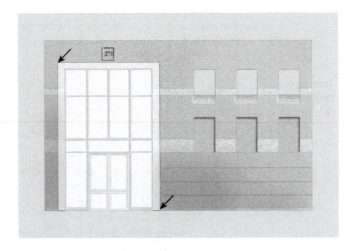

16. Apply an Inner Shadow effect to the Entry Shadow shape layer. In the Layer Style dialog box, set the following parameters: 50% Opacity, 20 px Distance, 10% Choke, and 25 px Size. Click OK to close. Figure 6.23 shows the entry shadow.

17. Save the file as Elevation3.psd. If you're going to continue working through the following sections, you can leave this file open for now.

FIGURE 6.23
Casting the entry's
inner shadow

Faking Reflection and Refraction

Building windows reflect the world around them and bend light as it passes through (refraction). A 3D program such as Autodesk VIZ can accurately calculate reflection and refraction of the surrounding environment using a time-consuming rendering process called raytracing.

Fortunately, you don't have to wait long in Photoshop because you can reasonably fake these optical phenomena by pasting photographic images into the glazed surfaces of the image. In this section, you'll learn techniques for making windows more realistic by varying the lighting intensity with a paint brush. We'll use liquify and warp techniques in reflected images to slightly hint at refraction that takes place in the real world.

Although reflection and refraction aren't as accurate in Photoshop as in a complete 3D model, you'll find that you can get reasonable quality in a short time. These faked techniques effectively convey the idea of glazing and still reflect a bit of a building site's context to the viewer.

I'm taking you through these steps because this is something that will most likely happen in a real project. You have spent a lot of time working on your elevation in Photoshop, only to discover that you need some additional line work from CAD. Or worse yet, the design has changed again at the last minute! You don't have to start over or worry once you see how easy it is to reimport additional image layers and integrate them into your project.

1. Before you dive in, you need to import a hidden layer from the original CAD file. Launch AutoCAD, and open the file `Elevation.dwg` from the companion CD.

2. On the Command line, type **LAYER** and press Enter to open the Layer Properties Manager dialog box. Click the lightbulb icon next to Elev-7 to turn on this layer (see Figure 6.24).

3. Click the lightbulb icons next to all the remaining layers to turn them off. A warning dialog asks you whether to keep the current layer on; click No. Click OK to close the Layer Properties Manager dialog box.

4. Press Ctrl+P to open the Plot dialog box. (Click OK if you see a warning dialog box.) Choose <Previous plot> from the Name drop-down list box in the Page Setup group. All the settings you used earlier in this chapter should appear. (If they don't, refer to the "Converting AutoCAD Drawings" section of this chapter, and use the settings given there in the Plot dialog box.) Click OK, and save the plot file as `Elevation-Model2.tif` on your hard drive. Close AutoCAD without saving.

FIGURE 6.24
Turning on a hidden layer in AutoCAD

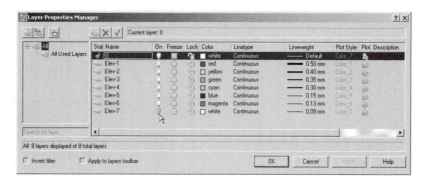

5. Launch Photoshop if it is not already running. Open the file `Elevation-Model2.tif` from your hard drive or from the companion CD. Press Ctrl+A and then Ctrl+C to copy the file's entire contents to the Clipboard. Once the file is on the Clipboard, you can close it without saving.

6. If you have `Elevation3.psd` open from the previous exercise, you can continue here; if not, open that file in Photoshop from the companion CD before continuing.

   The imported layer will contain both black and white pixels. You will use the Darken blending mode to show only the black pixels.

TIP Alternatively, you could erase the white pixels on the CAD Linework layer with the Magic Eraser.

7. Press Ctrl+V to paste the image from the Clipboard into your Elevation project. Rename Layer 1 to CAD Linework, and drag it to the top of the Layers palette if it is not already there. Change CAD Linework's blending mode to Darken.

8. Press V to select the Move tool. Drag the CAD Linework layer up until it is centered in the window openings (see Figure 6.25).

   Let's create a layer set to stay organized and make new layers for each of our tasks. We'll fill the window frames with black, apply layer style effects, and mask off the window area on a new layer, all in preparation for painting.

9. Create a new layer set called Windows. Then create a new layer called Frames. (This layer will appear in the set automatically.) Zoom into 100% magnification around the window area. Select the Paint Bucket tool, and make sure that Use All Layers is checked on the Options bar. Click inside each of the three window frames to fill them with black. Apply the following layer style effects to the Frames layer:

   Color Overlay Select a medium gray with HSB vales of 0,0,50.

   Bevel And Emboss Select Inner Bevel Style, Smooth Technique, 100% Depth, Up Direction, 5 px Size, and 0 px Soften

FIGURE 6.25
Reimporting CAD data: move the CAD line work up and center it in the window openings.

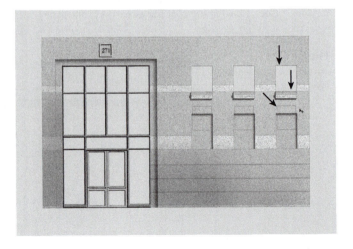

10. Create a new layer called Intensity. Select the Magic Wand tool; click the Add To Selection button on the Options bar. Click inside each of the three windows to create a selection. Convert the selection to a mask by clicking the Add Layer Mask button in the Layers palette. Click the Intensity layer thumbnail to select it.

11. Select the Brush tool in the toolbox, and build up a lighting intensity by painting in grayscale. There is really no right way to do this; feel free to make brush strokes however you see fit—the point is to create variation on the glass surface—but here is what I did:

♦ I choose a 250-pixel soft brush and used the square bracket keys to change sizes and hardness.

♦ I changed the foreground color to dark gray (HSB values of 0,0,25).

♦ I painted a few diagonal brush strokes across the windows.

♦ I changed the foreground color to light gray (HSB values of 0,0,75).

♦ I painted a few more brush strokes across the windows, obscuring all the blue areas (see Figure 6.26).

At this point, you could leave the windows as they are for an abstract look. For more realism, however, you'll paste a photograph of the sky into the window area in step 14. Before this, you will need to recall the window selection from the Intensity layer mask.

12. Select the Intensity layer mask thumbnail by clicking it in the Layers palette. Right-click this mask to open the context menu shown in Figure 6.27, and select Add Layer Mask To Selection. The marching ants appear in the window boundaries.

FIGURE 6.26
Painting lighting
intensity

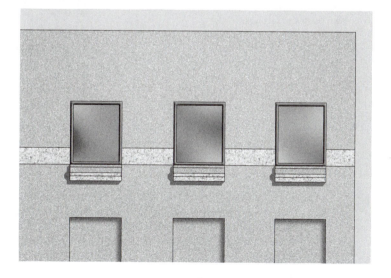

FIGURE 6.27
Recalling a selection
from a mask

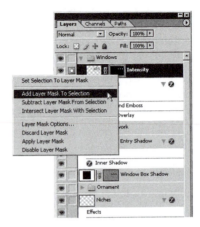

13. Open the file Sky.jpg from the companion CD. Press Ctrl+A and then Ctrl+C to select all and copy to the Clipboard. Close Sky.jpg without saving.

14. Choose Edit ➢ Paste Into; a new layer appears with a mask in the shape of the selection. In the Layers palette, rename this new layer Clouds. Press V to select the Move tool, and drag the clouds around until you find an aesthetically pleasing position for them inside the window boundaries. Change the blend mode of the Clouds layer to Soft Light, and set Opacity to 50% to partially reveal the Intensity layer below (see Figure 6.28).

FIGURE 6.28
The Clouds layer gets its
own mask and settings.

The glazing system in the entry area will also receive a photographic reflection. Instead of simply reflecting clouds, you can reveal a bit of the building site's context by reflecting the opposite side of the street in the glazing.

15. Press W to select the Magic Wand. Click inside each of the remaining window boundaries, including the glass panels in the door, to build a selection. Open the file Reflection.jpg from the companion CD. Choose Select All, and then choose Copy (press Ctrl+A and then press Ctrl+C), and then close Reflection.jpg. Paste the image from the Clipboard into the selection by pressing Shift+Ctrl+V (see Figure 6.29). Rename the new layer Reflection.

The image you pasted into the glazing selection in the previous step is too small; enlarge it by transforming the layer.

16. Press Ctrl+T to transform the Reflection layer. On the Options bar, click the Maintain Aspect Ratio button (the icon that looks like links in a chain). Click inside the Set Horizontal Scale text box to make it active. Press and hold the Up arrow key until the reflection image fills the glazing boundaries; the Width and Height values should reach at least 123%. Click the Commit button.

17. You can simulate refraction by liquifying the reflection and warping the image. Be careful not to go overboard with this tool; aim for subtle warping only: choose Filter ➢ Liquify to open the Liquify dialog box. Click the Forward Warp tool (the top tool on the Liquify dialog box toolbar). Put your mouse over the image and drag a short distance; the pixels warp and flow, as shown in Figure 6.30. Continue selecting other locations and dragging short distances to distort the straight lines between the buildings. Press Ctrl+Z if you make a mistake, and click OK when you are satisfied with the results.

NOTE   Refer to Photoshop Help for more information on the powerful (and fun) Liquify command.

Right now the glazing system looks more like a mirror because the reflection is at full intensity. Tone down the reflectivity with a black-to-white gradient.

18. Apply a Gradient Overlay layer style effect to the Reflection layer. In the Layer Style dialog box, set Opacity to 75% and Scale to 150%. Click OK. Figure 6.31 shows the final reflection and refraction.

19. Save the file as Elevation4.psd. If you're going to continue working through the following sections, you can leave this file open for now.

FIGURE 6.30
Warping a liquid image

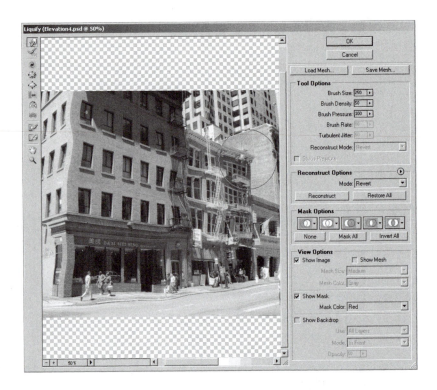

FIGURE 6.31
Reflection and refraction
complete

Adding Entourage

Adding human entourage gives the viewer a sense of scale, and adding vegetation can soften the building and provide context for the construction. You will use the entourage library developed in Chapter 4, "You and Your Entourage," to enhance this elevation.

It is wise to create a layer set when you anticipate creating a series of related layers; the added organization will help you navigate a crowded Layers palette.

1. If you have Elevation4.psd open from the previous exercise, you can continue here; if not, open that file from the companion CD before continuing.

2. Create a new layer set called Entourage: click the Create A New Set button in the Layers palette, double-click Set 1, and rename it.

3. Open the file EntourageLibrary.psd from the Chapter 4 folder on the companion CD.

4. Drag the WomanFront layer into the Elevation4 document window; it appears in the Entourage layer set. Minimize the EntourageLibrary.psd window for now; you will need it later in this section.

5. Select the Move tool in the toolbox, and drag the woman's feet to rest on the ground line. Press Ctrl+T for transform, and then hold down Shift to lock the aspect ratio. Drag one of the upper handles downward until the woman's eyes align with the third reveal. Press the Commit button on the Options bar. Drag the woman in front of the door, with her toes slightly below the ground line, as shown in Figure 6.32. Apply a Drop Shadow; in the Layer Style dialog box, set a 13 px Distance and 9 px Size.

6. Notice that the entourage (and her shadow) extends below the building. Let's hide this by adding a shape layer that also visually grounds the building. Select the Rectangle tool in the toolbox. On the Options bar, click the Shape Layers button and change the color swatch to medium gray. Drag out a long thin rectangle that aligns with the bottom of the building (see Figure 6.33).

FIGURE 6.32
Transforming human entourage

FIGURE 6.33
Grounding the building
with a shape layer

7. Time to add another piece of entourage from your library: the plum tree. Maximize the Entourage-Library window. Drag the PlumTree layer into the Elevation4 window. Close `EntourageLibrary.psd`. Press V to select the Move tool, drag the tree down to the top of the ground line, and center it. Press Ctrl+T, and scale the tree down and position it as shown in Figure 6.34.

The shadows of leaves from a deciduous tree can be pleasing. To accentuate the drama of filtering light through the leaves, you will treat these shadows in a special way. Start by generating shadows with an effect, and then convert the effect to a layer. You will later transform and distort the shadow layer separately from the tree.

FIGURE 6.34
Adding more entourage

8. Apply a Drop Shadow layer style effect to the PlumTree layer. In the Layer Style dialog box, set a 0 px Distance and a 2 px Size to generate crisp shadows that are directly behind the tree.

9. In the Layers palette, right-click the Drop Shadow effect under the PlumTree layer to open a context menu; select Create Layer. A warning dialog box appears, informing you that some effects cannot be reproduced with layers; click OK to close the dialog box.

10. In the Layers palette, click the PlumTree's Drop Shadow that was just generated in the previous step. Change the opacity of this layer to 40% to dim the shadows a bit (see Figure 6.35).

FIGURE 6.35
Lighten the tree's shadow by using the layer Opacity setting.

11. Press Ctrl+T and then right-click in the document window. Select Distort from the context menu. Drag the transform handles around to distort the shadow and separate them from the tree itself, as shown in Figure 6.36. Click the Commit button on the Options bar or press Enter when you are satisfied with the shadow form.

12. A more subtle way of illustrating entourage is to show *only* shadows. You might prefer this technique if you feel that the entourage diverts too much attention from the structure. Duplicate the existing tree (mirroring and distorting the new layer to make the copy seem different), and apply a Drop Shadow effect, as I described in Chapter 4. Then remove the tree itself and erase the shadow pixels that extend beyond the building.

FIGURE 6.36
Distorting the tree's shadow

13. The last items that can be attended to in this project are the sheet details. Add a title, logo, and scale bar to the sheet, referring to Chapter 5 for instructions if necessary. Figure 6.37 shows the final elevation image. A version of this image is provided in the color section.

14. Save your work as Elevation5.psd if you plan to refer to it again. This file is also provided on the CD for reference.

FIGURE 6.37
The completed elevation project

Summary

In this chapter you have taken a line drawing in AutoCAD and transformed it into an image that enhances the impression a viewer receives from the design. You were exposed to numerous tips and tricks that you can refer to when working on your own projects. The next chapter introduces you to the art of compositing: you'll layer images made in Autodesk VIZ and improve them dramatically with Photoshop.

Chapter 7

Creative Compositing

You will use both Adobe Photoshop and Autodesk VIZ in the compositing techniques presented in this chapter. In this context, *compositing* is the art of blending and enhancing images rendered in VIZ within Photoshop.

As you may know, one of the liabilities of solely using VIZ to create computer-generated imagery (CGI) is the huge amount of time usually required to calculate photo-realistic renderings. Compositing is a technique that speeds up this process by leveraging the power of Photoshop. Instead of spending time in VIZ designing realistic materials, simulating real-world light sources, and waiting for a lengthy rendering calculation, Photoshop adds real-time realism to basic 2D imagery output from VIZ.

The compositing process begins in VIZ, where we'll prepare a 3D model for rendering. Each object is separately matted and rendered in VIZ with an alpha channel to preserve the object boundaries in the images. This series of rendered images is then integrated in Photoshop into a composite whole. In the transfer, each VIZ object becomes a layer in Photoshop, and the alpha channels become layer masks.

To gain an understanding of how compositing works, you'll step through a high-rise building tutorial that shows you how to manually transfer objects from VIZ to masked layers in Photoshop. You'll save time processing the remaining objects in the scene by using MAXScript and an action that automate the transfer from VIZ into Photoshop.

Once the project is assembled in Photoshop, you'll add realism with many of the same layer style effect techniques presented in Chapters 5 and 6, plus you'll explore new creative compositing techniques. This chapter's topics include the following:

- Rendering in Autodesk VIZ
- Compositing in Photoshop
- Applying Effects to Masked Layers
- Working with the Environment
- Making Adjustments with Clipping Groups
- Adding to the Composite

Rendering in Autodesk VIZ

You will start the high-rise building tutorial in Autodesk VIZ 2005. A free trial version of Autodesk VIZ 2005 is available at www.autodesk.com. Install Autodesk VIZ 2005 on your computer even if you are accustomed to using other 3D software, because the techniques and automation presented in this chapter are specific to VIZ. After you understand the compositing process, you can adapt the procedures you learn in this chapter to your favorite 3D software package (such as 3ds max, formZ, Lightwave, Maya, and others).

TIP The building model is provided in additional file formats (.3ds, .dxf, and .wrl) on the companion CD for greater compatibility with other 3D programs.

Exploring the 3D Model

One of the strengths of compositing CGI in Photoshop is that you can use a basic 3D model to start the process. You'll save a lot of time in VIZ not having to worry about designing realistic materials, placing physically accurate light sources, building a highly complex model, or rendering with radiosity or mental ray because all the realism will be added with Photoshop. You need only begin with a simple massing model in VIZ, in a scene having the basic materials, lighting, and camera setup. It is important to familiarize yourself with the VIZ scene because its structure determines what you will be working on in Photoshop later in this chapter.

1. Launch Autodesk VIZ 2005.

2. Open the file Building.max from the companion CD. The Perspective viewport appears maximized in the VIZ interface (see Figure 7.1). Notice the various parts of the scene, including the model, light sources, and camera.

FIGURE 7.1
The 3D model in VIZ

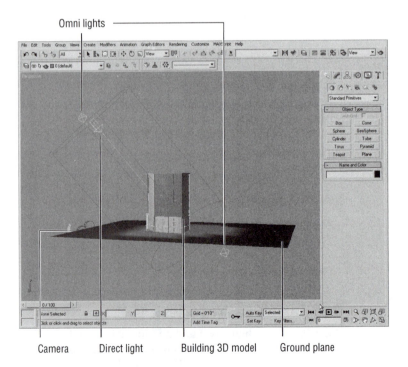

Omni lights illuminate in all directions, and two are used for basic or ambient light in the scene. These are set to render with a multiplier of 0.5 (each at half of normal intensity) so as not to wash out the scene with too much illumination. Because the omnis simulate ambient light, they are not set to cast shadows. One omni light source is below the ground plane; this acts as a backlight to round out illumination on the building.

A direct light is positioned in relation to the building as if it were the sun in the midafternoon. You will be using the direct light to cast shadows on the building later in this section.

NOTE If you are interested in making a more accurate lighting simulation, use the Sunlight system instead of a direct light in VIZ. The Sunlight system is an accurate sun-angle calculator that takes geographic location and time into account to locate the light source.

A single camera is also provided in the scene to get you started framing your composition. The building model itself is composed of several objects. To investigate this, look at objects by name:

3. Open the Select Objects dialog box (press H), as shown in Figure 7.2. All the objects in the scene are shown, including the lights and the camera. To display a listing of the geometrical objects only, click the None button in the List Types group, and then check Geometry to display this category in the list box.

FIGURE 7.2
Geometrical objects in the scene

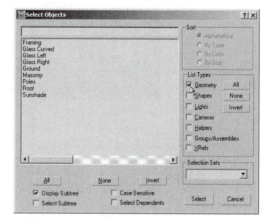

4. Click the first item in the list, in this case Framing, and then click the Select button to close the Select Objects dialog box. Right-click in the viewport, and choose Hide Unselected from the display quad.

5. Navigate to get a better view of the object. Drag the wheel button to pan, turn the wheel to zoom, and hold down the Alt key while dragging the wheel button to arc rotate. Figure 7.3 shows a better view of the Framing object. This object was initially made with the Railing tool (which can be found in VIZ on the Create tab of the Command Panel under AEC Extended) and later collapsed to an Editable Poly to save memory.

FIGURE 7.3
Framing object

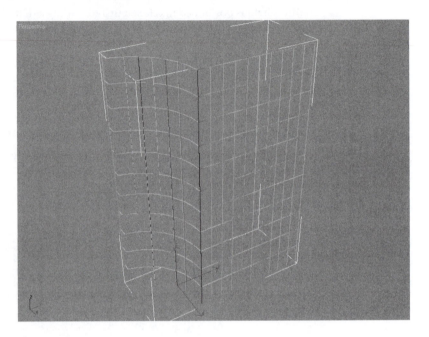

6. Right-click and choose Unhide All from the display quad. Press H and select the next object in the Select Objects dialog box (Glass Curved). Click the Select button and right-click in the viewport again. Choose Hide Unselected from the display quad so that you can see this object by itself. Repeat this step over and over until you have visualized each object (there are nine total); this is a good way to get familiar with the scene's organization and how its objects are named.

7. Right-click and choose Unhide All from the display quad. Take a quick look at the materials in the scene.

8. Open the Material Editor dialog box (press M), as shown in Figure 7.4. Most materials are as simple as possible, using only flat color. One material uses a Tiles map to add interest to the masonry surface. The editor contains six materials; click each one and investigate. Close the Material Editor dialog box when you are satisfied.

FIGURE 7.4
Investigating materials

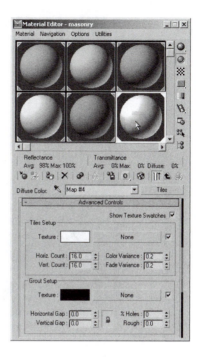

Composing the Scene

Now that you are familiar with the scene, it is time to set up the camera to create a composition that you will later render. You will need to adjust the camera angle and output size so that the composition takes in the entire building in two-point perspective.

Before you can truly compose the scene, you have to select an output size because the composition will relate to the image aspect ratio of the width and height values you select. You'll then need to see the image aspect in the viewport before you can settle on a composition.

1. Press C to enter the Camera viewport. The point of view changes as you leave the Perspective viewport and enter the Camera view (see Figure 7.5).

2. Right-click the viewport name (the word *Camera*) in the upper-left corner of the viewport. Choose Select Camera from this viewport menu (see Figure 7.6).

3. Select the Select And Move tool (press W). Notice that the Z transform type-in at the bottom of the user interface shows an elevation of 5~FT for the camera. Because the ground plane is at an elevation of 0, the camera height approximates eye level on the ground for most people. To make a realistic rendering of this building, you will be committed to rendering from this vantage point, rather than from a point hovering in space above the ground (as if the camera were in a helicopter). In this way, the rendering you make will truthfully represent what a person would see from the street.

FIGURE 7.5
The initial Camera view

FIGURE 7.6
Accessing the
viewport menu

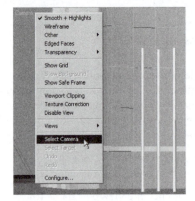

4. Open the Render Scene dialog box (press F10). Click the Common tab if it is not already selected. In the Output Size group, enter 768 for Width and 1024 for Height (values in pixels). Notice that the Image Aspect parameter reads 0.75, meaning this is the relationship you are selecting of width to height in your output (see Figure 7.7).

5. Right-click the viewport name and choose Show Safe Frame. The outer rectangle in Figure 7.8 displays the image aspect ratio of your chosen output size. You can disregard the inner rectangles as they are for live-action sequences.

Clearly there is a problem with the composition in Figure 7.8; about half the image shows the ground. Because you want to keep the camera on the ground in a realistic viewing location, you will need to rotate the camera upward to see the top of the building.

FIGURE 7.7

Render scene settings

FIGURE 7.8

Safe frame displayed in viewport

6. Press E to select the Select And Rotate tool. To accurately rotate the camera upward, do so numerically rather than by dragging the rotate gizmo in the viewport or by using the Pan Camera tool. Type **111** in the X transform type-in text box at the bottom of the user interface, and press Enter to rotate the camera upward from its initial setting of 90 degrees.

7. Do a quick render (press Shift+Q). The Rendered Frame Window (RFW) appears, and in a few seconds a rendering is processed. Figure 7.9 shows the three-point perspective rendering.

FIGURE 7.9
The three-point perspective rendering

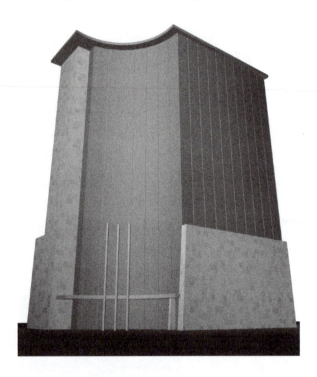

NOTE   See Chapter 1, "The Basics," for a description of two- and three-point perspective as they relate to tall buildings.

8. Two-point perspective forces the building's outer walls to appear as vertical lines: right-click in the Camera viewport. An additional choice appears under the tools 1 quad menu. Click Apply Camera Correction Modifier. Then click the Modify tab of the Command Panel, and notice that a modifier is applied to the Camera object. No adjustment is required unless the walls don't appear vertical.

WARNING   The Apply Camera Correction Modifier is available in the quad menus only when a camera is selected.

9. Do another quick render (press Shift+Q). Figure 7.10 shows the two-point perspective rendering. This composition has an acceptable balance between ground, building, and sky; it will be the basis of the project. A version of this image is in the color section.

10. Save your work as `BuildingComposed.max`. You are ready to start rendering the objects in this scene individually for later compositing in Photoshop.

FIGURE 7.10
Two-point perspective rendering

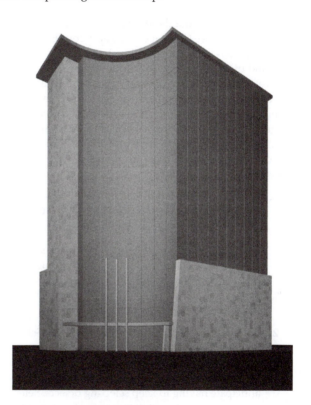

Rendering Matted Objects with Alpha Channels

You can't directly render each VIZ object separately as a 2D image and expect the pieces to fit together in Photoshop, because objects in any 3D scene obscure one another. For example, the glass objects in the composed rendering from the previous section are in front of, and therefore obscure portions of, the masonry that make up the back of the building. You don't have to worry about obscuration in 3D because VIZ handles spatial relationships automatically.

However, you do have to think about obscuration when you render 3D geometry to pixels, because spatial considerations are lost in Photoshop. There are two aspects to the solution of this problem in VIZ: matte objects and alpha channels.

Matte objects are invisible in any rendering, but they magically block geometry behind them. Therefore, matte objects are at the root of the solution to the 3D obscuration problem in a 2D rendering. In VIZ, you assign matte objects by applying the Matte/Shadow material to selected objects.

NOTE   Optionally, you can set matte objects to cast and/or receive shadows, even though they are invisible.

To preserve the boundaries of each rendered object for later compositing in Photoshop, you use alpha channels. (See Chapter 4, "You and Your Entourage," for more information on alpha channels.) Alpha channels are automatically calculated in every VIZ rendering, but they can only be stored on disk (and therefore transferred to Photoshop) in a few file formats, including .psd, .tif, and .tga.

We will use the Targa format (*.tga) in this chapter to store alpha channels. Targa images also feature optional compression for small file sizes. One peculiarity of VIZ is the requirement that the background be black to properly store anti-aliased object boundaries in the alpha channel; otherwise, a fringe of environment color can appear around the objects.

A black environment is not a problem because we will be compositing the background image in Photoshop, covering the black areas entirely. Let's set the environment color and then dive into the object-rendering work flow:

1. In VIZ, open the Environment And Effects dialog box (press 8). Click the Environment tab if it is not already selected (see Figure 7.11). Click the Background Color swatch to open the Color Selector. Drag the Whiteness slider to the top to select black. Close both dialog boxes.

   To render a single object, you'll need to assign the Matte/Shadow material to all the other objects in the scene. In this way, everything that is matted is invisible, and the object in question is obscured appropriately, should any other objects overlap it. Once you've selected everything but the object we are interested in, you can assign the Matte/Shadow material to the selection.

2. Choose Tools ➢ Selection Floater to open the Selection Floater dialog box, as shown in Figure 7.12. A floater is any dialog box that is modeless, meaning it stays open while you do other things and until you close it. The advantage to using the Selection Floater dialog box rather than the Select Objects dialog box (which is identical) is that the floating version stays open when you anticipate having to keep selecting objects. Select the Framing object by double-clicking its name. Click the Invert button at the bottom of the dialog box, and then click the Select button.

FIGURE 7.11
Set the black
environment.

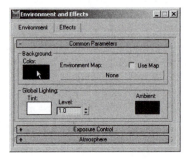

FIGURE 7.12
The Selection Floater
dialog box

FIGURE 7.12
The Selection Floater
dialog box

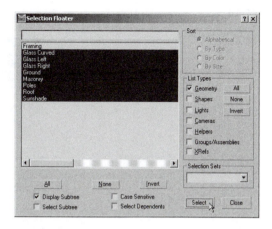

3. Press M to reopen the Material Editor dialog box, as shown in Figure 7.13. Scroll to an unused sample slot by clicking the Down arrow on the vertical scrollbar. To change the material type, click the button that is currently marked Standard.

FIGURE 7.13
Changing material
types in the Material
Editor dialog box

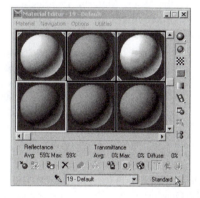

4. The Material/Map Browser dialog box appears (see Figure 7.14). Choose Matte/Shadow from the list of materials and click OK.

5. The Matte/Shadow material and its parameters appear in the Material Editor dialog box. Uncheck Opaque Alpha in the Matte group. When this setting is unchecked, the matted objects will not contribute to the alpha channel, so the rendering can be used for compositing. In the Shadow group, uncheck Receive Shadows and uncheck Affect Alpha; we will deal with shadows differently later in this tutorial.

FIGURE 7.14
The Material/Map
Browser dialog box

6. Click the Assign Material To Selection button on the Material Editor toolbar. Notice the white triangular corner tabs that appear in each corner of the material sample slot; these indicate the material is *hot*, or instanced in the scene.

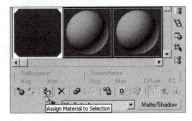

7. Do a quick render (press Shift+Q). The RFW appears, displaying the framing object in red. Click the Display Alpha Channel button on the RFW toolbar. The grayscale alpha channel displays, showing the boundaries of this object. Notice that the RFW indicates this is an RGB Alpha image, meaning there are a total of four channels held in the RFW (Red, Green, Blue, and Alpha), sometimes called RGBA.

8. Click the Save Bitmap button on the RFW toolbar. Navigate to the folder on your hard drive where you want to save the compositing renderings (I recommend making a folder called Output); click the Save As Type drop-down list box and select Targa Image File. Type **Framing.tga** in the File Name text box and click Save.

NOTE See Chapter 1 for a discussion of why RGBA images have 32 bits per pixel.

9. The Targa Image Control dialog box appears. Click the 32 Bits-Per-Pixel radio button. Check Compress for a smaller file size. Also, check Pre-Multiplied Alpha before clicking OK. Close the RFW.

WARNING The alpha channel must be premultiplied for efficient compositing in Photoshop; otherwise, transparency and anti-aliasing around the object boundaries are thrown off.

Congratulations, you have successfully rendered your first compositing image! We will repeat the object rendering process once more so you get some practice performing these steps manually.

10. Press Ctrl+Z to undo. This is an essential step in the object-rendering work flow! Undo doesn't count for the steps you performed in the RFW; in this case, it undoes the material assignment from step 6. The objects return to their original materials, and the white triangular corner tabs that appear in each corner of the Matte/Shadow sample slot disappear, meaning the material is now *cold* (or unused in the scene).

11. In the Selection Floater dialog box, click the next object (in this case, Glass Curved). Click Invert, and then click Select.

12. In the Material Editor dialog box, click Assign Material To Selection.

13. Press Shift+Q to do another quick render.

14. Click Save Bitmap in the RFW. Save the file in the same folder you used in step 8. Type **Glass Curved.tga** in the File Name text box and click OK.

WARNING Always use the same filename as object name to avoid confusion.

15. Click OK in the Targa Image Control dialog box to use the same settings as you did in step 9.

16. Close the RFW if it's in your way, and remember to undo once and only once; press Ctrl+Z to do this.

At this point you could repeat steps 11 through 16 for each object in the scene. Because this scene has only nine objects, this wouldn't take long. Feel free to do this to practice the object-rendering process until you understand why you are performing the steps—but the next section will show you why you don't have to do all the work.

Automating Output with MAXScript

One of the advantages of using Autodesk VIZ is the potential to use its powerful scripting language called MAXScript to reduce repetitive tasks. I'd like to give you a script that I've written to help with the more complex scenes you may be creating in your own projects. What if there are a few hundred objects in your 3D scene? Who would want to manually repeat the object-rendering steps that many times? In fact, by itself this MAXScript is worth the price of this book when you consider how much time it can save you.

Fortunately, you don't have to learn any MAXScript to take advantage of an automated object-rendering pipeline; you can just run my script. However, the script provided in the Chapter 7 folder on the companion CD is commented and easy to understand. If you have any interest in programming, this script might be an entry point for you to explore the benefits of solving tedious tasks with code.

1. Close the Selection Floater and/or Material Editor dialog boxes if they are still open from the previous section.

2. Click the Utilities tab of the Command Panel.

3. Click the MAXScript button to display a new rollout.

4. Click the Open Script button to open the Choose Editor File dialog box.

5. Navigate to the companion CD and open the file RenderMatte0.4.ms. A MAXScript window appears with color-coded text (see Figure 7.15). A version of this image appears in the color section.

FIGURE 7.15
RenderMatte
MAXScript

```
--define actions
    --Get Path button
    on pathgo pressed do (
        --get selected path as string
        global new_path = getSavePath()
    )
    --Start Rendering button
    on nowgo pressed do (
        --get all objects in an array
        scene_nodes = geometry as array
        --loop through all objects
        for i in scene_nodes do (
            --select the ith object in the scene
            select i
            --select inverse
            actionMan.executeAction 0 "40044"
            --turn undo recording on so that we can restore the original material later
            undo on (
                --assign material to selection
                $.material = MatteShadow opaqueAlpha:false affectAlpha:false receiveShadows:false
                backgroundColor = color 0 0 0
            ) -- end undo control
            --set Targa format to 32 bits/pixel, compressed, not split, store alpha
            targa.itgaio.setColorDepth(32)
            targa.itgaio.setCompressed(true)
            targa.itgaio.setAlphaSplit(false)
            targa.itgaio.setPreMultAlpha(true)
            --render as tga to chosen path
            render outputFile:(new_path + "\\" + i.name + ".tga") vfb:off
            --undo the matte material application
            max undo
        )--end for
        --select none
        actionMan.executeAction 0 "40043"
        --notify user of completion
        messageBox "Done" title:"Render Matte"
    )--end on
)--end utility
```

Read through the code and notice what is happening. The script starts by defining the user interface. An output path is then recorded, and the Start Rendering button starts looping through all the objects in the scene. Within the loop, an object is selected, and then the selection is inverted. Undo recording starts, and the Matte/Shadow material is assigned to the selection. The background color is set to black, the Targa options are set, and the file is saved as an RGBA image. An Undo restores the original materials. The next object is then processed in exactly the same way, and so on. At the end of the loop, the user is notified that the processing is done.

The script executes the same steps you performed manually in the last section. The great benefit is that now you merely have to start the processing and you can walk away from the computer while the processing takes place.

6. To interpret the code, choose File ➢ Evaluate All from the MAXScript window, and then close the MAXScript window. On the Utility tab of the Command Panel, click the Utilities drop-down list box in the MAXScript rollout and select Render Matte to display a new rollout.

7. You may have to scroll the panel upward to see the Render Matte rollout if your screen is set to a low resolution. You'll see a Render Matte rollout (see Figure 7.16) at the bottom of the Utility panel; inside this rollout, click the Get Path button.

FIGURE 7.16

The Render Matte rollout

WARNING Choose the output path before starting the rendering process. If you don't, the script will not save your renderings. Note that the renderings use the output size settings in the Render Scene dialog box.

8. Select a folder on your hard drive to save the renderings in the Browse For Folder dialog box and click OK. Then click the Start Rendering button once. When the renderings are completed, a small dialog box informs you that the processing is complete.

Figure 7.17 shows the Targa files output by the MAXScript in Windows Explorer; there will be one file per object in the 3D scene. Be patient while the renderings are processed; there is no progress bar to indicate how long it might take. The high-rise project should only take about a minute (there are nine objects), but complex projects can take much longer.

FIGURE 7.17
Rendered Targa files
output from MAXScript

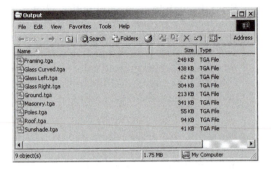

In your own projects, do a few test renders using the procedure in the earlier "Rendering Matted Objects with Alpha Channels" section. This will give you a sense for how long an average object takes to render. Multiply the number of objects in your scene by your best guess for an average frame time, and you'll have an idea how long the entire process will take. Then use the RenderMatte MAXScript to automate the process while you make better use of your time.

Rendering the Shadow Element

So far you have rendered only the objects themselves, but none of the shadows. Instead of rendering shadows on each object, it is more efficient to render the shadows all together in a single image that you can later composite in Photoshop. This way, you'll have global control over the shadows by being able to change the opacity of the shadow image layer.

In VIZ, you must first turn on shadow casting in at least one light source. You can then render the shadows in a separate pass by using the Render Elements feature. Let's see how this works:

1. Open the Select Objects dialog box (press H). In the List Types group, click the None button to deselect all categories. Then check Lights to display a listing of all the objects of this category. Double-click Direct Light to select this object and close the dialog box.

2. Click the Modify tab of the Command Panel. In the General Parameters rollout, check On in the Shadows group. Make sure Ray Traced Shadows is selected in the drop-down list box if it's not already.

TIP Ray traced shadows are the most accurate casting algorithm, and they show crisp edges.

3. Open the Render Scene dialog box (press F10). Click the Render Elements tab. Click the Add button and select Shadow from the list of elements (if not already present). Make sure Enable is checked.

4. Click the Browse button in the Selected Element Parameters group. In the Render Element Output File dialog box, navigate to the folder in which you stored your rendered images from the last section. The filename will automatically be Shadow.tga (see Figure 7.18); click OK.

5. Click the Render button at the bottom of the Render Scene dialog box. An RFW appears, and the building progressively appears in color as the scan lines are rendered. After the first rendering is complete, a second Shadow window appears. The shadow is completely black in RGB. You'll have to view the alpha channel to see the shadows against the black background. Click the Display Alpha Channel button in the RFW toolbar, as shown in Figure 7.19.

6. You don't have to save the shadow rendering manually because Render Elements did that automatically for you. Close both rendered frame windows. You are done with the 3D part of the tutorial because all the necessary images have been rendered. Exit VIZ without saving the scene.

FIGURE 7.18
Browsing a path for the shadow rendering

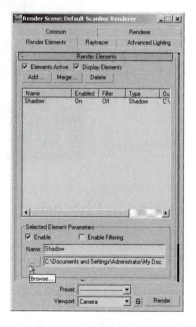

FIGURE 7.19
Displaying the shadow
rendering's alpha
channel

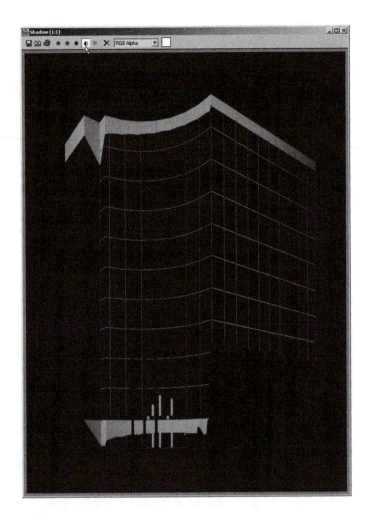

FIGURE 7.19
Displaying the shadow
rendering's alpha
channel

Compositing in Photoshop

Now that you have successfully rendered all the objects in VIZ for compositing, it is time to put them
all together in Photoshop. You will be manually converting alpha channels to layer masks first, and
then you'll create an action to automate the process to save time with larger projects. You'll transfer
each of the rendered images to a project document where you will organize the layers in preparation
for the effects you'll apply in the next section. Let's get started in Photoshop:

Converting Alpha Channels to Layer Masks

The alpha channels in the rendered images store information about the location of the 3D object
boundaries. Because alpha channels are in grayscale, white indicates where the object is fully opaque,
black indicates where there is no object, and gray pixels indicate partial transparency. You'll be

converting this alpha information into a selection. You'll then use the selection to create a layer mask that reveals only the pixels of the "object" itself. This is as close as you can get to having objects in Photoshop; you understand we are actually manipulating pixels in Photoshop that represent the real 3D objects from VIZ.

1. In Photoshop, open `Framing.tga` from among the renderings we built in the preceding section.

2. Click the Channels palette, and then click the Alpha 1 channel. The boundaries of the 3D object appear as white pixels on this channel.

3. At the bottom of the Channels palette, click the Load Channel As Selection button (first on the left). The marching ants surround the white pixels on the alpha channel.

4. Click the RGB channel. As you do so, notice that the Alpha 1 channel is turned off, but that the marching ants are still visible. Click the Layers palette.

   Now you have the object boundaries loaded as a selection. Notice that there is only one layer in the Layers palette, background. Unfortunately, you can't add a layer mask to the Background layer; a mask would hide part of the layer, and nothing can be behind the background by definition. To get around this situation, we convert the background to a normal layer.

5. Hold down the Alt key and double-click Background in the Layers palette; the Background layer converts to a normal layer called Layer 0.

6. Click the Add Layer Mask button at the bottom of the Layers palette. The selection is converted to a mask, and a gray-and-white transparency checkerboard pattern is visible outside the object boundaries. Rename Layer 0 to Framing. Leave the Framing document open for now.

   The Framing layer is finally ready for compositing! Only the pixels belonging to the former 3D object are visible on this layer because of the layer mask. We will repeat the process once so you get some practice performing these steps manually.

7. Open the file `Glass Curved.tga` from the same folder you browsed to in step 2.

8. Activate the Channels palette and click the Alpha 1 channel.

9. Click the Load Channel As Selection button and then click the RGB channel.

10. Activate the Layers palette. Hold down Alt and double-click Background.

11. Click the Add Layer Mask button.

12. Rename Layer 0 to the filename without the extension; in this case it is Glass Curved (see Figure 7.20).

FIGURE 7.20
The Layers palette
showing the alpha
channel converted to a
layer mask.

You could manually repeat steps 7 through 12 for each of the object images you rendered in the last section. Again, because there are only nine objects in the scene, this wouldn't take too long. However, whenever you will have to repeat a mindless series of steps, alarm bells should go off in your mind. This is your chance to create automation that does the tedious work, and it can save you lots of time in the long run. Why not let Photoshop do the mindless tasks so you have more time to do creative work?

Creating an Action to Automate Conversion

Fortunately, creating automation in Photoshop is easy, and no programming is required. Although it's not as powerful as a real scripting language such as MAXScript is inside VIZ, Photoshop can record a series of your steps and store them in an action. When the action is played, Photoshop automatically runs through the same list of prerecorded steps at the click of a button. Here's how to create your own action to convert an alpha channel to a layer mask:

1. Open the file Glass Left.tga from your hard drive.

2. Click the Actions palette. On the lower edge of the Actions palette, click the Create New Action button to open the New Action dialog box, as shown in Figure 7.21.

FIGURE 7.21
Naming a new action

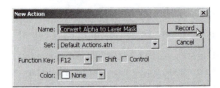

3. In the Name text box, type **Convert Alpha to Layer Mask**. Use the default Set if you like; otherwise select a custom action set from the Set drop-down list box if you already have made your own actions. Click the Function Key drop-down list box, and select the F12 key if it's not already in use. This allows you to execute this action with the click of a single button. Click Record.

4. Activate the Channels palette and click Alpha 1 Channel.

5. Click the Load Channel As Selection button.

6. Click the RGB channel.

7. Activate the Layers palette. Hold down Alt and double-click Background.

8. Click the Add Layer Mask button.

9. Click the Stop Playing/Recording button on the Actions palette. Look at the Actions palette and expand the steps to examine the recording you've just made (see Figure 7.22).

FIGURE 7.22

A recorded Action

Photoshop has no way to grab the filename from within an action. Therefore, you'll have to type the appropriate layer name each time. Such is the price we pay for not having a real scripting language inside Photoshop.

10. Rename Layer 0 to Glass Left. Leave this file open.

Congratulations on recording an action that has the potential to save you a lot of time in your own projects! Let's try using your newly created tool on the next rendered image.

11. Open the next file from your hard drive; in this case, it is `Glass Right.tga`.

12. Press the F12 key. The action you recorded plays, and the alpha channel is successfully converted to a layer mask.

13. Rename Layer 0 to the filename without the extension; in this case, rename it to Glass Right.

14. Repeat steps 11 through 13 for each of the six remaining rendered images. Minimize (but do not close) each image as you complete this step.

15. Leave Photoshop and all documents open for work in the next section.

Transferring Masked Layers to a Project

The next step is to integrate all the files into a single document. You will do this by dragging and dropping masked layers with the Move tool. You'll be able to perfectly snap the layers into their proper positions because all the rendered images have exactly the same document size. You'll then precisely match all the pieces in Photoshop and be ready to start altering the layers with effects in the next section.

1. Create a new document (press Ctrl+N). In the New dialog box, enter **CompositingProject.psd** in the Name text box. Type 768 pixels for Width and 1024 pixels for Height. Set Resolution to 72 pixels/inch, Color Mode to RGB Color with 8 bits per channel, and Background Contents to White (see Figure 7.23). Click OK to create the new document window.

NOTE   If you'd like to be able to print the compositing project in a large size, you will have to go back into VIZ and render a greater number of pixels. See Chapter 1 for information on setting image size, resolution, and document size.

FIGURE 7.23

Creating a new document

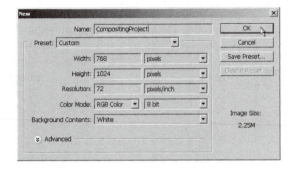

2. Open all the Targa images you rendered in the last section, if they are not already open. Choose Window ➢ Framing.tga to maximize the Framing document window. Minimize all other windows except for the CompositingProject itself.

3. Select the Move tool (press V). Drag from the Framing window and drop into the Compositing Project window. The Framing layer is transferred but is not in the correct location yet.

4. While you're in the Compositing Project window, drag the Framing layer around both horizontally and vertically until you "feel" it snap into position. There will be a positive stop in both directions, and you'll know the layer has come to rest in the correct location.

5. Repeat steps 2 through 4 for each of the remaining rendered images. You will end up with a CompositingProject that contains all the other images as masked layers. Figure 7.24 shows the Layers palette after all the rendered images have been integrated into a single document.

6. Close all the documents without saving except for CompositingProject.

FIGURE 7.24

The Layers palette with composited renderings

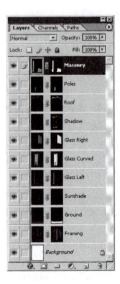

Organizing Layers

Before we start applying layer style effects in the next section, it is worth spending some time organizing the layers of the CompositingProject document. Taking time to organize the layers is especially warranted in a more complex project if you have dozens or hundreds of layers.

You can organize layers in the Layers palette in four ways: descriptive naming, ordering, using colors, and categorizing with layer sets. Of these four, you have already applied descriptive names to each layer in the previous sections, actually beginning with naming the objects in VIZ. Also, you might have noticed that I've been routinely assigning colors throughout the preceding chapters, but layer color is affected by arranging layer sets. Let's take a look at how you can keep the Layers palette organized.

There are 10 layers and only 7 colors, so if you want to color every layer, some repetition is necessary. It doesn't really matter which colors you choose for particular layers; the colors are used only to visually differentiate the layers within the Layers palette and provide a visual mnemonic for you while you work with this project. That said, try to find some logic for the colors that you choose if possible.

In this project, the glass layers are related, so they could have the same color. The shadow layer is a somewhat special layer because it doesn't represent a 3D object like the other layers. For these reasons, I recommend using blue for all three glass layers and setting the Shadow layer's color to red.

1. Right-click the Shadow layer name in the Layers palette and choose Layer Properties from the context menu. In the Layer Properties dialog box, choose Red from the Color drop-down list box and click OK.

2. Similarly, give the three glass layers a blue color.

3. Layer order is significant whenever pixels overlap. In this project, only the Shadow layer has pixels that overlap other layers; therefore, it should be at the top of the Layer stack so it can be seen. Drag the Shadow layer to the top of the Layers palette, if it is not already. The shadow will be revealed in the document window if it was previously hidden below other layers.

    The most important purpose for reordering layers is to reveal obscured pixels. A secondary purpose is to organize that Layers palette. You might want items at the bottom of your composition to appear at the bottom of the layer stack, for example. It's really a matter of personal preference, and more complex projects can warrant additional thought.

    If you have a series of related layers, it makes sense to put them together within a layer set. Photoshop CS now supports nested layer sets, making organized folks very happy (myself included admittedly). Let's see how this works in our relatively simple project.

4. Click the Create A New Set button at the bottom of the Layers palette. Drag the Framing, Glass Right, Glass Curved, and Glass Left layers into the new set. Rename Set 1 to Curtain Wall. Notice that the layers you dragged into the set are indented so you can tell that they are part of it.

5. Create another layer set inside the first set and call it Glazing. Drag Glass Left, Glass Curved, and Glass Right into the Glazing set. Leave the Framing layer above the Glazing set but still within the Curtain Wall set. Reorder the remaining layers according to Figure 7.25.

    But look! When you created the layer sets, you lost any layer color that was on the layers you dragged into the sets. However, you can give the entire set a color.

FIGURE 7.25
The Compositing Layers
palette

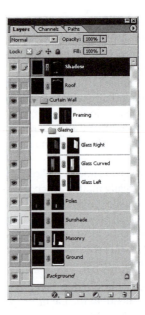

6. Right-click the Curtain Wall layer set and choose Layer Set Properties. Give the set a violet color in the Layer Set Properties dialog box. Notice that the nested set assumes this color as well.

7. Right-click the Glazing nested layer set and choose Layer Set Properties from the context menu. Give this set a blue color.

Refer to the color section for a version of Figure 7.25 showing the colors I've chosen for this project. Feel free to use your own colors. You can even give individual layers within a layer set their own colors, but you have to draw the line somewhere.

A project this small probably doesn't warrant this amount of attention to its organization within the Layers palette, but it is good to learn these skills for when you are working on bigger projects. For example, if you must maintain a particular layer order due to blending modes or pixel coverage, you might find that some related layers are discontiguous. In that case, you won't be able to group them into a layer set, but you can use the layer-color technique to indicate their relationship. Good layer organization translates to more efficient work in Photoshop.

TIP You might want to choose similar colors for your Photoshop layers as compared with the flat material colors used in VIZ. This is a solid strategy for maintaining organization continuity across applications.

8. Press Ctrl+S to save CompositingProject for the first time. Click Save in the Save As dialog box to save the file in Photoshop's native format. If you're going to continue working through the following sections, you can leave this file open for now.

Applying Effects to Masked Layers

You've come a long way to arrive at what is essentially the start of the creative part of compositing. Layer style effects are a powerful way to transform the appearance of the composition. In the following steps, you will use many of the skills you picked up when working with plans and elevations earlier in the book. However, you won't have to fill in transparent areas with black as you did when working with CAD drawings of plans and elevations.

NOTE Refer to Chapter 5, "Presenting Plans," and Chapter 6, "Elevating the Elevation," for a review of applying layer style effects.

The layers in the compositing project already reveal rendered pixels in the appropriate areas by virtue of their layer masks. Therefore, all that is required is for you to experiment by applying various layer style effects to get the look you want for each layer.

Although the parameters in the following steps are given with exact values, you can experiment and find your own combination of parameters that makes the masked layers look best in your opinion. One of the best things about layer style effects is the immediate visual feedback you get when adjusting the parameters; so keep tweaking until you are satisfied. Let the exact values be your guide and starting point.

Throughout these steps, you can open the Layer Style dialog by double-clicking just to the right of the layer name or by clicking the Add A Layer Style button at the bottom of the Layers palette and choosing a style.

1. If you have `CompositingProject.psd` open from the previous exercise, you can continue here; if not, open that file from your hard drive before continuing. This file is also provided on the companion CD if you are jumping in here.

2. Select the Ground layer in the Layers palette and open the Layer Style dialog box. Apply the following effects:

   Pattern Overlay Use the Parchment pattern from the Artist Surfaces library at 99% Scale, Overlay Blend Mode, and 60% Opacity.

   Gradient Overlay Select Overlay Blend Mode, 25% Opacity, and select the Black, White gradient from the Gradient Picker. Check Reverse, Linear Style, Angle 35°, and 125% Scale. Drag in the document window to adjust the gradient if desired.

   Color Overlay Select a pure white color, Screen Blend Mode, and 10% Opacity.

   The Pattern Overlay effect adds texture to the original flat rendering color. Gradient Overlay adds slight lighting variation on the ground surface, getting darker in the background. Color Overlay is used creatively here to brighten the other effects, rather than overlay a new color as is usually done. Figure 7.26 shows the pertinent effect parameters for the Ground layer.

FIGURE 7.26
Ground effects

3. Select the Masonry layer. Open the Layer Style dialog box and apply the following effects:

Pattern Overlay   Select Overlay Blend Mode, 22% Opacity, select the Concrete pattern from the Texture Fill library, and set a 63% Scale.

Gradient Overlay   Select Overlay Blend Mode, 35% Opacity, select the Black, White gradient, and uncheck Reverse, Linear Style, 125° Angle, and 150% Scale.

Color Overlay   Select a pure yellow with HSB values of 60,100,100 in the Color Picker, set Overlay Blend Mode, and 10% Opacity.

The same set of three effects is used on this layer as in the last step. This time Color Overlay is used in a more traditional way to warm the masonry with a toned-down yellow hue. The Gradient Overlay gives some shading to the wall surfaces. Pattern Overlay combines nicely with the original subtle checkerboard texture that was rendered in VIZ.

4. Select the Sunshade layer. Once again, apply layer style effects:

Color Overlay   Choose a dark gray (HSB values of 0,0,30), and leave Normal Blend Mode set at 100% Opacity.

Bevel And Emboss   Select Inner Bevel Style, Smooth Technique, 51% Depth, Up Direction, 7 px Size, and 5 px Soften.

Color Overlay is used here to completely replace the original color. A bevel is added to give the sunshade a more rounded, three-dimensional appearance. See Figure 7.27 for this layer's effects.

FIGURE 7.27
Sunshade effects

5. Select the Poles layer. Apply more effects as usual.

Gradient Overlay   Choose Normal Blend Mode, 100% Opacity, Black, White gradient, and check Reverse, Radial Style, 90° Angle, and 130% Scale. Drag the mouse down in the document to move the gradient center to the top of the poles.

Bevel And Emboss   Select Inner Bevel Style, Smooth Technique, 300% Depth, Up Direction, 4 px Size, and 6 px Soften.

Contour   Click the Contour Picker and select the Gaussian contour thumbnail, check Anti-aliased, and set Range to 17%.

In this case, Gradient Overlay replaces the original yellow color with shades of gray. You beveled to round out the poles and the Contour effect to tweak shading within the bevel.

Because the building glass reflects the outside world, we'll skip the layers in the Glazing set for now and return to them in the "Working with the Environment" section, later in this chapter. You will use a new technique on the Framing layer. Here you will use a layer style effect that extends beyond the boundaries of its mask.

6. Select the Framing layer. Open the Layer Style dialog box and apply the following effects:

Outer Glow   In the Structure group, select Screen Blend Mode, 70% Opacity, 0% Noise, and click the solid color swatch to open the Color Picker. Select a pure blue color (HSB values 240,100,100) in the Color Picker. In the Elements group, select Softer Technique, 9% Spread, and 60 px Size. In the Quality group, change Range to 75%.

Gradient Overlay   Choose Normal Blend Mode, 100% Opacity, check Reverse, select Radial Style, 90° Angle, and 140% Scale.

Color Overlay   Click the color swatch and select pure white from the Color Picker. Set Overlay Blend Mode with 50% Opacity.

The Outer Glow effect bleeds blue beyond the Framing layer mask, effectively colorizing the glazing. The Gradient Overlay adds specular shine to the framing, and the Color Overlay brightens the metal. Figure 7.28 shows the pertinent effect parameters for the Framing layer.

NOTE   The blue color from the Outer Glow effect employed here bleeds out and affects surrounding areas beyond the Framing itself. You'll learn how to fix this in the "Adding to the Composite" section later in this chapter.

FIGURE 7.28
Framing effects

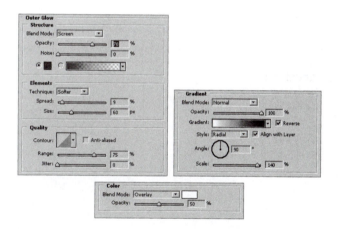

7. Select the Roof layer. When you apply a Color Overlay effect, you'll lose the subtle shading that was rendered on this layer. Re-create this shading with an Inner Shadow effect. Stroke is added at the end to outline the edges of the roof. Apply effects as follows:

Color Overlay   Leave Blend Mode set to Normal, and leave Opacity at 100%. Choose a light gray color with HSB values of 0,0,75.

Inner Shadow   Bring Opacity down to 30%, and leave everything else with default settings.

Stroke   Set a 1 px Size, Center Position, and click the color swatch and select a medium gray color from the Color Picker with HSB values of 0,0,50.

Figure 7.29 shows the last effects you'll need to apply in this tutorial.

FIGURE 7.29
Roof effects

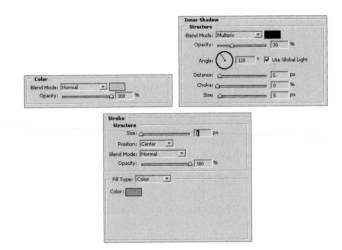

8. Click the Shadow layer at the top of the Layers palette. Turn down its opacity to 60%. The shadows are all instantly lightened. Figure 7.30 shows the result of all the effects you've applied in this section.

9. Save your work as CompositingProject2.psd. If you're going to continue working through the following sections, you can leave this file open for now.

FIGURE 7.30
The layer style effects
applied

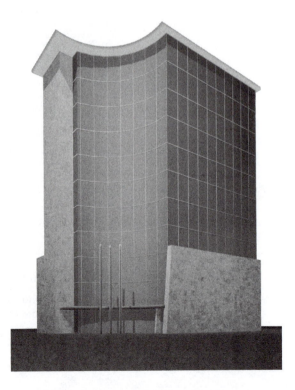

Working with the Environment

When you were preparing the 3D model in VIZ, you had to use a black background color for the environment because of the necessity to create anti-aliased alpha channel renderings. Later, when you brought those renderings into Photoshop, you converted their alpha channels to layer masks, leaving transparency around each of the objects. Therefore, white pixels currently surround the building because the Background layer is white.

Now all you have to do to see an environment surrounding the building is to replace the background with a photographic image. In addition, to create a more realistic composition, we can copy and reflect the photographic environment, confining the pasted layers to the building's glazing using clipping groups. Let's see how it is done:

1. If you have CompositingProject2.psd open from the previous exercise, you can continue here; if not, open that file from your hard drive before continuing.

2. Open the file Clouds.jpg from the companion CD. This is the photographic image you'll use to place the building in its environment.

3. Press Ctrl+A and then Ctrl+C to copy all the pixels from the cloud image to the Clipboard. Close Clouds.jpg.

4. In the CompositingProject2 window, click the background layer in the Layers palette. Press Ctrl+V to paste the image from the Clipboard onto a new layer called Layer 1.

5. The cloud image in Layer 1 is larger than your canvas size, so you can move it around to find the best fit for the building's surrounding environment. Select the Move tool (press V) and drag Layer 1 around until you are satisfied with its appearance in relation to the building.

NOTE If your photographic image were smaller, you could use Free Transform (Ctrl+T) to scale it up so it would cover the needed area. However, you'll get the best results when using environment images with at least the same or greater pixel size as compared to your compositing project.

6. When you are satisfied with the position of the environment in the previous step, you can trim away the excess pixels on Layer 1 to make the file smaller. Choose Image ➤ Trim, click the Top Left Pixel Color radio button in the Trim dialog box, and click OK.

   Adjust the exposure of the cloud image so it matches the rest of the composition by using a layer blending mode technique.

7. Duplicate Layer 1 by pressing Ctrl+J, making a new layer called Layer 1 Copy. Change the blending mode of Layer 1 Copy to Screen. Adjust its opacity to 35% to brighten the underlying underexposed layer.

8. Click the link icons next to Layer 1 and the Background layer to link these two layers with Layer 1 Copy.

TIP   Use Multiply blending mode on a duplicate layer to darken an underlying overexposed layer.

9. Click the triangle button on the Layers palette and choose Merge Linked from the palette menu. The two temporary layers disappear, and you are left with a new cloudy Background layer.

Next, let's reflect the clouds in the glazing. You'll start by copying the background and mirroring the reflection. Then to confine the reflection to appear only in the windows, you'll create a clipping group. (See Chapter 1 for a review of clipping groups.)

10. Select the Background layer (now containing the cloudy sky image). Duplicate the Background layer (press Ctrl+J). Rename the new layer Reflection.

11. Choose Edit ➢ Transform ➢ Flip Horizontal to mirror the Reflection layer.

12. Drag the Reflection layer inside the Glazing layer set, just above the Glass Right layer (see Figure 7.31).

13. Hold down the Alt key and position your mouse on the interface between layers Glass Right and Reflection. Click when you see the clipping group cursor appear. The Reflection layer then features a downward arrow pointing to the underlined Glass Right layer, which is acting as the base of the clipping group. The reflection image now is revealed through Glass Right's layer mask.

TIP   If you move the Reflection layer, it stays within the boundaries of the glazing because it is part of a clipping group.

14. Click the Reflection layer if it is not already selected, and change its opacity to 40% to dim the reflection; otherwise the glazing would be a perfect mirror. Click the Glass Right layer, and change its opacity to 75% to brighten the reflection slightly.

15. You can use effects on the clipped layer, just as you can on normal layers. Apply a Gradient Overlay layer style effect to the Reflection layer. Choose Overlay Blend Mode, 75% Opacity, select Black To White gradient, check Reverse, choose Linear Style, and set a –27° Angle.

Two other glass layers can use a similar treatment. To save time, duplicate the existing Reflection layer and then set up new clipping groups.

FIGURE 7.31

Dragging the Reflection layer into the Glazing layer set

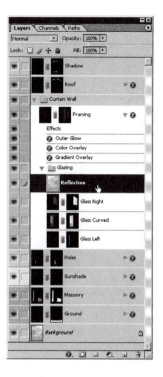

16. Click the Reflection layer and press Ctrl+J to duplicate it. Notice that the copied layer is not part of the clipping group, but retains the layer style effect. Rename this new layer Reflection2 and drag it between the Glass Right and Glass Curved layers.

17. Create a new clipping group. Hold down the Alt key and position your mouse on the interface between layers Reflection2 and Glass Curved. Click when you see the clipping group cursor appear.

18. Adjust Gradient Overlay to show the shading running vertically along the curved glass surface. Double-click the *f* icon of the Gradient Overlay effect under the Reflection2 layer. In the Layer Style dialog box, change the Angle to 90°, uncheck Reverse, and click OK.

19. Make another copy of the reflection and set up a new clipping group for Glass Left. Click the Reflection2 layer and press Ctrl+J to duplicate it. Rename this Reflection3, drag it down in the Layers palette, and drop it just above Glass Left.

20. Set up a clipping group between the Reflection3 and Glass Left layers. Figure 7.32 shows the Glazing layer set after all the reflection clipping groups are set up.

21. Use the opacity of the various reflection layers to shade the various planes of the building differently. Select the Reflection3 layer and change its opacity to 50%. Select the Reflection2 layer and set its opacity to 65%.

FIGURE 7.32
The Glazing layer set
with clipping groups

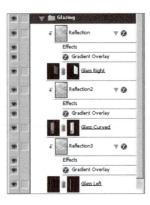

22. To simulate refraction and the imperfections of glass, you can optionally distort the reflection layers. Select the Reflection layer. Choose Filter ➤ Distort ➤ Glass. The Filter Gallery dialog box opens showing the Glass filter. Change the Distortion slider to 4 and the Smoothness to 5 (see Figure 7.33). Click OK to apply the filter.

23. Select the Reflection2 layer and press Ctrl+F to reapply the last-used filter (Glass). Select the Reflection3 layer and press Ctrl+F again.

24. Save your work as CompositingProject3.psd. If you're going to continue working through the following sections, you can leave this file open for now.

FIGURE 7.33
Distorting the glass

Making Adjustments with Clipping Groups

You might remember from Chapter 1 that you can edit adjustment layers in the layer stack (as compared with adjustments). Adjustment layers are preferable because they allow you to try things out without having to commit to them. You can change your mind later and alter the parameters of an adjustment layer or throw it away without permanently affecting the pixels of your image.

Normally, adjustment layers affect all the layers below them in the Layers palette. That's fine if you want to increase the brightness of many layers at once, for example. Just add a Brightness/Contrast adjustment layer, and it will affect everything below it in the layer stack.

On the other hand, what if you want the increased flexibility of an adjustment layer, but want to affect only a single layer? Simple—create a clipping group with the adjustment layer and a masked layer. Here's how this works:

1. If you have CompositingProject3.psd open from the previous exercise, you can continue here; if not, open that file from your hard drive before continuing.

2. Select the Masonry layer. Add a Brightness/Contrast adjustment layer by clicking Create New Fill or Adjustment Layer at the bottom of the Layers palette. In the Brightness/Contrast dialog box, drag the Brightness slider to +15, drag the Contrast slider to +30, and click OK.

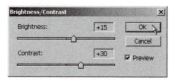

3. Notice that the Masonry layer looks better, but the Ground and Background layers were affected and look too bright. Hold down the Alt key and position your mouse on the interface between the Brightness/Contrast adjustment layer and the Masonry layer. Click when you see the clipping group cursor appear. Now the adjustment layer only affects the Masonry layer.

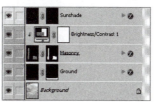

4. Select the Ground layer. Apply a Hue/Saturation adjustment layer. Drag the Saturation slider to –50 and Lightness to +10. Click OK to close the Hue/Saturation dialog box.

5. Create a clipping group between the Hue/Saturation adjustment layer and the Ground layer.

6. Leave the file open for work in the next section.

Adding to the Composite

Layer styles and adjustments are great because they maintain flexibility for you in the compositing process. You can always go back and tweak as your composition evolves. At some milestone in your process, you can create composite layers that contain collections of work that you have built up from multiple layers. Because a composite layer is an aggregation of work on multiple layers, you lose the ability to edit parameters you may have enjoyed previously.

However, the benefit of aggregating content on fewer layers is the ability to affect the composite whole more readily (plus the simplification of the Layers palette). Let's start cleaning up the Curtain Wall layers by merging them in a composite layer.

1. Continue working here on the `CompositingProject3.psd` file from the last section.

2. Select the Curtain Wall layer set, right-click its eye icon in the Layers palette, and choose Show / Hide All Other Layers. Now only the layers in the Curtain Wall set are visible. You can readily see the blue glow that extends beyond the glazing system; you may remember this was originally created by the Outer Glow effect on the Framing layer.

3. Create a new layer and drag it above and out of the Curtain Wall layer set. Rename it Curtain Wall Composite.

4. Press Alt+Shift+Ctrl+E to stamp all visible layers onto the current layer (see Figure 7.34).

FIGURE 7.34

The composite layer stamped from all visible layers

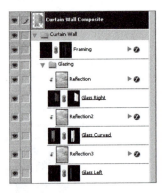

To fix the outer glow problem, you'll need to build up a selection from all the masks of the layers in the Curtain Wall layer set. Later, you'll create a new mask from this super-selection.

5. Right-click the layer mask thumbnail on the Framing layer. Choose Add Layer Mask To Selection from the context menu.

6. Repeat step 5 on each of the following layers: Glass Right, Glass Curved, and Glass Left. By adding each of these layer masks to the selection, you are building a super-selection containing all the masks in the layer set.

7. Select the Curtain Wall Composite layer and click the Add Layer Mask button at the bottom of the Layers palette. The selection turns into a mask that hides the outer glow pixels.

8. Turn all the layers on. Right-click the eye icon of the Curtain Wall Composite layer, and choose Show/Hide All Other Layers from the context menu.

9. Click the eye icon on the Curtain Wall layer set to toggle it and turn off all the layers it contains.

   Next, you'll add a lens flare to the composite layer (see Chapter 3, "Digital Darkroom Skills").

10. Select the Curtain Wall Composite layer if it's not already selected. Make sure its layer thumbnail is selected, not its layer mask thumbnail.

11. Choose Filter ➢ Render ➢ Lens Flare. In the Lens Flare dialog box, click the 50-300mm Zoom radio button, and click a point high up on the glass in the preview area, as shown in Figure 7.35. Click OK to close the Lens Flare dialog box when you're finished.

12. Drag the Opacity slider down to 80% in the Curtain Wall Composite layer. The entire curtain wall mixes a bit with the background.

TIP To further embellish the image, you could optionally add some entourage from the library started in Chapter 3.

   Now that the project is nearly complete, create a master composite layer representing all of your work to date. This composite layer will live at the top of the Layers palette.

13. Create a new layer and drag it to the top of the Layers palette. Rename this layer Master Composite.

FIGURE 7.35
Adding a lens flare to the composite layer

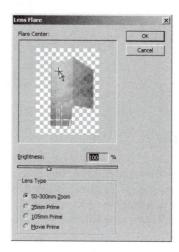

14. Press Alt+Shift+Ctrl+E to stamp all visible onto the new layer. All the other layers are irrelevant at this point. Still, it is best to keep the underlying layers in case future changes need to be made to this file; this is why we avoided flattening all the layers into one.

15. Choose Filter ➤ Texture ➤ Grain. Select a low intensity in the Filter Gallery dialog box; drag the slider to 10 and click OK.

TIP A slight amount of grain or noise helps correct problems with color banding common in inkjet printers.

Figure 7.36 shows the final project image. A version of this image is in the color section.

FIGURE 7.36
The completed
compositing project

Summary

You have taken a 3D model from Autodesk VIZ and greatly enhanced its appearance in Adobe Photoshop though the art of compositing. Hopefully this chapter has introduced you to new avenues for creative expression in your own work. The compositing techniques presented here offer exciting image-based alternatives to the lengthy photo-realistic rendering process of a 3D program. In the next chapter you'll learn artistic options for illustrating architecture.

Chapter 8

Illustrating Architecture

For many years photo-realism has been aggressively marketed by software companies, in trade magazines and in computer graphics circles. A 2004 survey at www.cgarchitect.com shows that the architectural visualizations created most often, by a wide margin, are photo-realistic renderings.

Although it is certainly true that a photo-realistic 3D rendering can be spectacular and at best is indistinguishable from a photograph, liabilities to this style are worth considering. Every facet of a photo-realistic rendering must be specified, including 3D geometric detail, materials that correctly simulate real-world optics, texture map coordinates, photometric luminaires, and so on. As simulations of reality, photo-realistic imagery can be so accurate that nothing is left to the imagination.

But it can actually be troublesome to show clients imagery in the early design development stages that is too realistic or pinned down, especially when the intent is to share a common vision and dialogue, not to debate the index of refraction of the glazing, for example.

Non–photo-realistic (NPR) illustrations convey a visual feel for a space when something softer and less determined is called for. NPR illustration stimulates the imagination and draws attention to the essential design ideas of your composition without attempting to be an accurate reality simulation.

This chapter is about illustrating architecture with NPR techniques that encompass both VIZ and Photoshop. You will start in Autodesk VIZ with a 3D model and render special channels (ObjectID, Normal, and Zdepth) that are useful in maintaining three-dimensionality and object-selectability in a rendered 2D image. Where appropriate, you'll also use some of the compositing skills presented in Chapter 7 to render and convert specific objects and shadows in VIZ to masked layers in Photoshop. You'll improve your illustration skills in the following areas:

- ◆ Illustrating a 3D Model
- ◆ Integrating and Painting in Photoshop
- ◆ Working in Black and White
- ◆ Reproducing Grayscale Images with Colored Inks

Illustrating a 3D Model

Start the illustration project in Autodesk VIZ 2005. As mentioned in Chapter 7, a free trial version of Autodesk VIZ 2005 is available at www.autodesk.com. The techniques and automation presented in this chapter are specific to VIZ, and I recommend you use the program or its trial version to walk through these exercises even if you are accustomed to using other 3D software. After you understand this illustration process, you can adapt the procedures to your favorite 3D software package (such as 3ds max, formZ, Lightwave, Maya, and others).

TIP   The model used in this chapter is provided in additional file formats (`.3ds`, `.dxf`, and `.wrl`) on the companion CD for greater compatibility with other 3D programs.

Rendering in VIZ

You'll be making several renderings of the 3D model in VIZ to ultimately integrate into the illustration project for work in Photoshop. All the renderings made in this chapter will be generated from exactly the same point of view, although each will contain different forms of image data.

Although the rendering process presented here has some similarities to the compositing process , presented in Chapter 7, there are important differences. Instead of rendering each object as a separate image, you'll render special image channels that allow you to select, mask, and illustrate specific surfaces in Photoshop.

The first step when opening the sample file is to examine it and get a sense of the massing and spatial qualities of the design. The 3D model I'll use here is inspired by William Wurster's Gregory Farmhouse design in Santa Cruz, California (1926). It is a simple residential design centered on an open courtyard featuring spatial sophistication.

Once you visualize the 3D model, render an overall shot of the structures and tree, including an alpha channel, to delineate all the object boundaries at once. Make a similar rendering without the tree so that the building is easier to illustrate. To later composite the tree on top of the building, you need to render the tree separately as a matted object. The shadows will also be rendered as a separate element for compositing.

1. Launch Autodesk VIZ 2005.

2. Open the file `Farmhouse.max` from the Chapter 8 folder on the companion CD. Figure 8.1 shows the 3D model from a bird's-eye perspective. Notice the camera at eye level on the ground. Use the navigation tools in VIZ to get a feel for the model.

FIGURE 8.1
The 3D model

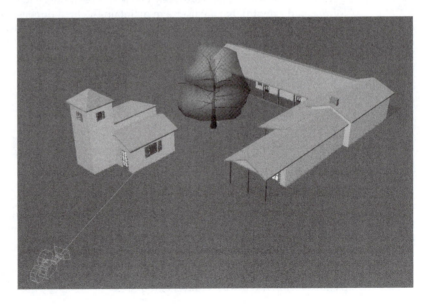

TIP When exploring any 3D model for the first time, examine its objects, modifiers, materials, lights, and so on. You can learn a lot by noticing how other artists structure their scenes.

3. Press C to enter the Camera viewport.

4. Right-click the viewport label (the word *Camera*) in the upper-left corner of the viewport. Choose Show Safe Frame from the Viewport menu. This feature displays concentric rectangles in the viewport. The outermost rectangle reveals the aspect ratio and cropped edge of the composition (see Figure 8.2). This is the point of view you'll be using in the illustration project. A version of this image is in the color section.

5. Press F10 to open the Render Scene dialog box (see Figure 8.3). Notice the Output Size is already set to 1024 × 768; the Width and Height parameters here control the output size for the entire illustration project.

6. Click the Render button to open the Rendered Frame Window (RFW). The image progressively renders as the scan lines are processed; this should only take a few seconds (see Figure 8.4).

NOTE The scene uses a black environment background color to ensure that object boundaries are properly anti-aliased in the alpha channels of composited images.

Notice that the RFW shows RGB Alpha in its drop-down list box, indicating that VIZ automatically renders the standard color channels plus an alpha channel that stores the object boundaries in a grayscale channel (see Chapter 7, "Creative Compositing").

FIGURE 8.2
The camera view

FIGURE 8.3
The Render Scene
dialog box

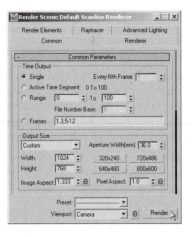

FIGURE 8.4
The Rendered Frame
Window

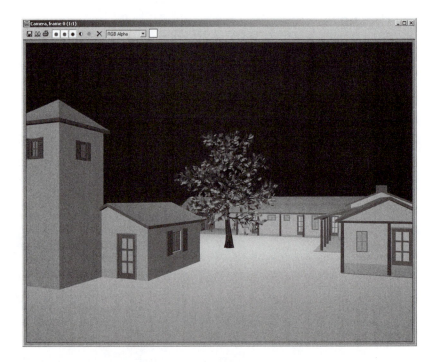

7. Click the Save Bitmap button in the RFW. Navigate to a project folder on your hard drive and select Targa Image File from the Save As Type drop-down list box in the Browse Images For Output dialog box. Type in the filename FarmhouseandTree.tga and click the Save button to open the Targa Image Control dialog box (see Figure 8.5). If they are not already selected, click the 32 Bits-Per-Pixel radio button, check Compress, and check Pre-Multiplied Alpha. Click OK to save the file.

FIGURE 8.5

The Targa Image Control dialog box

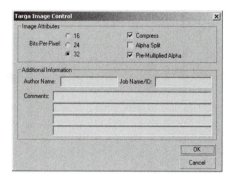

The oak tree that the courtyard is built around gets in the way of illustrating the background structure in Photoshop. The tree's many leaves and complex form make it difficult to mask without rendering it as a separate object. Let's turn off the tree for now and make another rendering.

8. Click the tree to select it; the leaves appear because the AEC Foliage object is set to stay in Viewport Canopy mode only when the object is unselected in order to save memory.

9. Right-click in the viewport to open the quad menus. Select Hide Selection from the display quad; the tree disappears.

10. Press Shift+Q to quickly render the scene again. The RFW appears; save the rendering as Farmhouse.tga with the same Targa options used previously.

The next step is to render the tree matted against all the other objects in the scene, as you did in Chapter 7. Use the Matte/Shadow material on everything but the tree.

11. Press M to open the Material Editor, and then press Ctrl+A to select all the objects. Click the Assign Material To Selection button in the Material Editor (see Figure 8.6). Since the Matte/Shadow material is the current material, it is assigned to the objects in the scene. In the Matte/Shadow Basic Parameters rollout, make sure that Opaque Alpha, Receive Shadows, and Affect Alpha are unchecked.

FIGURE 8.6

Assigning Matte/Shadow material

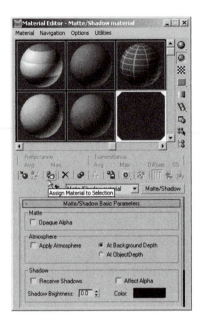

12. Click the Display tab of the Command Panel. Click the Unhide All button in the Hide rollout to again display the tree.

13. Press Shift+Q or click the Quick Render button on the main toolbar to generate another rendering. In the RFW save the image as `Tree.tga`, accepting the Targa options that save a premultiplied alpha channel. Close the RFW and Material Editor if they are open.

14. Press Ctrl+Z to undo until the original materials reappear on the objects in the viewport. Click the Unhide All button again.

15. Press H to open the Select Objects dialog box to turn on shadow casting in the sun before rendering the shadow element. Click Sun01 under Compass01 (part of the Sunlight system) and then click Select. Click the Modify tab of the Command Panel and check On in the Shadows group of the General Parameters rollout. Make sure that Area Shadows is selected in the dropdown list box.

NOTE   Area shadows are softer the further they are from the casting edge.

16. Press F10 to open the Render Scene dialog box if it is not already open. Click the Render Elements tab and open the rollout if necessary. Click the Add button and select Shadow from the Render Elements dialog box. Then click OK.

17. In the Render Scene dialog box, click the Browse button in the Selected Element Parameters group to open the Render Element Output File dialog box. Type the filename Shadow.tga and click Save. Click OK in the Targa Image Control dialog box. Figure 8.7 shows the resulting Render Scene dialog box.

    Render elements are post-processing effects that appear after the entire color image is rendered. Choose not to show the RFW because you are only interested in the shadows right now.

18. Click the Common tab in the Render Scene dialog box. Scroll down if necessary and clear Rendered Frame Window in the Render Output group because you don't need to see the color rendering.

19. Click the Render button. Be patient as the rendering proceeds. (It should take a few minutes.) When the processing is complete, a Shadow RFW window appears that is all black (black shadows against a black environment background color). Click the Display Alpha Channel button to see the shadow mask (see Figure 8.8).

20. Close the Shadow RFW, but keep the file open in VIZ.

FIGURE 8.7

The Render Elements tab in the Render Scene dialog box

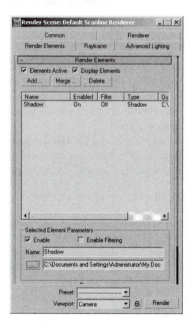

FIGURE 8.8
Rendering the Shadow
element

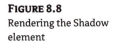

Rendering Special Image Channels with MAXScripts

3D programs generate what I'm calling special image channels internally during the process of calculating a rendering. ObjectID, Normal, and Zdepth are examples of special image channels in VIZ; these will later aid in maintaining pseudo–three-dimensionality and object-selectability in Photoshop. You will eventually render these channels as image files and then composite them as channels in the illustration project.

These channels represent data that separates the objects (ObjectID), determines which way all the geometrical surfaces in the model are oriented (Normal), and calculates the distance each object is from the picture plane (Zdepth).

NOTE   The Zdepth channel can alternatively be rendered as a render element.

VIZ's graphics buffer (G-Buffer) stores object numbers that identify nodes to be included in postprocessing effects. In other words, ObjectIDs are just a means to mark certain objects for postprocessing.

Accessing special image channels is an advanced topic in VIZ, so I've written a pair of MAXScripts that automate this process for you. We will assign unique ObjectIDs to every object in the scene with a MAXScript called ObjectIDAssigner. Then every object will be included on the ObjectID image channel when we render the scene using a second MAXScript called ChannelRenderer (along with other channels). Let's give it a whirl. So that you are aware of what the first MAXScript is automating, let's first take a look at object channels as they are stored in the G-Buffer.

   1. Click the Tree object in the viewport. Right-click and choose Properties from the transform quad.

2. On the General tab of the Object Properties dialog box (see Figure 8.9), notice that the Object Channel (also known as the ObjectID) is set to 0. You would have to set this to a nonzero value to include this object in the G-Buffer. Don't change anything yet, however; click Cancel.

FIGURE 8.9

The Object Properties
G-Buffer Object Channel

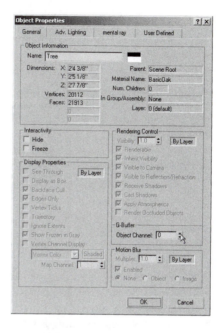

To differentiate the objects in the G-Buffer, you would have to give each and every object in the scene a unique ObjectID, a tedious process. Instead, use the ObjectIDAssigner MAXScript; it assigns sequential ObjectIDs to each object automatically.

3. Click the Utilities tab of the Command Panel. Click the MAXScript button in the Utilities rollout.

4. Click the Open Script button, and then select the file ObjectIDAssigner0.2.ms from the companion CD to open a MAXScript window showing the code (see Figure 8.10). Within this window, choose File ➢ Evaluate All. Then close the window.

Now that the code has been evaluated, it is part of VIZ. Run the utility.

5. In the MAXScript rollout, select ObjectID Assigner from the Utilities drop-down list box.

6. Click the Assign button once; that's it.

FIGURE 8.10
The ObjectIDAssigner
MAXScript window

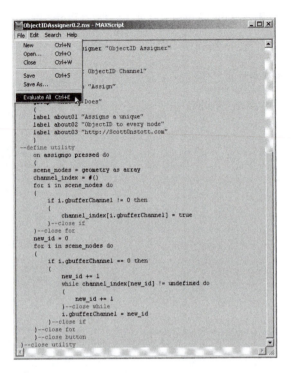

7. To verify that objects have unique ObjectIDs, choose an object at random and check its properties: Click the roof object in the viewport. Right-click and choose Properties. Verify that the object has a nonzero Object Channel number. Click Cancel.

8. Now use the second MAXScript to render the special image channels discussed earlier: Click the Open Script button in the MAXScript rollout and select the file ChannelRenderer0.3.ms from the companion CD. Figure 8.11 shows the MAXScript window. Even if you don't understand the language, scan the code to get a sense of what this script is doing; you will probably understand more than you might suppose. Choose File ➢ Evaluate All from the MAXScript window. Then close the window.

ChannelRenderer saves the ObjectID, Normal, and Zdepth image channels as Portable Network Graphics files (called ping, or .png, files) when it is applied as a render effect.

9. Choose Rendering ➢ Effects. Click the Add button, select ChannelRenderer from the list, and click OK.

10. Click the Get Path button (see Figure 8.12) in the Channel Renderer rollout at the bottom of the Environment And Effects dialog box. Select the project folder on your hard drive where you'd like to save the three .png images.

11. Click the Render button in the Render Scene dialog box and wait until the rendering is complete. Close all the open dialog boxes. Close VIZ without saving the file.

FIGURE 8.11

The ChannelRenderer
MAXScript window

FIGURE 8.12

Choosing where to save
the rendered images

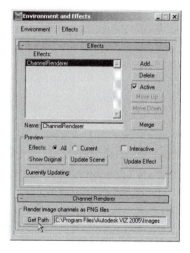

Now you have rendered the special channels and elements needed for masking in preparation for painting. Just as with house painting, most of the effort goes into the prep work. You'll integrate these files into Photoshop and use them to mask off areas that you'll eventually paint.

Figure 8.13 shows all the rendered files you have made for this project in VIZ. Once you've completed these steps, you should have the following files:

Filename	Description
Normal.png	Represents all the surfaces in the model in different gray tones regardless of material or object membership
ObjectID.png	Reveals each object in rendering as a distinct grayscale value
Zdepth.png	Represents 3D space in grayscale, with objects in the foreground fading from white to black as they recede from the picture plane
Farmhouse.tga	Four-channel (RGB plus alpha) render of all buildings (without tree)
FarmhouseandTree.tga	Four-channel (RGB plus alpha) render of all buildings plus tree
Shadow.tga	Render of shadows only
Tree.tga	Render of tree matted against all other objects

FIGURE 8.13
Rendered files

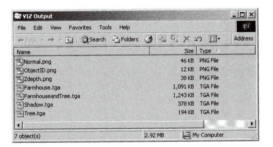

Integrating and Painting in Photoshop

When painting a house, most of the work goes into preparing the building's surfaces to receive paint and masking off the rest of the surfaces you want to protect. Digitally illustrating a 3D model is much the same. Before you can paint, you'll need to integrate the various files generated in VIZ into a single Photoshop document. You'll then create new layers, mask them off, and organize them before you apply digital paint with a brush.

Integrating the Renderings

You generated multiple images in VIZ showing different aspects of the 3D model, rendered from the same point of view. How you integrate these depends on how you will use them in Photoshop to create the illustration: in some cases, you will composite the renderings as masked layers, and in others you will save them as channels.

COMPOSITING MASKED LAYERS

You can composite the Farmhouse, Tree, and Shadow renderings the way you learned in the last chapter; with layer masks coming from their alpha channels. In addition, you will paste a photograph of a cloudy sky into the background.

1. Launch Photoshop if it is not already open. Open the file `Farmhouse.tga` from your hard drive. All the renderings are also provided in the VIZ Output subfolder within the Chapter 8 folder on the companion CD in case you are jumping in here.

2. Choose File ➤ Save As and change the Format drop-down list box to Photoshop in the Save As dialog box. Save the file as `Farmhouse.psd` in the project folder on your hard drive. Make sure Alpha Channels is checked in the Save Options group and then click Save. This file will be your working illustration project document into which you'll integrate other images.

TIP You can use the Convert Alpha To Layer Mask action recorded in Chapter 7 in place of steps 3 through 6. If you assigned the F12 function key to the action then, you can now use that shortcut to execute the action.

3. Select the Channels palette. Click the Alpha 1 channel.

4. Click the Load Channel As Selection button at the bottom of the Channels palette to display the marching ants. Click the RGB channel.

5. Select the Layers palette. Hold down the Alt key and double-click the Background layer to convert it to a normal layer called Layer 0.

6. Click the Add Layer Mask button at the bottom of the Layers palette. The selection is converted into a layer mask, and the sky turns transparent in the document window (see Figure 8.14).

FIGURE 8.14
Masking the farmhouse with its alpha channel

7. Rename Layer 0 to the name of the file (Farmhouse in this case). Click the Layer thumbnail to select it and deselect the layer mask. This layer is ready to be integrated into your illustration project.

Open the rendering of the isolated tree, and convert its alpha channel into a layer mask before integrating it into the Photoshop document.

8. Open `Tree.tga` and repeat steps 3 through 7, renaming the resulting layer to Tree.

9. Drag the Tree layer from `Tree.tga` into `Farmhouse.psd`. Then use the Move tool (shortcut key V) to drag the Tree layer until it snaps into position both horizontally and vertically.

10. Open `Shadow.tga` and repeat steps 3 through 7, renaming the resulting layer to Shadow.

11. Drag the Shadow layer from `Shadow.tga` into `Farmhouse.psd`. Then use the Move tool (shortcut key V) to drag the Shadow layer until it snaps into position both horizontally and vertically (see Figure 8.15).

Paste a photograph of a cloudy sky behind the other layers and transform it to fit the composition.

12. Close `Shadow.tga` and then open `Clouds.jpg` from your hard drive.

13. Press Ctrl+A and then Ctrl+C to select all the pixels and copy them to the Clipboard. Close `Clouds.jpg`.

14. Create a new layer and rename it Sky. Drag this layer to the bottom of the Layers palette. Press Ctrl+V to paste the contents of the Clipboard onto the Sky layer.

15. Press Ctrl+T to activate the Free Transform command. On the Options bar, click the Maintain Aspect Ratio button and then click inside the Width text box. Set Width to 77% (press and hold the Down arrow key, or type **77** and press Enter). Notice that Height also reads 77% because you maintained the aspect ratio. Click the Commit button.

16. Press V to select the Move tool. Drag the Sky layer and center it from right to left. Then drag it up so the lower edge of the clouds are just below the buildings, as shown in Figure 8.16. Make sure not to reveal the edge of the background in the final composition.

FIGURE 8.15
Compositing Farm-
house, Tree, and Shadow
layers

FIGURE 8.16
Transforming the photo-
graphic background

PASTING IMAGES INTO CHANNELS

In contrast to compositing masked layers, the renderings containing special image channels from VIZ will be literally integrated as channels in Photoshop. These special channels are not meant to be composited directly as layers in the final illustration, but will act as aids during the illustration process that you will repeatedly refer to. Let's get started integrating the images as channels in Photoshop.

1. Open the file ObjectID.png from your hard drive (see Figure 8.17). This image reveals each object in the rendering as a distinct grayscale value. It may be hard to tell objects apart when their grayscale values are similar, but later you will be able to select these object areas separately using the Magic Wand.

FIGURE 8.17
The ObjectID channel

2. Press Ctrl+A and then Ctrl+C to copy all the ObjectID pixels to the Clipboard. Close ObjectID.png.

3. Select Farmhouse.psd and click the Channels palette.

4. Click the Create A New Channel button at the bottom of the Channels palette and then press Ctrl+V to paste the pixels from the Clipboard onto the new channel.

5. Rename the Alpha 2 channel ObjectID. Hereafter you'll be able to select this channel by pressing Ctrl+5 without having to select the Channels palette.

6. Open the file `Normal.png` from your hard drive (see Figure 8.18). This image represents all the surfaces in the model in different gray tones, regardless of material or object membership. You will use this channel to help create selections for masking in the next section.

7. Press Ctrl+A and then Ctrl+C to copy all the Normal pixels to the Clipboard. Close `Normal.png`.

8. Select `Farmhouse.psd`, click the Create A New Channel button at the bottom of the Channels palette, and then press Ctrl+V to paste the pixels from the Clipboard onto the new channel.

FIGURE 8.18
The Normal channel

9. Rename the Alpha 2 channel Normal. Hereafter you'll be able to select this channel by pressing Ctrl+6 without having to select the Channels palette.

10. Open the file `Zdepth.png` from your hard drive (see Figure 8.19). This image represents 3D space in grayscale, with objects in the foreground fading from white to black as they recede from the picture plane. You will use this channel later in this chapter to create a fog or a shadow that accentuates the spatial quality of the illustration.

NOTE The Z in Zdepth refers not to the spatial world Z axis (which is up), but to the axis that runs along the camera-target vector, away from the picture plane.

11. Press Ctrl+A and then Ctrl+C to copy all the Zdepth pixels to the Clipboard. Close `Zdepth.png`.

12. Select `Farmhouse.psd`, click the Create A New Channel button at the bottom of the Channels palette, and then press Ctrl+V to paste the pixels from the Clipboard onto the new channel.

FIGURE 8.19
The Zdepth channel

FIGURE 8.19
The Zdepth channel

13. Rename the Alpha 2 channel Zdepth. Hereafter you'll be able to select this channel by pressing Ctrl+7 without having to select the Channels palette.

14. Press Ctrl+D to deselect. Then press Ctrl+~ to select the RGB channels (see Figure 8.20).

15. Click the Layers palette. Note that no new layers have been created while you have been adding data to the Channels palette. Press Ctrl+S to save your work. If you're going to continue working through the following sections, you can leave this file open for now.

FIGURE 8.20
The Channels Palette

You'll be using both the ObjectID and Normal channels to make selections that will be converted to painting masks. The alpha channel provides the outline of all the structures, so it is always useful for masking a background image. You can optionally use the Zdepth channel to create a 3D fog that gets thicker in the distance.

Masking and Painting Surfaces

Now that all the renderings from VIZ have been integrated into a working Photoshop document, you are ready to start masking and painting. This tutorial must follow a particular sequence of steps to be useful. However, I encourage you to experiment and play as you illustrate; make up your own steps once you get a feel for it. Don't be afraid to throw layers away and try different combinations of masks, colors, brushes, and brush strokes to get what you are looking for.

MASKING WITH CHANNELS

In the following steps, we'll use the special channels pasted into the document in the previous section to make selections. Often the ObjectID and Normal channels are both used to select a particular surface that you'd like to protect with a mask. The selection is then converted to a masked layer, ready to receive paint. You'll mask a couple of layers manually before saving an action that automates some of the prep work to save time.

1. If you have `Farmhouse.psd` open from the previous exercise, you can continue here; if not, open it from your hard drive before continuing. This file is also provided on the companion CD if you are jumping in here.

2. Click the Layers palette if it is not already selected. Toggle the Shadow and Tree layers off by clicking their eye icons. Select the Farmhouse layer. Create a layer set by clicking the Create A New Set button at the bottom of the Layers palette, and rename the new set to Walls.

   Select one of the wall surfaces in the tower using the Normal channel.

3. Click the Channels palette. Select the Normal channel or press Ctrl+6. Press W to select the Magic Wand tool. On the Options bar, click the New Selection Mode button, type **20** into the Tolerance text box, and check Anti-aliased and Contiguous. Clear the Use All Layers option.

4. Click a point inside the tower wall, as shown in Figure 8.21. The marching ants appear on the selected wall surface.

   Notice that part of the window is selected. We can subtract these areas from the selection using the information contained in the ObjectID channel.

5. Press Ctrl+5 to select the ObjectID channel. Click the Subtract From Selection button on the Options bar.

6. Click inside the window and shutter area that is within the current selection. You'll have to click three times to remove each shutter and the glass from the selection (see Figure 8.22).

FIGURE 8.21
Click with the Magic
Wand in the Normal
channel, within the wall.

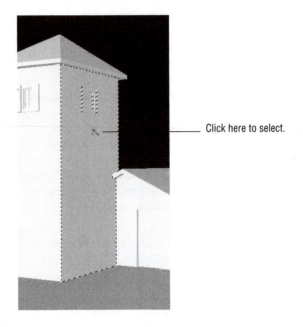

Click here to select.

FIGURE 8.22
Subtracting from
the selection using the
ObjectID channel: click
within the window
pane and each of the
shutter areas.

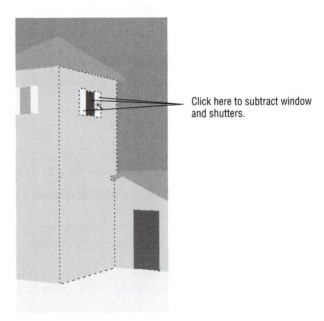

Click here to subtract window
and shutters.

7. Click the Layers palette. Press Ctrl+~ to select the RGB channels. Notice that you didn't have to be on the Channels palette to change channels. Create a new layer and then add a layer mask; click the Create A New Layer and Add Layer Mask buttons at the bottom of the Layers palette. The selection disappears once the mask is created. Deselect the layer mask by clicking the layer thumbnail; this step is necessary prior to painting or the paint goes on the mask.

NOTE   You will be creating many layers as you mask individual surfaces to receive paint. It would be too much to give each one of these layers a descriptive name. Therefore, organize at a higher level with named layer sets instead.

The masked layer you made in the previous step is ready to receive paint. However, let's hold off on painting a while longer until we mask a few more layers and learn how to automate the prep work.

Remember that the ObjectID channel shows distinct shades of gray for each object in the 3D scene. You can select every pixel of a particular shade of gray using the Magic Wand with zero tolerance in noncontiguous mode.

8. Press Ctrl+5 to select the ObjectID channel. Press W to select the Magic Wand. On the Options bar, click New Selection mode, set Tolerance to 0, and clear Contiguous.

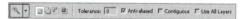

9. Click a point on the wall of the structure in the background, as shown in Figure 8.23.

FIGURE 8.23
Selecting an object using
the Magic Wand

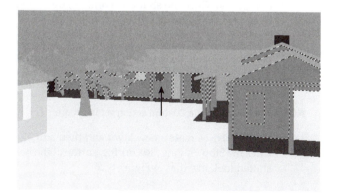

10. Press Ctrl+~ to return to the RGB channels. Create a new layer and then add a layer mask. Click Layer 2's layer thumbnail to prepare it to receive paint.

    Let's automate the repetitive steps with an action. Before you begin recording, you'll have to make another selection on a special channel because this step won't be part of the action.

11. Press Ctrl+6 to select the Normal channel. On the Options bar, click the New Selection button, change Tolerance to 20, and check Contiguous.

12. Hold down the Shift key and click two points inside the wall surfaces, as shown in Figure 8.24.

FIGURE 8.24
Selecting additional
Normal surfaces

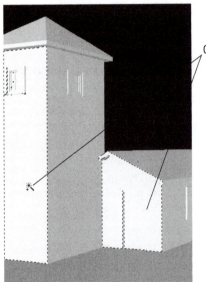

Click once on each of these surfaces.

13. Press Ctrl+5 to select the ObjectID channel. On the Options bar, click the Subtract From Selection button. Click the shutters, window, door, and roof edge inside the selection to remove these areas (see Figure 8.25).

14. Click the Actions palette. Click the Create A New Action button to open the New Action dialog box. In the Name text box, type **Prepare for Painting**. Choose Custom from the Set drop-down list box if it's available; otherwise, choose Default Actions. Select F12 as the Function Key and check Shift. Click Record.

NOTE We created the Custom action set in Chapter 7.

15. Press Ctrl+~. Create a new layer and then add a layer mask. Click Layer 3's layer thumbnail. Click the Stop Playing/Recording button at the bottom of the Actions palette, and your palette should look like that in Figure 8.26.

FIGURE 8.25

Subtract these areas from the selection with the ObjectID channel.

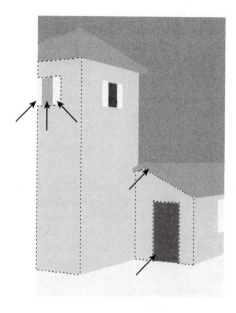

FIGURE 8.26

After recording the Prepare For Painting action

16. Now much of the prep work is automated. For each layer you want to mask, make a selection and play the action: Use the Normal (Ctrl+5) and/or ObjectID (Ctrl+6) channels to make a selection, adding or subtracting from its boundary with the Magic Wand as you see fit. Press Shift+F12, and you'll be ready for painting.

The rest of this project's masking is left for you to complete. I recommend making layer sets for roof, windows, doors, posts, and ground. (You'll need these sets to continue following along with the instructions later in this chapter.) Fill the layer sets with sequentially named layers as you mask surfaces. You can either mask these layers now or wait until after you have done some painting in the next section.

CHOOSING COLORS AND BRUSHES AND APPLYING PAINT

Creative freedom in the illustration project really begins when you choose a paint color and a brush. Although selecting a discrete color palette is a decision that limits this freedom, doing so can lead to a distinctive visual style. You'll load a custom color swatch library containing a preselected color palette for the illustration.

An almost limitless combination of brush parameters gives you a wide range of painted expression, including shape, hardness, spacing, textures, dual brush tips, scattering, and dynamic properties, plus flow and airbrush capabilities. In this tutorial, you'll use an off-the-shelf brush from one of the brush libraries that come with Photoshop. On to the fun part!

1. Create a background layer to act as the paper that you paint on: Create a new layer, and drag it to the bottom of the layer stack. Press D to set the default colors, and then press Ctrl+Delete to fill the layer with the background color (white). Choose Layer ➢ New ➢ Background From Layer.

TIP You can optionally fill the background with a color and/or texture to simulate real canvas or watercolor paper, for example.

2. Press B to select the Brush tool. Drag the Brushes palette out of the palette well, making it a floating palette. Click the triangle button in the upper-right corner of the floating Brushes palette, and choose Dry Media Brushes from the palette menu. Click OK in the warning dialog box. Scroll to the bottom of the Brushes Presets and click Pastel Medium Tip (see Figure 8.27). Drag the Master Diameter slider to 50 px.

FIGURE 8.27
The Floating Brushes palette

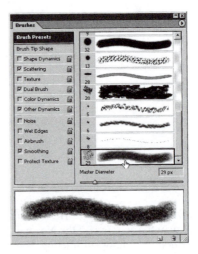

3. Click the Swatches palette. Click the triangle button at the top right, and choose Replace Swatches from the palette menu. Browse to the Chapter 8 folder on the companion CD, select the file `Project Color Swatches.aco`, and click the Load button in the Replace dialog box.

The custom swatches contain three versions (dark, medium, and light) for each of the following hues: red, yellow, green, blue, and gray. These are separated by black spacer swatches, so the colors we are interested in line up in columns in the Swatches palette (see Figure 8.28).

FIGURE 8.28
The custom color swatches for the farmhouse scene

NOTE   Before you begin painting, spend some time choosing a color palette in your own projects; add these colors to the Swatches palette and save it as a swatch library. Alternatively, you might find color inspiration by opening a piece of art you'd like to emulate and using the eyedropper to sample its colors.

4. Click the eye icons of the Farmhouse and Sky layers in the Layers palette to toggle them off. Select Layer 1 in the Walls layer set. Press the backslash key (\) to toggle rubylith mode on. This mode displays the currently selected layer's mask in transparent red and is helpful to visualize which portions of a layer are masked (rubylith) and which are revealed (white).

5. Click the Dark Red swatch to load this color into the foreground swatch in the toolbox. On the Options bar, change Flow to 50%. Make a few brush strokes on the surface that is revealed through the mask (see Figure 8.29). Be careful not to completely cover the surface; try to leave some white areas that do not have any paint applied.

FIGURE 8.29
Making brush strokes

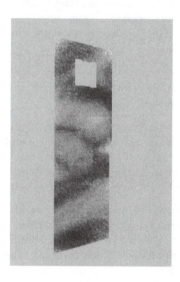

6. On the Options bar, turn Opacity down to 50% and make another few brush strokes. Paint applied with lower opacity appears lighter.

7. Press X to exchange the foreground and background swatches in the toolbox so that white is in the foreground. Make additional brush strokes, and notice how they seem to remove paint from the surface (because you are painting in white). Press the backslash key (\) to toggle rubylith mode off.

8. Select the next layer (Layer 2). Press the backslash key (\) again to toggle rubylith mode on; this time it displays the mask from the current layer.

9. Press X to exchange the foreground and background swatches again. Select a color from the Swatches palette (Light Red in this case). Change Opacity back up to 100%, and leave Flow at 50%. Paint a few brush strokes on the new layer.

10. Change Opacity to 50%, and paint again with lighter strokes. Press X, and then make white brush strokes to effectively remove paint from the layer (see Figure 8.30).

FIGURE 8.30
Painting another masked layer

In general, start by painting at 100% opacity and 50% flow. Then, decrease opacity to paint in lighter shades of the same hue. If you go too far and build up too much paint on the layer so that it looks like a flat color, paint in white to remove color from the masked layer. For more variation, change the brush size and hardness by pressing the left and right square bracket keys in combination with the Shift key.

TIP Select a different preset brush shape or design your own in the Brushes palette for very different looking strokes.

Digital painting is really an art form that takes practice to perfect. There is no "right way" to paint; you are free to experiment and find a methodology that works for the look you desire. All your masked layers ensure that you will never "paint outside the lines." However, if you want paint to spill out beyond its masked border, just click the layer mask thumbnail and paint in white to increase the borders within which you can paint.

11. Continue painting each prepared masked layer, repeating steps 8 through 10 for each one. Use the colors available in the Swatches palette, and vary your painting technique to avoid areas of flat color where too much paint can build up. Figure 8.31 shows one possible result. Your results will be different because it is impossible to exactly duplicate the nuances of brush strokes.

USING LAYER STYLE EFFECTS

As you learned in Chapter 5, "Presenting Plans," Chapter 6, "Elevating the Elevation," and Chapter 7, layer style effects are a powerful way to add character to your compositions. Illustrations can also benefit from judicious use of these effects. Let's add texture and shading to the ground plane using pattern and gradient overlays.

1. Press Ctrl+5 to switch to the ObjectID channel. Use the Magic Wand to make a selection; press W and use a Tolerance of 20, with Anti-Aliased and Contiguous checked. Click in the ground area in front of the building.

2. Press Shift+F12 to prepare this selection as a masked layer with your action recorded in the Masking With Channels section.

FIGURE 8.31
The painted Illustration

FIGURE 8.31
The painted Illustration

3. Press D to set the default colors. Press Alt+Backspace to fill the layer with black.

4. Drag the new layer into the Ground layer set. If you haven't yet made this layer set, do so now. Rename the layer Grass.

5. Apply layer style effects; double-click just to the right of the name Grass in the Layers palette to open the Layer Style dialog box. Apply the following effects (see Figure 8.32):

   Pattern Overlay   Apply the Green With Fibers pattern from the Color Paper pattern library. Use 100% Scale and 100% Opacity.

   Gradient Overlay   Overlay Blend Mode, 100% Opacity, Black To White gradient, clear Reverse, Linear Style, 90° Angle, 100% Scale.

FIGURE 8.32
Layer style effects

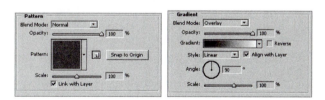

Change the opacity of the Grass layer to 75% after you apply the layer style effects.

FINISHING TOUCHES

There are just a few finishing touches to add before the illustration is complete: the tree, shadows, the sky backdrop, and some fog.

1. Toggle the Tree layer on. The rendered 3D tree looks out of place in the illustration. Notice that there are also white halos around the leaves. Right-click the Tree layer mask and select Add Layer Mask To Selection from the context menu.

2. You can eliminate the white halos around any composited layer by enlarging and feathering the selection that defines its mask. Choose Select ➢ Modify ➢ Expand, enter **2 pixels** in the Expand dialog box, and click OK.

3. Choose Select ➢ Feather. Enter **1 pixel** in the Feather dialog box and click OK. This softens the expanded selection border.

4. Create a new layer and add a layer mask. Click the layer thumbnail and rename the new layer Painted Tree.

5. Toggle the Tree layer off and make sure the Painted Tree layer is selected. Paint the tree using shades of green from the Swatches palette and the brush of your choice. Figure 8.33 shows the result.

FIGURE 8.33
Painting the tree

6. Toggle on the Shadow layer by clicking its eye icon in the Layers palette. Select the Shadow layer and turn down its opacity to 75% to tone down the shadows slightly.

7. Right-click the mask thumbnail on the Farmhouse layer. Select Add Layer Mask To Selection from the context menu. Press Shift+Ctrl+I to invert the selection.

8. Select the Sky layer and toggle off the Farmhouse layer. Click the Add Layer Mask button at the bottom of the Layers palette, and then click the layer thumbnail to select it. The Sky layer fits within the composition without overlapping other layers.

    It looks a bit strange to have a photographic sky in the illustrated scene. You can make the sky take on a hand-painted look with artistic filtering.

9. Choose Filter ➢ Filter Gallery to open the Filter Gallery dialog box. If there are any effects in the effect layer stack, delete them by clicking the Delete Effect Layer button, repeatedly if necessary (see Chapter 1, "The Basics"). Click the Create New Effect Layer button, expand the Brush Strokes folder, and select Accented Edges. Set Edge Width to 1, Edge Brightness to 33, and Smoothness to 4.

10. Click the Create New Effect Layer button again. Select the Angled Strokes filter in the Brush Strokes folder. Set Direction Balance to 28, Stroke Length to 25, and Sharpness to 6.

11. Once more click the Create New Effect Layer button. Expand the Artistic folder and select the Dry Brush filter. Set Brush Size to 2, Brush Detail to 4, and Texture to 1.

12. Add additional effect layers and/or tweak the settings given in steps 9 through 11 if desired to produce a hand-illustrated look for the Sky layer. You can zoom in and out by holding down the Alt and/or Ctrl keys while clicking in the preview window of the Filter Gallery dialog box. When satisfied, click OK (see Figure 8.34).

Use the Zdepth channel to create a fog that gets thicker as it recedes from the picture plane.

13. Click the Channels palette and select the Zdepth channel. Click the Load Channel As Selection button at the bottom of the Channels palette. The marching ants appear to describe a boundary, but be aware that some pixels (beyond that boundary) are partially selected according to the grayscale values in the channel.

14. Click the RGB channel and then click the Layers palette. Select the Shadow layer at the top of the layer stack, and then click the Create A New Layer button at the bottom of the Layers palette. Rename this new layer Fog.

15. Click the Add Layer Mask button at the bottom of the Layers palette. Press Ctrl+I to invert the mask. Click the Fog layer thumbnail. Press D to set the default colors. Press Ctrl+Delete to fill the Fog layer with white.

FIGURE 8.34
The Filter Gallery

16. Turn the opacity of the Fog layer down to 75% to reduce the density of the fog. Figure 8.35 shows the completed illustration. A version of this image is in the color section.

17. Save your work as `Farmhouse2.psd`. If you're going to continue working through the following sections, you can leave this file open for now.

Congratulations on completing the illustration! Hopefully this tutorial has provided you with inspiration to illustrate your own projects with Photoshop. Once you practice masking with the special channels, it becomes second nature, and you'll be able to "paint within the lines" and create illustrations from 3D models easily.

FIGURE 8.35
The completed illustration

Working in Black and White

Black and white is a medium that is often neglected in presentations today considering the level of public fascination with photo-realistic 3D color renderings. However, black and white remains a powerful medium with benefits worth considering for your projects. Black-and-white images focus attention on form and composition because color is removed from the picture.

Rather than simply convert an RGB image to grayscale, you'll have more control over the conversion process using a Channel Mixer adjustment layer. You'll see how to add drama to a grayscale image by mixing channels creatively.

Sketchy black-and-white illustrations can sometimes convey emotion more effectively than glossy photo-realistic color presentations. You can simulate the look of hand-drawn black-and-white ink drawings, etchings, and engravings using a combination of Sketch filters. Let's take a look.

1. If you have `Farmhouse2.psd` open from the previous exercise, you can continue here; if not, open that file from your hard drive before continuing. This file is also provided on the companion CD if you are jumping in here.

2. Make sure the top layer in the Layers palette is selected; in this case it is Fog. Click the Create New Fill Or Adjustment Layer button at the bottom of the Layers palette to apply a Channel Mixer adjustment layer.

3. Check Monochrome at the bottom of the Channel Mixer dialog box. Drag the Red channel slider to +100%, Green to +60%, and Blue to –60% (see Figure 8.36). This combination subtracts the blue component from the other two channels. Furthermore, notice that the sum of all three channels is exactly 100%.

FIGURE 8.36

The Channel Mixer adjustment Layer

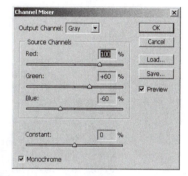

You have flexibility with the Channel Mixer. As long as the sum of the red, green, and blue channels adds up to 100%, the image will maintain the same exposure level. However, each image has different data stored on its three color channels, so you'll have to experiment in your illustration by mixing the three channels in a way that is aesthetically pleasing to your eye.

4. Try mixing Red at +40%, Green at –40% and Blue at 100%. Try another combination that sums to 100% until you are satisfied with the results that appear in the document window. Click OK to close the Channel Mixer dialog box.

5. Create a new layer and rename it Composite B&W. Press Alt+Shift+Ctrl+E to stamp all the visible layers onto this layer without flattening. This layer contains a record of all your work to date.

Let's explore artistic possibilities by applying Sketch filters to your black-and-white composite image. It's always a good idea to duplicate a layer before you alter it, so you can easily dispose of it (without altering your compositing) if you don't like the results.

6. Press Ctrl+J to duplicate the Composite B&W layer. Rename this layer Filtered. Choose Filter ➢ Filter Gallery to open the Filter Gallery dialog box. If there are any effects in the effect layer stack, delete them by clicking the Delete Effect Layer button, repeatedly if necessary. Click the Create New Effect Layer button, expand the Sketch folder, and select Halftone. Set Size to 1, Contrast to 9, and Pattern Type to Dot.

7. Select the Graphic Pen filter. Set Stroke Length to 6, Light/Dark Balance to 52, and Stroke Direction to Right Diagonal.

8. Add additional effect layers and/or tweak the settings given in steps 6 and 7 if desired to produce a traditional artistic look for the Filtered layer. When satisfied, click OK (see Figure 8.37).

If you think the filters applied in the last step are okay, but perhaps too much of a good thing, try using Fade to reduce their cumulative effect.

9. Choose Edit ➢ Fade Filter Gallery. Drag the Opacity slider down to 35% to partially fade out the filters you applied in steps 6 through 8.

10. Save your work as `Farmhouse3.psd`. Figure 8.38 shows the black-and-white illustration. If you're going to continue working through the last section, you can leave this file open for now.

FIGURE 8.37
The Filter Gallery
sketch filters

FIGURE 8.38
The filtered black-and-
white Illustration

Reproducing Grayscale Images with Colored Inks

Anyone who has studied traditional photography is probably aware of the beauty of old-fashioned photographs. For example, sepia-toned prints have a pleasing antique feel and warmth that is uncommon in computer graphics. You can simulate this effect in Photoshop using Duotone color mode.

In Photoshop, Duotone color mode collectively represents monotone, duotone, tritone, and quadtone prints. These terms refer to the practice of printing grayscale images with one- to four-colored inks.

Photoshop does not maintain separate channels for these inks like it does in RGB and CMYK modes. Instead, the tonal information in duotones come from a single channel containing 256 value levels only (similar to grayscale). Each ink is allocated a portion of the tonal range in the Duotone Options dialog box using curves. Let's take a look at how this works.

1. If you have `Farmhouse3.psd` open from the previous exercise, you can continue here; if not, open that file from your hard drive before continuing. This file is also provided on the companion CD if you are jumping in here.

2. Click the Layers palette if it is not already active. Click the triangle button, and select Flatten Image from the palette menu. Click OK in the warning dialog box to discard hidden layers.

WARNING   You cannot convert directly from RGB to Duotone color mode without first converting to grayscale in order to discard the additional color channels.

3. Choose Image ➤ Mode ➤ Grayscale. Click OK to the warning dialog box asking whether you want to discard color information. The black-and-white image was stored with RGB channels previously, and now it has only one Gray channel carrying the tonal information.

4. Click the Channels palette. Notice that in addition to the Gray channel, special channels still appear from the previous exercise. Delete the Alpha 1, ObjectID, Normal, and Zdepth channels by dragging and dropping them on the Trash icon at the bottom of the Channels palette.

5. Choose Image ➤ Mode ➤ Duotone to open the Duotone Options dialog box. Select Tritone (three inks) from the Type drop-down list box. Click the Load button to open the Load dialog box, as shown in Figure 8.39. Navigate through your file system to the `Photoshop CS` folder and load the following preset file:

    `\Presets\Duotones\TRITONE\Process Tritones\BMY sepia 1.ado`

FIGURE 8.39
Loading a set of duotone options

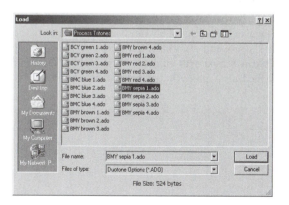

6. The preset file loads three ink colors and curves into the Duotone Options dialog box (see Figure 8.40). You can alter the inks by clicking their color swatches and choosing new colors from the Color Picker if desired.

FIGURE 8.40
The Duotone Options
dialog box

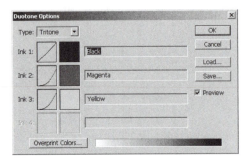

7. Click the curve thumbnail next to Ink 3 (Yellow). The Duotone Curve dialog box (see Figure 8.41) lets you determine which potion of the tonal range this ink will print. Type **50** in the 60% text box to increase the strength of yellow ink in the midtones. Click OK, and then click OK again to close both dialog boxes.

FIGURE 8.41
Set the strength of an
ink in the Duotone Curve
dialog box.

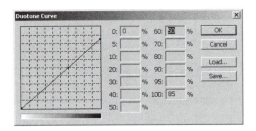

You are left with a pleasing sepia-toned image that can be reproduced with black, magenta, and yellow inks on a professional printing press. If you want to print this image on an RGB printer, convert from Duotone color mode to RGB to preserve the tint.

Summary

You have been exposed to many non–photo-realistic illustration techniques in this chapter, including advanced masking of 3D model surfaces and methods of applying digital paint. In addition, black-and-white and duotone illustrations were considered and explored. Your options for presentation have increased with this knowledge and hopefully will expand your artistic potential using Photoshop. In the last chapter you will focus on issues related to showing your hard work to clients electronically.

Chapter 9

Showing Work to Your Clients

Showing work to your clients can be a stressful yet often rewarding experience. Soliciting client feedback through a visual design presentation could result in project approval or call for further refinement. Depending on where you are in the continuing design process, you might choose to display work in a variety of formats at different times, based on the strengths of each medium.

Printed media is an excellent way to get your point across, in large-format boardroom presentations and in smaller marketing packets or brochures. But in some circumstances glossy prints may seem too finalized (or too expensive) to a client.

If you want to show a quick progress snapshot, e-mailing an image to your client might be the way to go. But filling mailboxes with large files can be bad manners; there are specific tricks to preparing images for effective e-mail. You can also consider building a project website or an online gallery, easily accessible by anyone to whom you send a link. Although creating an entire site is beyond the scope of this book, in this chapter you'll learn how to create optimized graphic web pages and even rollover effects with ImageReady for improved online marketing of your designs. And I'll discuss slide shows: whether in Photoshop itself or as Acrobat PDF presentations, they're another time-tested way to present images.

This chapter concludes with an important section on intellectual property. You'll find tips on adding metadata and watermarks, password protecting, and encrypting secure access levels to your confidential data.

- ◆ Producing Prints
- ◆ E-Mailing Images
- ◆ Generating Web Photo Galleries
- ◆ Creating Optimized Web Pages with ImageReady
- ◆ Presenting Slide Shows
- ◆ Protecting Your Intellectual Property

Producing Prints

So you have completed your masterpiece and want to print it? It can be satisfying to see your hard work emerge from the printer. Not to spoil your moment, but hold the press! The rapid adoption of personal computers by the masses had some thinkers speculating that the digital age would be "the end of paper." Instead, stark reality has shown an exponential rise in paper consumption. The reason is highly correlated with the habit of impulsively printing without due consideration.

Before you send your file to a printer, there is a work flow to follow that reduces the need to print a document many times before it meets your expectations. If you follow the printing work flow presented in this section, you should be able to digitally proof and preview and end up printing your final document only once.

This book assumes that you are printing on a desktop or floor model printer such as an inkjet, a laser, a thermal, an electrostatic, or a dye-sublimation device. In general, these devices accept input in the form of RGB color data.

TIP   Do not convert your document to CMYK if printing on a consumer or professional-level digital print device. These are designed to receive RGB data and internally convert to the device color space (based on the number of inks used).

However, if you are planning to use a commercial printer (using offset lithography, gravure plate setter, prepress, or any other image setter technology), contact the technical people at the service bureau and agree on a custom work flow. Often commercial printers want you to convert to CMYK color mode, but not necessarily so (see Chapter 2, "Working with Color").

Let's get started with the printing work flow on a desktop printer.

1. Open the file Illustration.tif from the companion CD. You will print the illustration from Chapter 8 in this tutorial.

    The next three steps are not strictly necessary in order to print, but they are recommended if you are serious about color accuracy.

2. Ensure that you have a color-accurate system. You might need to characterize or calibrate your monitor, output device, and/or print media for accurate color rendition. See Chapter 2 for more information.

3. Once you are satisfied with your color environment, soft-proof the document to see how it will look in the output color space on the screen. See Chapter 2 for a tutorial.

4. If you perceive that changes should be made before printing, color correct the image next (see Chapter 3, "Digital Darkroom Skills").

    The next step will set the image resolution for the planned print quality. Traditionally, web graphics are shown at 72 pixels/inch, and printed work has a minimum of at least 200 pixels/inch resolution. If the image's pixel dimensions allow you to still reach your target document size, using greater resolution (300 dpi on up) yields higher print quality up to the resolution limit of your printer. See Chapter 1, "The Basics," to review these relationships.

5. Choose Image ➢ Image Size to open the Image Size dialog box. Clear Resample Image if it is already checked. Change the height parameter to 3 inches. Notice that Width automatically changes to 4 inches and that Resolution changes to 256 pixels/inch (see Figure 9.1). This resolution is sufficient for printing at a good quality level, although the document size is still quite small. Click OK.

    If you find that increasing the resolution to print quality results in a document size that is too small for you needs, the best solution is to go back to the source of your image and acquire more pixels. The source of your image may be a digital photo, drawing, or 3D model, for example.

FIGURE 9.1

Trading document
size for resolution

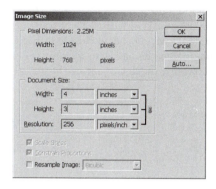

If the image source is a photo (see Chapter 3 and Chapter 4, "You and Your Entourage"), you might be able to adjust your digital camera's settings to capture more pixels or use a better camera (with more megapixels). Either way, reshoot the photo to start with more information from the real world.

TIP Photoshop's Photomerge command (choose File ➢ Automate ➢ Photomerge) allows you to stitch together multiple low-resolution images, resulting in a seamless higher document size composite. Stitch multiple telephoto images together to yield an image that covers your desired field of view, and then trade the large document size for higher resolution.

If the image source was an AutoCAD plan or elevation drawing (see Chapter 5, "Presenting Plans," or Chapter 6) or an Autodesk VIZ 3D model (see Chapter 7, "Creative Compositing," and Chapter 8, "Illustrating Architecture"), you might have to go back and basically start over to end up printing a large document at sufficient resolution. Convert the source drawing or 3D scene to an image having a greater number of pixels in the source application, and then proceed to colorize, composite, or illustrate the project in Photoshop.

Not having to start your project over is why it is so important to plan ahead for a target pixel size at the beginning of your project. However, perfect forethought is not always possible, and you can find yourself faced with resampling to reach a larger document size at the last minute.

Remember that resampling an image to much larger pixel dimensions does not generally increase the quality of the image. When you add pixels through resampling, the existing pixel colors are interpolated to yield the new pixel colors. For example, using the Image Size command to double document size (while holding resolution constant) usually results in a blurrier image compared with the original, because a large number of pixel colors had to be "guessed" by an algorithm in Photoshop.

One trick might be extremely helpful to you to reduce the amount of "guessing" when resampling. Instead of resampling in huge jumps (such as doubling), try increasing the document size by 10% at a shot. This way, Photoshop doesn't have to interpolate (guess) many pixels at each jump, so it can base each interpolation more on "real" data. Let's try this technique next.

6. Choose Image ➢ Image Size again to open the Image Size dialog box. Check Resample Image. Change the Width drop-down to Percent, and type **110** in the Width text box. Then click OK. Height will probably be close to 110, but might be slightly off due to inaccuracies in Photoshop's internal mathematics (to the result of the discrete pixel size). Figure 9.2 shows how you are increasing the document size by 10% while holding the resolution constant.

FIGURE 9.2

Resampling at 110%

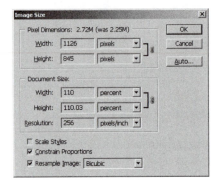

7. Continue incrementally boosting the document size until you reach your target document size. In this case, repeat step 6 five more times, using 110% for Width in each iteration. Figure 9.3 shows where you'll end up after boosting the printed size: with pixel dimensions of 1814 × 1362.

FIGURE 9.3

The image size after incremental small increases

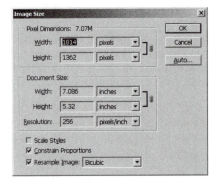

TIP Repetitive steps are a sign that you should record an action. Try recording step 6 as an action that you can quickly replay with a keystroke (see Chapter 7).

The resulting image will be crisper and less pixelated than an image that was resampled up to this size from the smaller original in one shot. The document now measures more than 7 by 5 inches at reasonable print resolution, so we are ready to open the relevant print dialog boxes. The dialog boxes you'll have to open are seemingly organized backward, because you'll have to open a slew of them to make your first settings.

8. Choose File ➢ Print With Preview or choose Alt+Ctrl+P to open the Print dialog box (see Figure 9.4). This dialog box will remain open in this tutorial until the document is sent to the printer.

FIGURE 9.4
The Print dialog box

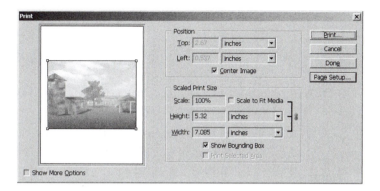

9. Click the Page Setup button to open the Page Setup dialog box, as shown in Figure 9.5.

FIGURE 9.5
The main Page Setup
dialog box

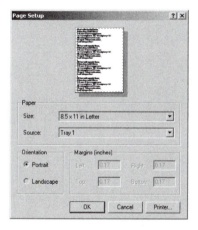

NOTE You could choose File ➢ Page Setup before Print With Preview in step 8 if you want to separate these steps, but that is not necessary.

10. Before you set anything in the Page Setup dialog box, select the print device, because the information that is in Page Setup depends on the printer driver you select: Click the Printer button in the lower-right corner to open the small Page Setup dialog box. Click the Name drop-down and select your printer driver (see Figure 9.6). I'll select EPSON Stylus C60 Series because that is the printer driver I will be using on my system. (Yours will most likely be different.)

FIGURE 9.6
The small Page Setup
dialog box

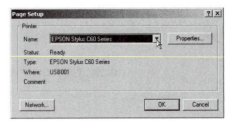

NOTE Click the Network button in step 10 if your printer is a node on a local area network (LAN), rather than physically connected to your computer.

11. Click the Properties button in the smaller Page Setup dialog box to open a dialog box that is specific to your print device. Figure 9.7 shows the EPSON Stylus C60 Series Properties dialog box.

FIGURE 9.7
The printer Properties
dialog box

At this point you are about as deep as possible into the nested set of print dialog boxes. Ironically, this is where you'll start altering settings for your print job. (This system could stand to be redesigned in a future release of Photoshop, to make the printing work flow smoother and more intuitive.) One by one you can close dialog boxes, making any needed changes along the way, until you return to the Print dialog box that you initially opened.

12. Make any adjustments you'd like to the printer properties now. I will choose Premium Glossy Photo Paper from the Media Type drop-down list box. Choose the type of media you'll be printing using the specific driver on your system. Also disable your printer driver's color correction system if it hasn't been done already (see Chapter 2). We use Photoshop for color correction exclusively in this book.

13. Click OK, and then click OK again to close the printer properties and small Page Setup dialog boxes.

14. In the large Page Setup dialog box, click the Landscape radio button to set the print orientation. Select a relevant paper size and source if necessary. (I'll choose letter-sized paper and use the sheet feeder.) Click OK to close the large Page Setup dialog box.

Remember that the image resolution set in step 5 was 256 pixels/inch. You have a little wiggle room, so you can scale the image up slightly and still maintain an adequate resolution of at least 200 pixels/inch.

15. Make sure that Center Image is checked if it is not already. At 100% scale, the width and height parameters are as you left them in the Image Size dialog box in step 7. Position your mouse over one of the bounding box handles in the preview area and drag the image outward, increasing the print size. Release the mouse button when the scale parameter reads approximately 120% (see Figure 9.8).

FIGURE 9.8

Dragging the bounding box in the Print dialog box

Set color management options so that Photoshop's Color Management Module (CMM) can translate from the working profile embedded in the document into the print space of your specific device. This way you'll maintain accurate color from screen to printed page.

16. Click Show More Options in the lower left corner of the Print dialog box. Choose Color Management from the drop-down menu immediately below this checkbox (see Figure 9.9). Note that the source space is set to the document's embedded profile, which is Adobe RGB (1998) in this case. Choose your printer's color profile. I'll choose EPSON Stylus C60 Series from the Profile drop-down list box. Set Intent to Perceptual and make sure Use Black Point Compensation is checked.

FIGURE 9.9

The color management options in the Print dialog box

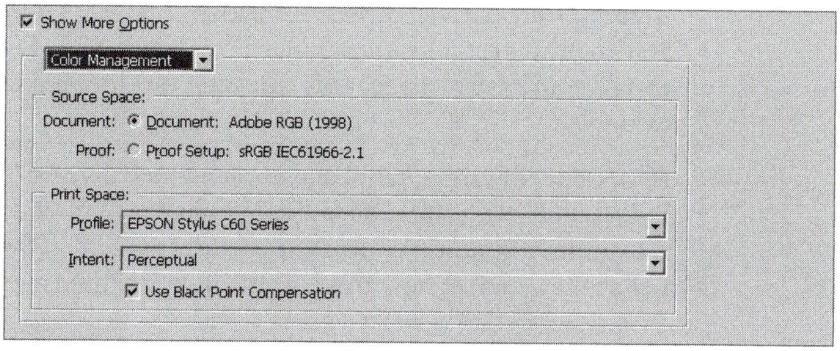

17. A lesser-known feature of Print With Preview is a set of additional button functions that are useful when you have multiple prints to make with different settings. Hold down the Alt key and observe the buttons in the Print dialog box change functions. As you might expect, Print One prints one copy of the image; Reset sets the original parameters back into the dialog box without closing it. The Remember button saves the print options without closing the dialog box. Don't click anything, and let go of the Alt key; this step was simply for your information.

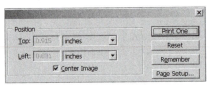

At long last we are ready to send the document to the printer. Pause a moment to be sure this is what you really want (breathe) and then proceed.

18. Click the Print button to open a smaller Print dialog box that belongs to the operating system (see Figure 9.10). Click OK to send the file to the printer, and you are done!

FIGURE 9.10

The Windows Print dialog box

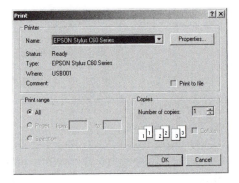

TIP Increasing the number of copies in the Windows Print dialog box is the best way to get duplicates, because the data is sent to the printer only once, and the printer is then responsible for repeating the print job. Repeatedly sending one print job at a time is much less efficient because the entire print data set must be transmitted each time. The time saved is significant when printing larger images.

If your printer driver supports PostScript (check your printer documentation), you may be able to print vector graphics such as text and shape layers at much higher resolution than the rest of your raster image. This can keep text looking crisp in an otherwise blurry image, for example.

PostScript is a printer language implemented at the driver level allowing text and shape layers to be sent to the printer as separate image layers. These vector layers are sent at the printer's maximum resolution while the raster data is sent at the lower level that you specify normally. Let's take a look at how this is controlled in Photoshop.

19. Reopen Print With Preview (press Alt+Ctrl+P). Make sure Show More Options is checked, and change the drop-down list box immediately below it to Output (see Figure 9.11). If the printer driver you selected supports PostScript, check Include Vector Data at the bottom of the Print dialog box. (This will be grayed out if not supported.) Choose a method from the Encoding drop-down list box that your printer supports. (Consult your network administrator if necessary.)

FIGURE 9.11
Including vector data in
Postscript output

WARNING   Most inkjets do not support PostScript. However, many laser and electrostatic printers do.

20. Close Illustration.tif without saving.

A few final conveniences are worth mentioning. After you go through the printing work flow, the settings you changed in the nested printing dialog boxes remain there until you change them. Therefore, you can quickly print an additional copy (with the same settings) by choosing File ➢ Print One Copy or by pressing Alt+Shift+Ctrl+P. If you want more than one copy, choose File ➢ Print to open the Windows Print dialog box where you can adjust the number of copies. Be warned that this is exactly how you might waste print media if you are not careful. I recommend going through Print With Preview so you'll be visually aware of what you are sending to the printer each time.

E-Mailing Images

Sending an image by e-mail is perhaps the most expedient way to communicate visually at a distance. However, remember that clients are often technically challenged and probably will not have Photoshop on their machines, let alone know how to use it or any other image-viewing software.

Therefore, before you e-mail an image to someone who will be frustrated because they can't view it, read this section. It contains information about how to use e-mail techniques that reach the lowest common digital denominator: e-mail client software. If you prepare an image for easy viewing in an e-mail program such as Microsoft Outlook or Mozilla Thunderbird, the recipient will immediately see the image when they open the e-mail message.

Let's see how you can prepare an image to be sent as an attachment that can be viewed by anyone who knows enough about computers to check their e-mail.

1. Open the file ClientProof.tif from the companion CD. This image is from the Hollyhock project in Chapter 5.

2. Open the Save For Web dialog box (choose File ➢ Save For Web, or press Alt+Shift+Ctrl+S). Click the Original tab to view the source document in the preview area (see Figure 9.12).

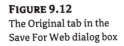

FIGURE 9.12
The Original tab in the
Save For Web dialog box

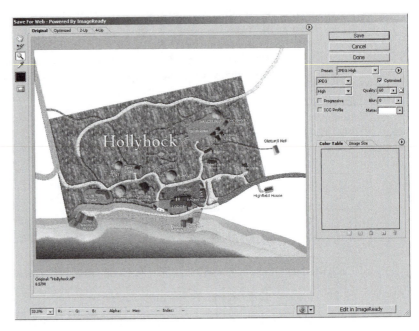

To be safe, don't assume that the recipient of your e-mail message knows how to download, save, or view attachments. (Imagine e-mailing something to your grandmother or grandfather if that helps.) Instead, the image you attach must fit within the recipient's message window (or "pane" as it is called in some client programs).

To guarantee that the recipient of your e-mail message can view the image in their message window, you must greatly reduce the size of most images, to a recommended 8″ width at 72 ppi, or approximately 575 pixels. The image height isn't as critical because you can assume that the recipient can use scrollbars, but ideally the height should be a mere 360 pixels, more or less.

Feel free to adjust these specifications based on your judgment of how techno-literate the recipient is, but assuming ignorance is safer. Better to have the client request another higher resolution attachment than to have them upset that they can't see the whole image on their screen.

3. Click the Image Size tab in the lower-right portion of the Save For Web dialog box. This tab is like a shortcut to the Image Size dialog box. (You could do Image Size first and then Save For Web, but this integrated tab is convenient.) Change the width parameter to 575, make sure Constrain Proportions is checked and that Quality is Bicubic, and click the Apply button.

4. Select the 4-Up tab; the dialog box splits into four sections, each a different version of the image (see Figure 9.13). Each section can display different compression settings. Press Z to select the Zoom tool, and click in any section until the zoom level at the bottom left of the dialog box indicates 200% magnification. Hold down the spacebar, and drag the image to an area where you can see a variety of tonal detail, structures, text, and paths.

FIGURE 9.13

The 4-Up tab in the Save For Web dialog box

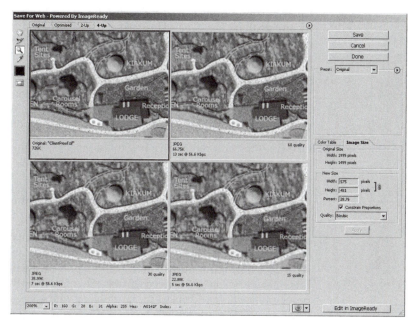

TIP   If your e-mail recipient is technologically savvy, post a high-res image on your FTP site and have them download it. Exchanging data is a nonissue with technical people.

CHOOSING A COMPRESSION FORMAT

The Save For Web dialog box allows you to compress images in three major graphics formats: Graphics Interchange Format (GIF), Portable Network Graphics (PNG), and Joint Photographic Experts Group (JPEG or JPG). Each format has its strengths and weaknesses:

GIF images are best for images with a few flat colors, such as pictures of text or simple graphics. GIF images use Lempel-Zif-Welch (LZW) lossless compression, so there is no degradation in image quality and small file size. GIF images can be compressed more by including fewer indexed colors. In addition, GIF images can preserve transparency but not alpha channels. Note that the GIF image format is proprietary.

PNG images were developed as a free alternative to GIF. Lossless PNG images are superior to GIF, especially in the 24-bit version that supports greater color depth and anti-aliased transparency. Older browsers do not support PNG images so it is a judgment call to use these images as you may be excluding some people.

JPEG images are best used to display photographs or other continuous tone images on the Web. They use lossy compression that sacrifices image quality for smaller file size. Highly compressed JPEG files have smaller sizes and lower image quality.

Choose a compression format and adjust its settings to optimize the image for reasonable quality and small file size. The 4-Up arrangement allows you to compare versions with different compression settings. Compressed images are efficiently transmitted over the Internet and take less time to transfer using less bandwidth.

5. Select the upper-right section in the Save For Web dialog box by clicking in the view. Click the triangle button just above the right corner of the current section to open the preview pop-up menu. Choose Standard Windows Color to simulate the color space of this operating system. Open the preview pop-up menu again and select Standard/Download Time (56.6 Kbps Modem/ISDN).

6. Open the Preset drop-down list box and select JPEG High if it is not already. The selected section shows a quality level of 60 and a file size of 66.75 KB. This image would take 13 seconds to download over a 56K modem.

7. Click the lower-left section to select it. Open the Preset drop-down list box and select JPEG Medium if it is not already. Click the lower-right section and change it to the JPEG Low preset.

8. Visually compare the four sections in the Save For Web dialog box. Choose the JPEG Medium version in the lower-left corner because it offers a reasonable quality level while taking only 7 seconds to download. Click in the lower-left preview window, and then click the Preview In Browser button along the lower edge of the Save For Web dialog box. Your default web browser program launches and displays the image along with suggested HTML code and image statistics (see Figure 9.14). Close the web browser window when you're finished previewing the image.

FIGURE 9.14
Previewing in the web browser

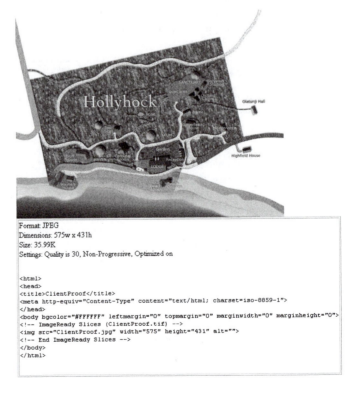

9. Click the Save button and save the file as `ClientProof.jpg` on your hard drive. Save For Web always creates a new file on your hard drive, leaving the original file untouched.

10. Close `ClientProof.tif` without saving.

You might also want to include a short disclaimer at the bottom of your e-mail (in addition to any confidentiality or copyright notices) to avoid potential misunderstandings. Sometimes AOL users can't see images in the body of the message. Such text might read something like this:

If you do not see the image in the body of this message, please double-click the attachment to view it in your browser. This image was optimized for viewing on a computer monitor and is not intended to be printed. Note also that the image on your monitor is not color accurate and is meant for proof only.

11. Open your e-mail client program and create a new message. Attach the JPG version of the image, write your message, and optionally include a disclaimer. Send the message.

WARNING   Attaching many images to an e-mail message is not only considered bad netiquette, but the message can be bounced back if it exceeds the recipient's mailbox quota. If you want to share lots of images, generate a web photo gallery (see the next section) or project site instead.

Generating Web Photo Galleries

Photoshop can generate a web photo gallery from a set of images. This type of gallery is an interactive interface for viewing images using a web browser. By posting the gallery on a web server, you maintain a centralized storage location for the images on the Internet. E-mail a gallery link to your clients, team members, or consultants, or make the URL available to the general public to suit your project's needs.

TIP   A network administrator can password protect a gallery URL if you want to maintain confidentiality.

A series of gallery styles comes with Photoshop CS; check the following folder:

`C:\Program Files\Adobe\Photoshop CS\Presets\Web Photo Gallery`

These are customizable HTML templates that web designers can alter to adjust the look of the web photo gallery.

Let's create a web photo gallery of images from earlier chapters of this book.

1. Open the File Browser (press Shift+Ctrl+O).

2. Using the controls in the File Browser, navigate to the Web Photo Gallery folder under Chapter 9 on the companion CD.

3. The sequential order of the thumbnail images in the File Browser determines the order images will appear in the web photo gallery. Drag the thumbnails to reorder the images if desired. Arrange the "before" images earlier than their corresponding "after" images in the File Browser. Figure 9.15 shows one such sequence.

4. Press Ctrl+A to select all the thumbnails in the File Browser. You can optionally use the Ctrl key to deselect individual images to exclude them from the web photo gallery. Choose Automate ➢ Web Photo Gallery in the File Browser to open the Web Photo Gallery dialog box.

5. Select Horizontal Neutral from the Styles drop-down list box. Notice the preview image on the right side of the Web Photo Gallery dialog box. Type your contact e-mail address in the E-Mail text box (optional). Click the Use drop-down list box, and choose Selected Images From File Browser. You can alternately select an entire folder for inclusion by clicking the Browser button. Click the Destination button, and select a folder on your hard drive where you want Photoshop to place the web files it will create.

NOTE   You can control the order of images in a web photo gallery by using selected images from the File Browser; they appear in the order you see them in the File Browser. However, you cannot do this by selecting an entire folder in the Web Photo Gallery dialog box.

6. Under the General options, change the Extension to .html if your web server runs Linux or to .htm if your web server runs a version of Windows Server. Choose Banner from the Options drop-down list box. Type **Enhancing CAD Drawings with Photoshop** into the Site Name text box. Type your name in the Photographer text box if desired. Click OK to close the Web Photo Gallery dialog box (see Figure 9.16).

7. Be patient as Photoshop automatically opens, resizes, and captures each image in turn. After a few moments, your web browser will launch (see Figure 9.17). Preview your new photo gallery locally. In the example, you can click each of the thumbnails at the bottom of the gallery to jump to a larger version above. Each larger image has navigation arrows that allow you to navigate between images in the gallery. If you'd like to make any changes, repeat steps 3 through 6 until you are satisfied with how the gallery functions.

FIGURE 9.16
The Web Photo Gallery
dialog box

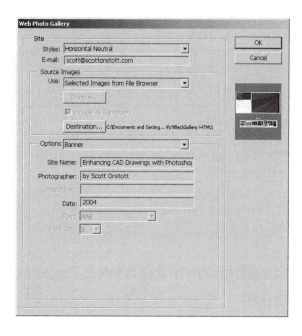

FIGURE 9.17
Photoshop opens your
gallery in a browser.

NOTE The logo in Figure 9.17 was customized. You can change it and much more in the template's HTML code. HTML coding—and therefore web gallery customization—is beyond the scope of this book. Refer to *HTML Complete* (Sybex, 2003) for more in-depth information about the Hypertext Markup Language.

8. Use an FTP program to upload the files and subfolders Photoshop generated for the gallery to your web server. Look in the destination folder you selected in step 5 to locate the relevant files and folders.

TIP Check out `filezilla.sourceforge.net` for a full-featured open-source FTP client and FTP server for Windows.

9. Use an Internet browser and surf to the URL of the gallery to verify that it is online. E-mail the URL of the new gallery to its intended audience.

10. Close the File Browser and web browser.

Creating Optimized Web Pages with ImageReady

You can reap marketing benefits for your project by making an interactive gallery with rollover effects. When it comes to displaying work online, Adobe ImageReady is the tool of choice for producing optimized graphics. ImageReady is Photoshop's sister product designed to produce web graphics at screen resolution (72 pixels/inch). You used ImageReady briefly in Chapter 7 and will use more of its features in this section to create optimized web pages. The process begins by cutting a sample file into slices—rectangular areas that divide an overall image into parts. You'll optimize each slice and then create rollovers using the slices, adjusted layers, and layer style effects. Rollovers control the web page's behavior when a visitor finally interacts with it in a web browser.

Creating and Optimizing Slices

Dividing an image into slices has many advantages when displaying visual information in a web page. Each slice can have different compression settings, so better overall optimization can be achieved (quality level versus file size). Slices can host rollovers and advanced animation effects. Furthermore, transmitting multiple smaller images rather than one large image is more efficient. Let's start by editing a sample file in ImageReady.

1. Open the sample file `Slices.psd` in Photoshop from the companion CD (see Figure 9.18). The file shows imagery from many of the chapters in this book.

2. Click the Edit In ImageReady button at the bottom of the Photoshop toolbox or press Shift+Ctrl+M.

   Wait a few moments for ImageReady to launch. Four tabs are at the top of the document window: Original, Optimized, 2-Up, and 4-Up. These are the same tabs seen in the Photoshop Save For Web dialog box. (See the section "E-Mailing Images" earlier in this chapter.)

FIGURE 9.18
A slices file

Enhancing CAD Drawings
with Photoshop

Image Slices and Rollovers

3. Click the Optimized tab. Select the Optimize palette and choose JPEG Medium from the Preset drop-down list box. The entire image in the document window is displayed with the chosen compression setting.

There are several kinds of slices in ImageReady: layer-based, user, auto, table, and subslices. We will create layer-based slices and later use the Slice tool to make user slices. Auto slices fill the spaces in between the other types and are created automatically. If there is overlap between slices, those areas are considered subslices.

NOTE Table slices are an advanced web design topic that you can read more about in the Image-Ready Help.

Layer-based slices divide image areas using the outer borders of layers. You will create several layer-based slices now.

4. Right-click the Site Plan layer, and choose New Layer Based Slice from the context menu. Repeat this process and create new layer-based slices on the Illustration, Compositing, and Glass layers.

Notice how the slices are identified in the document window. Layer-based slices have a solid edge, and auto slices fill the in-between spaces with dotted edges. Each slice is numbered and labeled.

5. Click the Slice tool in the toolbox, or press K. Drag rectangular windows around the kitchen plan, elevation, and two text layers to create corresponding user slices (see Figure 9.19).

Auto slices are identified by grayed-out labels that show the link symbol; auto slices are linked to layer-based and/or user slices and fill the in-between spaces (with white pixels in this example).

FIGURE 9.19
Layer-based, user, and auto slices

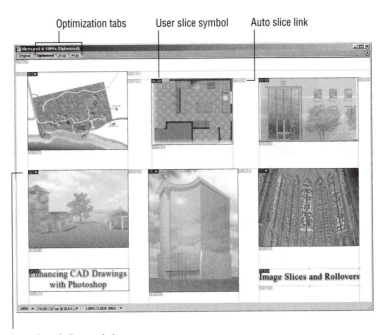

Optimization tabs   User slice symbol   Auto slice link

Layer-based slice symbol

Now that you've sliced the image, apply different optimization settings to selected slices to reduce the overall file size (and loading time) of the web page. JPEG compression is preferable for continuous tone images, and GIF is better for text (see the "Choosing a Compression Format" sidebar earlier in this chapter).

6. Choose the Slice Select tool in the ImageReady toolbox, or press O. Click slice 20 (text layer) and select the Optimize palette. Choose GIF 32 No Dither from the Preset drop-down list box. The text slice is reduced to displaying 32 shades of gray in indexed color mode for greater compression.

7. Click slice 21, and then choose GIF 32 No Dither from the Preset drop-down list box. Text renders more clearly with a lossless compression format.

8. Optionally, click any layer-based or user slice and change its compression settings using the Optimize palette. This is like having Photoshop's Save For Web command available for each slice.

Creating Rollovers

Rollovers are image areas that change when you interact with them in a web browser. Most commonly, rollovers are used with text buttons; the image changes when you roll your mouse over it, for example. Rollovers are managed by *rollover states*. Each rollover state enables a different behavior that is triggered by a person interacting with the web page in a web browser. The possible rollover states include normal, over, down, selected, out, up, click, custom, and none.

In this tutorial, you will create sepia-toned versions of the thumbnail images on new layers. Then, you'll assign different rollover states to the slices using both the new layers and layer style effects. Use both the Layers palette and the Web Content palette together to create rollovers. Let's create the sepia-tone effect first.

1. Using the Slice Select tool, click slice 03 (see Figure 9.19 in the previous section). The Site Plan layer is automatically selected in the Layers palette. Duplicate this layer by pressing Ctrl+J. A new layer is created called Site Plan copy, with the same information as the source layer.

2. Press Shift+Ctrl+U to desaturate the Site Plan copy layer. The site plan appears in grayscale in the document window while all the other slices appear as they were before. Slices are really independent images shown within the same document window.

3. Use the Colorize feature of the Hue/Saturation adjustment to impart a sepia-tone color cast to the desaturated layer: Choose Image ➤ Adjustments ➤ Hue/Saturation to open the Hue/Saturation dialog box. Adjustment layers are not present in ImageReady. Check Colorize, drag the Hue slider to 35, and drag the Saturation slider to 25 (see Figure 9.20). Click OK, making the current layer a sepia-toned version of the Site Plan layer.

FIGURE 9.20

ImageReady's Hue/
Saturation dialog box

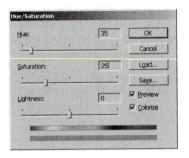

4. Now make the rollover: Select the Web Content palette, and notice that the current slice is already selected. (The Slice Select tool did this automatically.) Click the Create Rollover State button at the bottom of the Web Content palette (see Figure 9.21). The over state is created and indented under the selected slice in the Web Content palette.

FIGURE 9.21

Creating a rollover state
in the Web Content
palette

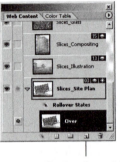

Create rollover state

5. Toggle the visibility of layers while in the over rollover state: click the Layers palette and toggle off the visibility of the Site Plan copy layer. Now the original color version of the Site Plan layer is visible in the document window. When the mouse is over the image, a color version is displayed in the browser.

6. Repeat the process to make additional rollover states: Repeat steps 1 through 5 for each layer-based slice (slices 13, 15, and 17 in Figure 9.19).

   Add sepia-toned over rollover states to the user slices that are images (kitchen plan and elevation thumbnails). First, add an over rollover state for the kitchen plan.

7. Select slice 6. Notice how the Slice Select tool does not automatically select a layer for user slices. Manually select the Kitchen Plan layer in the Layers palette.

8. Press Ctrl+J and Shift+Ctrl+U to duplicate the Kitchen Plan layer and desaturate it.

9. Press Ctrl+U to open the Hue/Saturation dialog box. Check Colorize and type **35** and **25** for Hue and Saturation, respectively. Click OK.

10. Select Slices_06 in the Web Content palette. Click the Create Rollover State button at the bottom of the Web Content palette. Toggle the Kitchen Plan copy layer off in the Layers palette.

11. Now add an over rollover state for the Elevation thumbnail: Repeat steps 7 through 10 for slice 8 and the Elevation layer.

So far you have made over rollover states for each thumbnail image by toggling the appropriate sepia-toned layers while the over state was selected in the Web Content palette. You can make changes by applying layer style effects for a specific rollover state. Apply a stroke effect next.

12. Select slice 03. Click the Create Rollover State button at the bottom of the Web Content palette; a new state appears called Down. The Down state appears in the web browser when the mouse button is held down.

13. Toggle off the Site Plan copy layer in the Layers palette. Select the Site Plan layer and apply a Stroke layer style effect. Click the Color swatch and select bright red from the Color Picker. Close the Color Picker, change Size to 3 pixels (see Figure 9.22), and click OK.

FIGURE 9.22
The Layer Style dialog box in ImageReady

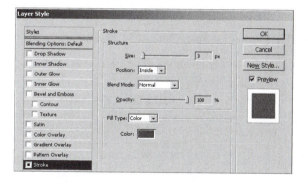

The Layer Style dialog box looks slightly different in ImageReady; there are square icons in the check boxes, for example. Even though there are slight cosmetic differences, the functionality of the Layer Style dialog box is much the same as in Photoshop.

The layer style you applied in the previous step affects only the currently selected rollover state.

14. Click the over rollover state in the Web Content palette. Notice how the Stroke effect disappears from the Site layer in the Layers palette. It is like having a whole new Layers palette for each rollover state.

15. Select the Slice palette. Type **Large_Site_Plan.html** in the URL text box. You can optionally add anchor tags to the HTML markup by entering data in the URL field for the slice.

NOTE Hyperlinking is something that is normally done in web design software such as Adobe GoLive or Macromedia Dreamweaver, but you can add basic links to a web page in ImageReady if desired.

16. Optionally, create another web page called `Large_Site_Plan.html` featuring an enlarged and optimized image of the site plan project (see Chapter 5). This web page was referenced by slice 03 in the previous step.

17. Save your work as `Slices2.psd` in ImageReady. If you're going to continue working through the following section, you can leave this file open for now.

Viewing the Optimized Web Page

After creating slices and rollover states, preview the web page in a browser locally and see how it functions before posting it to a web server.

1. If you have `Slices2.psd` open in ImageReady from the previous exercise, you can continue here; if not, open that file from your hard drive before continuing. This file is also provided on the companion CD if you are jumping in here.

2. Choose File ➢ Save Optimized As, or press Ctrl+Shift+Alt+S. Type **Slices_and_Rollovers** in the File Name field of the Save Optimized As dialog box. Choose HTML And Images in the Save As Type drop-down list box. Leave Settings set to Default and Slices set to All Slices. It is possible to save only the user slices or to save in XHTML, for example. Navigate to a project folder on your hard drive and make a Web Page subfolder. Click Save.

TIP Do not put spaces or unusual characters in the filenames of web pages.

3. If you see a warning dialog box, click OK to truncate lengthy filenames for compatibility with Macintosh browsers.

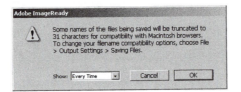

4. Open Windows Explorer and navigate to the folder on your hard drive where you saved the optimized HTML and images in step 2. Double-click `Slices_and_Rollovers.html` to launch your default browser. (This is also provided on the CD in the Web Page subfolder.) All the slices are stored in an images subfolder. Figure 9.23 shows the web page displayed in a browser (Mozilla Firefox in this case). A version of this image also appears in the color section.

FIGURE 9.23

A web page displayed in a browser

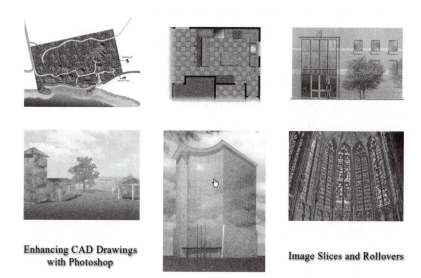

Enhancing CAD Drawings
with Photoshop

Image Slices and Rollovers

5. Notice how each of the thumbnail images appears in sepia tone in the browser. Move the mouse over the thumbnails and observe them each colorize when the mouse triggers the over rollover state in the slices. The slices return to sepia tone when the mouse is moved away. Hold the mouse button down on top of the Site Plan thumbnail and observe the stroke corresponding to the down rollover state appear.

6. If you're not quite satisfied with the behavior of the web page, go back and add rollover states as desired. Choose File ➤ Save Optimized when done. Preview the web page again locally to make sure it is okay. Upload the web page and the images subfolder (containing all the slices) to your web server. Test it by surfing to the proper URL, and verify that it works as expected in your target browsers.

7. Close your web browser and close ImageReady, but leave Photoshop open if you're going to continue working through the following sections.

Presenting Slide Shows

Slide shows, an effective means for presenting a series of still images, can be made in several formats to suit the intended viewing environment. Obviously, you can use Photoshop's File Browser to locate and open multiple images for viewing. However, using Photoshop in a production capacity leaves something to be desired when presenting images (unless your intent is to actually edit the images during the show or to demonstrate various Photoshop techniques using the palettes and toolbox).

Let's take a look at the two primary modes for creating slide shows: an in-Photoshop demonstration, and an Acrobat PDF presentation.

An In-Photoshop Demonstration

For impromptu meetings at your computer monitor, you can use Photoshop itself to present images to a client. Images are displayed against a black background, without the toolbox or palettes appearing on the screen, and the slides are manually advanced using the keyboard.

1. Press Shift+Ctrl+O to open the File Browser.

2. Using the controls in the File Browser, navigate to the Web Photo Gallery folder under Chapter 9 on the companion CD.

3. Select All (press Ctrl+A). Double-click any one of the images to open all selected in document windows (see Figure 9.24). Close the File Browser. Make sure the rulers do not display. (Press Ctrl+R to toggle them off if necessary.)

FIGURE 9.24
Opening multiple files through the File Browser

WARNING If you do not close the File Browser, it will appear as a slide in your presentation.

4. Press F to switch to Full Screen Mode With Menu Bar. The window of the top document itself disappears, but its content appears against a neutral gray background. The neutral background is appropriate for making decisions about color, but not necessarily for presentation.

5. Hold down Shift and click the Full Screen Mode button near the bottom of the toolbox. Now the image appears against a black background that is better for formal presentation. Holding down Shift while making this change alters the mode of all the images that are currently open; they are all in Full Screen mode now.

6. Hide the toolbox and palettes by pressing the Tab key. Now the image is presentable against a black background. The Windows taskbar is also hidden. (Press Alt+Tab to switch tasks if necessary.)

7. Advance to the next slide by pressing Ctrl+Tab. Repeat this to advance to the next slide. Press Ctrl+Tab at intervals you choose to set the speed of the slide show. When you get to the last slide, pressing Ctrl+Tab again loops around to the first slide.

TIP You can advance slides in reverse order by pressing Shift+Ctrl+Tab.

When the slide show is over, you'll need to know how to get Photoshop back to "normal."

8. Press Tab to toggle the toolbox and palettes on. (Shift+Tab toggles only the palettes on and off.)

9. Press F, and then press F again for each image to return it to Standard Screen Mode. Leave all the files open.

Acrobat PDF Presentation

If you have plenty of time to prepare for a client meeting, you might use an LCD projector or another suitable viewing method. For such a slide show presentation, you can author an Acrobat PDF file that displays images in Full Screen mode against a black background, complete with timed advance and optional special effects transitions between slides. The PDF presentation offers the additional benefit of encapsulating the entire slide show in a single file that you can electronically transfer (FTP) or possibly e-mail to a client (if it is small enough).

1. Choose File ➤ Automate ➤ PDF Presentation to open the PDF Presentation dialog box (see Figure 9.25). Check Add Open Files. Alternately, click the Browse button and select image files to be included. Click the Presentation radio button, and make sure View PDF After Saving is checked. Set the options in the Presentation Options section to advance every 15 seconds and to loop after the last page. Click the Transition drop-down list box, and notice the many special effect animated transitions that can be selected. Choose Dissolve and then click Save to open the Save As dialog box.

FIGURE 9.25
The PDF Presentation options

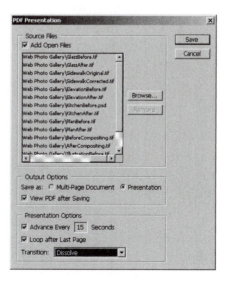

2. Navigate to the project folder on your hard drive and type the filename **Slide show.pdf**; click Save to open the PDF Options dialog box.

3. Choose JPEG Encoding if it is not already selected. Open the Quality drop-down list box, and select Medium. Make sure Image Interpolation is checked and click OK to generate the PDF file.

4. After a few moments, Adobe Acrobat launches and displays the slide show document in Full Screen mode. The slide show plays automatically; be patient as the slides will advance every 15 seconds (interval set in step 1). After viewing a few slides, manually advance to the next slide by pressing the Right arrow key; pressing the Left arrow key moves back one slide.

WARNING If you do not have Acrobat already installed on your system, download the free Reader from the companion CD.

5. Press the Esc key to switch to Single Page mode (see Figure 9.26). Choose View ➢ Full Screen or press Ctrl+L to return to Full Screen mode at any time.

6. Close Adobe Acrobat and all open files in Photoshop.

Not only can a PDF be an excellent way to present a slide show in-house, but your client can transfer, view, and print the PDF file. Be aware that once the PDF leaves your hands, you can no longer control its viewing environment or lighting, monitor calibration, and establish printing options, so misunderstandings about color can occur at the client's office. It is best to educate clients about these issues and warn them that the PDF is only a draft if color accuracy is important to your project (see Chapter 2).

FIGURE 9.26
An Acrobat slide show in Single Page mode

Protecting Your Intellectual Property

You can employ several strategies to protect your intellectual property. The first is embedding descriptive metadata that identifies the copyright holder. Metadata has the tangential benefit of providing a means to search for visual data with keywords—essential if your firm has thousands of digital photographic assets, for example. Metadata also encodes many useful details about an image such as when and where the shot was taken, with what camera, and how (specific camera settings).

Watermarks, both visible and hidden, can be used at the next level of protection. A visible watermark is a copyright symbol or a company logo that is faintly superimposed over an image, ensuring that the viewer is aware of its intellectual provenance. The downside to using a visual watermark is that it competes with the visual imagery itself and can distract from the image's worth as a communication tool. Hidden watermarks (also called digital copyright) are essentially imperceptible to the human eye; encrypted code is added as digital noise to the image. Hidden watermarks may positively identify a digital image as belonging to a specific copyright holder, but do not appear when printed.

The highest level of security is password protecting your imagery with PDF technology. You can also restrict access so that an image can be viewed and printed but not copied or altered, for example. After reviewing the options, the choice of how to protect your intellectual property (or to rely on trust) is your own strategic decision.

Adding Metadata

Metadata is information about image data; it describes and categorizes visual imagery with text, making it easily searchable. Librarians and professional photographers like metadata because it allows them to find the veritable needle in a digital haystack. Be aware that metadata is only useful if someone takes the time to embed meaningful information in metadata tags.

You might like metadata for the ability to embed your copyright and URL in image files so that unknown admirers of your imagery can find you on the Web. In addition, many types of metadata store useful factual information about the shooting settings, Camera Raw adjustments, and even GPS coordinates (if the camera was so equipped). Let's take a look at an image that already has metadata stored so that you can learn how to add metadata to your own images.

NOTE   Only the following file formats support metadata both on Windows and the Mac OS: PSD, PSB, TIFF, JPEG, EPS, and PDF.

1. Open the File Browser (press Shift+Ctrl+O).

2. Using the controls in the File Browser, navigate to the Chapter 9 folder on the companion CD.

3. Select `LookingEast.tif` and examine the Metadata palette within the File Browser (see Figure 9.27).

4. The File Properties category shows basic facts about the image, such as its pixel size, file size, color depth, and color profile. Expand the IPTC (International Press Telecommunications Council) category.

FIGURE 9.27

The Metadata palette in the File Browser

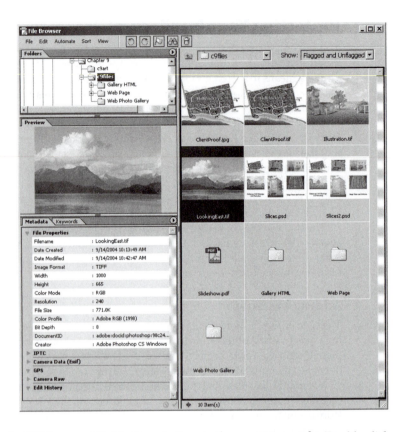

5. Some fields under IPTC are modifiable: Description, Author, and Copyright. Double-click Description to highlight it, allowing you to edit the text. Don't change anything here; this is just for your information. You can add this information to your own images using the Metadata palette.

6. Expand Camera Data (Exif) in the Metadata palette; this data was generated by the digital camera and automatically embedded in the file. This data includes camera make, model, exposure time, shutter speed, f-stop, ISO speed, lens focal length, and much more. None of the Exif data is modifiable.

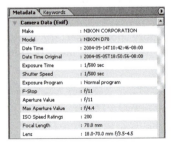

7. Choose File ➤ File Info from the File Browser menu bar or press Alt+Shift+Ctrl+I to open the File Info dialog box with the filename in the title bar (see Figure 9.28). You can enter data directly in this dialog box as an alternative to using the Metadata palette. In general, you can do more in the File Info dialog box as compared with the Metadata palette, although the Metadata palette is more convenient.

FIGURE 9.28

The File Info dialog box

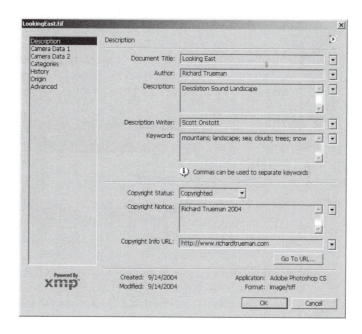

TIP   You can also access the File Info dialog box once an image is opened in Photoshop by choosing File ➤ File Info from Photoshop's menu bar.

Perhaps the most important parts of the File Info dialog box are the Copyright fields in the Description category. Here you can choose Copyrighted, Unknown, or Public Domain in the Copyright Status drop-down list box. You can enter text in the Copyright notice, and type a web address in the Copyright Info URL field. Viewers of this image can go to the URL, assuming that they are aware to look for embedded metadata hidden within image files.

Notice that keywords were entered (mountains, landscape, sea, clouds, trees, snow). Keywords allow you to search for an image within the File Browser much as you would for a web page on the Internet. Let's do a search for "landscape" in the File Browser and see what turns up.

8. Click OK to close the File Info dialog box. Choose File ➤ Search from the File Browser menu bar to open the Search dialog box (see Figure 9.29). Choose Other Metadata from the drop-down list box. Type **landscape** in the Criteria text box. You can enter additional criteria when making a more specific search by clicking the plus button.

FIGURE 9.29

The Search dialog box

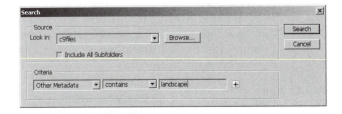

9. Click Search to close the Search dialog box. The Search Results appear under a node of the same name in the File Browser (see Figure 9.30). The search turned up LookingEast.tif because it has the keyword "landscape" embedded in its metadata.

FIGURE 9.30

Search results in the File Browser

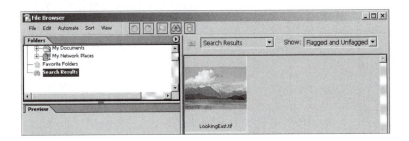

NOTE The metadata stored by Photoshop CS is in XMP (Extensible Metadata Platform) format, which is a variety of XML (Extensible Markup Language). It is possible to extract the embedded metadata and store it as an .xmp file. Advanced users should read more about XMP files in Photoshop Help.

10. Close the File Browser.

Adding Watermarks

The primary strength and limitation of metadata is that anyone can change it. Metadata is useless to viewers who aren't aware of its existence and is easily changed by those who aim to steal your intellectual property. Watermarks offer more secure evidence of ownership because they are difficult (if not impossible) to eliminate.

OVERLAYING A VISIBLE WATERMARK

Visible watermarks are meant to be faintly evident in the overall image, so they don't distract too much attention from the image itself. Care should be taken to place the watermark over a detailed central portion of the image so it is more difficult to remove the watermark through cropping or retouching. Usually visible watermarks are the copyright symbol itself (©), text, or a logo. Let's see how to integrate a logo as a visible watermark.

1. Open the file Illustration.tif from the companion CD.

2. Choose the Custom Shape tool in the toolbox. On the Options bar, click the Shape Layers button if it is not already selected. Open the Custom Shape Picker and select the logo that was

added to this library in Chapter 4. If you skipped Chapter 4, choose the copyright symbol in the Custom Shape Picker instead.

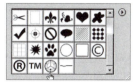

3. Hold down the Shift key to constrain the aspect ratio of the custom shape, and drag it out over the center of the illustration (see Figure 9.31).

4. In the Layers palette, double-click the shape layer thumbnail to open the Color Picker. Select medium gray (HSB values of 0,0,50). Click OK to close the Color Picker. Change the blend mode of the Shape 1 layer to Hard Light. The logo disappears because hard light blending works for grays that differ from medium gray.

5. To make the logo appear dimensional, add a bevel that will create grayscale variation on the shape layer: Add the Bevel And Emboss layer style effect to the Shape 1 layer. Change Depth to 300%, Size to 4 px, and Soften to 4 px. Click OK to close the Layer Style dialog box.

FIGURE 9.31
The logo added as a shape layer

6. Tone down the watermark by changing the opacity of the Shape 1 layer to 25% (see Figure 9.32). A version of this image is in the color section.

7. Choose File ➢ Save For Web. Save the image with medium compression as `Illustration.jpg`. This is the image you can distribute by e-mail or on the Web.

WARNING Do not distribute versions of your images that include layers, or it would be easy to remove the visible watermark simply by throwing away the appropriate layer.

8. You can now drag and drop the shape layer into other documents to quickly add an instant visible watermark. Close `Illustration.tif` without saving.

EMBEDDING A DIGITAL WATERMARK

Hidden, or digital, watermarks are added to images with the Digimarc filter in Photoshop. Digimarc technology works by adding a small amount of noise to the original image. This noise is visually so insignificant that you can hardly tell it is there. However, the added noise isn't random; encrypted data is cleverly encoded in the shifted colors of the pixels themselves. In this way, a nefarious hacker can't strip the hidden watermark from the file, because the watermark is actually part of the image data set.

To identify you as the copyright holder of images containing digital watermarks, Digimarc operates a fee-based subscription service that maintains your digital identity. Let's see how it works.

WARNING You cannot apply a watermark to a document that contains multiple layers. Flatten the image first, or use an image that was saved for the Web.

1. Open the file `ClientProof.jpg` from the companion CD.

FIGURE 9.32
A visible watermark
added

E 9.38
F Security
)ox

(PDF Security dialog box)

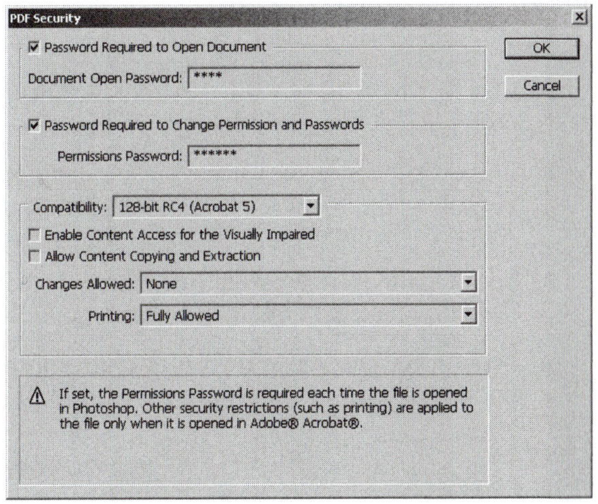

9. Adobe Acrobat launches. Type **1234** and click OK in the Password dialog box. The original image is visible inside Acrobat.

0. Close all files without saving.

The document is now completely secure and ready to be sent to your client. Be sure to make a note he passwords used in steps 4 and 5, as there is now no way to open or change the PDF document hout them.

ımmary

his chapter you explored numerous ways to show work to clients. Now you can choose the best ans of communication for your situation. Whether it be prints, e-mailed images, a web photo gal-
/, an optimized web page, or a slide show, your clients are bound to be impressed by your facility h Photoshop. All the while, you're able to safeguard your intellectual property so no problems se.

This brings you to the end of this book. I hope you have enjoyed learning the techniques and tips e had to offer and find creative ways to use Photoshop in your daily practice.

If you have comments regarding this book, please feel free to contact me. Thanks for choosing *iancing CAD Drawings with Photoshop*.

—Scott Onstott

Scott@ScottOnstott.com

http://www.ScottOnstott.com/

2. Choose Filter ➢ Digimarc ➢ Embed Watermark to open the Embed Watermark dialog box. Choose Copyright Year from the drop-down list box, and enter the year in the adjacent text box. Make sure Restricted Use and Do Not Copy are checked, and change Target Output to Web. Drag the slider toward the more visible and more durable end of the range, and check Verify (see Figure 9.33).

FIGURE 9.33
The Embed Watermark
dialog box

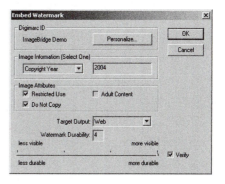

3. Click the Personalize button in the Embed Watermark dialog box to open the Personalize Digimarc ID dialog box. Enter your ID number and PIN (see Figure 9.34). If desired, visit www.digimarc.com/register to subscribe to the service and get your own digital identity. Enter your data, or click Cancel if you do not want to opt in at this time.

FIGURE 9.34
The Personalize
Digimarc ID dialog box

(Personalize Digimarc ID dialog box)

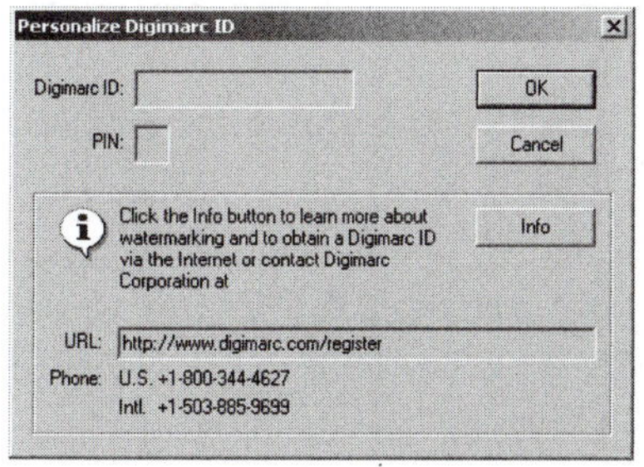

You can still embed a digital watermark even if you do not have a digital ID using the Image-Bridge Demo (set by default). The watermark will be embedded, but you will not be identified as the copyright holder unless you subscribe to the service.

The strength of a watermark depends on the dynamic range of the image itself. Strong water-marks can withstand a great deal of retouching before they are completely wiped out. The image would be so altered by the time the hidden watermark is lost that it wouldn't be of any value.

4. Click OK in the Embed Watermark dialog box. A verification dialog box appears showing that this particular image has a medium-strength watermark. Click OK. If you are prompted to check for an updated version of the Digimarc plug-ins at any time, choose Remind Me Later.

5. You can check any image to view its watermark information (if any is present). Choose Filter ➢ Digimarc ➢ Read Watermark to open the Watermark Information dialog box, as shown in Figure 9.35. Note that the Digimarc ID shows as ImageBridge Demo here, not as a specific identity. If a real digital ID were used, you could click the Web Lookup button to view the ID holder's contact information. Click OK.

6. Close `ClientProof.jpg` without saving.

FIGURE 9.35

Reading a digital watermark

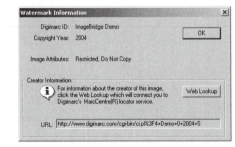

Securing Your Data

Acrobat files offer the highest level of security with password protection and access level permissions. Creating a multipage PDF presentation can be the safest way to go if you are worried about security. Let's see how easy it is to secure your data.

1. Open the file `Slices.psd` from the companion CD.

NOTE If you do not have Acrobat already installed on your system, download the free Reader from the companion CD.

2. Choose File ➢ Automate ➢ PDF Presentation to open the PDF Presentation dialog box, as shown in Figure 9.36. Click Add Open Files. Also choose Multi-Page Document and View PDF After Saving. Click Save to open the PDF Options dialog box, type **Security.pdf**.

3. In the PDF Options dialog box, as shown in Figure 9.37, choose JPEG encoding with Maximum quality. Check Image Interpolation and PDF Security. Click the Security Settings button to open the PDF Security dialog box.

4. Check Password Required To Open Document. Type the password **1234** in the Document Open Password text box. (Use a password that is much more difficult to guess in a real project.)

5. Check Password Required To Change Permission And Passwords, and type the password **654321** in the Permissions Password text box below. (Obviously, you should use a better password in a real project.) This is the administrator's password that is required to change the open password given in step 4.

WARNING If you use a permissions password, you will have opened in Photoshop; you won't have to enter it in Acrobat, h

6. Choose 128-bit RC4 (Acrobat 5) from the Compatibil encryption of the same caliber as used in online bank

7. Choose None from the Changes Allowed drop-down Click the Printing drop-down list box, and select Ful Allowed are also choices.) Click OK. Figure 9.38 show

8. You are immediately asked to confirm both the open passwords and click OK in the PDF Options dialog b

Because you checked View PDF after Saving in step the open password as the document is opened in Ac

FIGURE 9.36

Creating a multipage PDF presentation

FIGURE 9.37

PDF Options dialog box

Index

Note to the reader: Throughout this index **boldfaced** page numbers indicate primary discussions of a topic. *Italicized* page numbers indicate illustrations.

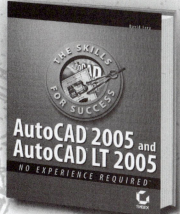
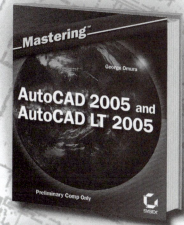
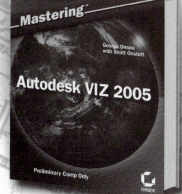

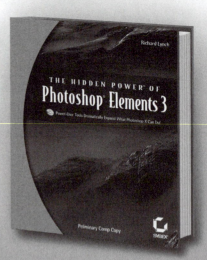

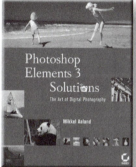

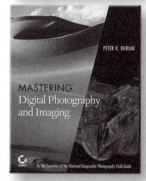

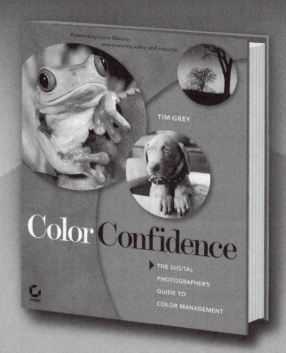

On the CD

This book's companion disk is an auto-run CD-ROM that includes the convenient Sybex interface. Just insert the CD into your CD-ROM drive and you'll be able to access all the project files, tools, and software that's included.

TIP   Visit this book's page at www.sybex.com, where we will post all updates to the text and projects.

Instructional videos   Almost an hour of screen-captured computer videos describe important techniques from each chapter.

Native CAD and VIZ files   Follow along in your CAD and 3D modeling software, and compare your work to the author's finished versions.

Sample images   Try out the book's techniques on all the main image formats.

Time-saving scripts   The companion CD also contains AutoLISP and MAX-Script programs used in tutorials involving AutoCAD and Autodesk VIZ.

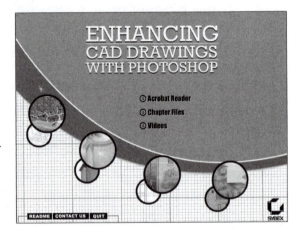

Adobe Photoshop   Even if you don't already own Photoshop, you can still use this book: Test-drive Photoshop CS with the free demo version.

Adobe Reader   See how effective PDF presentations are by viewing them in this free version of Acrobat.